PLANNING CONTROL
PHILOSOPHIES, PROSPECTS AND PRACTICE

CROOM HELM SERIES IN GEOGRAPHY AND ENVIRONMENT
Edited by Alan Wilson, Nigel Thrift, Michael Bradford and Edward W. Soja

CONCEPTS AND TECHNIQUES IN URBAN ANALYSIS
Bola Ayeni

URBAN HOUSING PROVISION AND THE DEVELOPMENT PROCESS
David Drakakis-Smith

URBAN TRANSPORT PLANNING
John Black

DAVID HARVEY'S GEOGRAPHY
John L. Paterson

PLANNING IN THE SOVIET UNION
Judith Pallot and Denis J.B. Shaw

CATASTROPHE THEORY AND BIFURCATION
A.G. Wilson

THEMES IN GEOGRAPHIC THOUGHT
Milton E. Harvey and Brian P. Holly

REGIONAL LANDSCAPES AND HUMANISTIC GEOGRAPHY
Edward Relph

CRIME AND ENVIRONMENT
R.N. Davidson

HUMAN MIGRATION
G.J. Lewis

THE GEOGRAPHY OF MULTINATIONALS
Edited by Michael Taylor and Nigel Thrift

URBANISATION AND PLANNING IN THE THIRD WORLD SPATIAL PERCEPTIONS AND PUBLIC PARTICIPATION
Robert B. Potter

OFFICE DEVELOPMENT: A GEOGRAPHICAL ANALYSIS
Michael Bateman

URBAN GEOGRAPHY
David Clark

RETAIL AND COMMERCIAL PLANNING
R.L. Davies

INSTITUTIONS AND GEOGRAPHICAL PATTERNS
Edited by Robin Flowerdew

MATHEMATICAL PROGRAMMING METHODS FOR GEOGRAPHERS AND PLANNERS
James Killen

THE LAND PROBLEM IN THE DEVELOPED ECONOMY
Andrew H. Dawson

GEOGRAPHY SINCE THE SECOND WORLD WAR
Edited by R.J. Johnston and P. Claval

THE GEOGRAPHY OF WESTERN EUROPE
Paul L. Knox

THE GEOGRAPHY OF UNDERDEVELOPMENT
Dean Forbes

REGIONAL RESTRUCTURING UNDER ADVANCED CAPITALISM
Edited by Phil O'Keefe

MULTINATIONALS AND THE RESTRUCTURING OF THE WORLD ECONOMY
Michael Taylor and Nigel Thrift

THE SPATIAL ORGANISATION OF CORPORATIONS
Ian M. Clarke

THE GEOGRAPHY OF ENGLISH POLITICS
R.J. Johnston

WOMEN ATTACHED: THE DAILY LIVES OF WOMEN WITH YOUNG CHILDREN
Jacqueline Tivers

THE GEOGRAPHY OF HEALTH SERVICES IN BRITAIN
Robin Haynes

POLITICS, GEOGRAPHY AND SOCIAL STRATIFICATION
Edited by Keith Hoggart and Eleonore Kofman

PLANNING IN EASTERN EUROPE
Andrew H. Dawson

PLANNING CONTROL:
Philosophies, Prospects and Practice

Edited by M.L. Harrison and R. Mordey

CROOM HELM
London • Sydney • Wolfeboro, New Hampshire

© 1987 M.L. Harrison and R. Mordey
Croom Helm Ltd, Provident House, Burrell Row,
Beckenham, Kent, BR3 1AT

Croom Helm Australia, 44-50 Waterloo Road,
North Ryde, 2113, New South Wales

British Library Cataloguing in Publication Data

Planning control: philosophies, prospects
   and practice. — (Croom Helm series in
   geography and environment)
   1. Regional planning — England 2. Real
   estate development — England
   I. Harrison, M.L.   II. Mordey, R.
   333.3'8   HT169.G7

ISBN 0-7099-3790-3

Croom Helm, 27 South Main Street,
Wolfeboro, New Hampshire 03894-2069, USA

Library of Congress Cataloging-in-Publication Data

Planning control.
   (Croom Helm series in geography and environment)
   Bibliography: p.
   Includes index.
   1. Land use — Government policy — Great Britain.
2. Real estate development — Government policy — Great
Britain. 3. Regional planning — Government policy — Great
Britain. 4. Land use — Law and legislation — Great
Britain. I. Harrison, M.L. (Malcolm L.) II. Mordey,
R. (Richard) III. Series.
HD596.P53   1987   333.73'17'0941   86-24079
ISBN 0-7099-3790-3

Printed and bound in Great Britain by Mackays of Chatham Ltd, Kent

CONTENTS

The Contributors
Preface by John Finney
Acknowledgements

PART ONE. SETTING THE SCENE

1. INTRODUCTION
   M.L. Harrison 3
2. DEVELOPMENT CONTROL AND THE DEVELOPMENT
   PROCESS: AN INTRODUCTORY REVIEW
   B.J. Pearce 11
3. PROPERTY RIGHTS, PHILOSOPHIES, AND THE
   JUSTIFICATION OF PLANNING CONTROL
   M.L. Harrison 32
4. SOME CURRENT ISSUES IN THE LAW ON
   DEVELOPMENT CONTROL IN ENGLAND AND WALES,
   WITH PARTICULAR REFERENCE TO THE ROLE OF
   THE COURTS AND JUDICIAL REVIEW
   M. Purdue 59
5. DEVELOPMENT CONTROL IN SCOTLAND
   E. Young and J. Rowan-Robinson 73

PART TWO. THE SYSTEM IN OPERATION: SOME
SPECIFIC TOPICS

6. PLANNING GAIN: AN AID TO POSITIVE
   PLANNING?
   I. Simpson 101
7. DESIGN CONTROL
   P. Booth 121
8. PLANNING CONTROL AND THE CONVERSION OF
   PROPERTY FOR SMALL BUSINESS USE
   H. Green and P. Foley 141

9. COMPUTERS IN DEVELOPMENT CONTROL AND
   RESEARCH
   E.J. Judge 160
10. ENFORCEMENT: THE WEAKEST LINK IN THE
   PLANNING CHAIN
   J. Jowell and D. Millichap 175
11. DEVELOPMENT CONTROL, PUBLIC
   PARTICIPATION AND THE NEED FOR
   PLANNING AID
   R. Mordey 195

PART THREE.   SOME ISSUES FOR THE FUTURE

12. CONCLUSIONS AND FUTURE PROSPECTS
    R. Mordey 219

Abbreviations of law reports, etc. 225
Selected readings and sources 227
Index 233

THE CONTRIBUTORS

Philip Booth, Lecturer in the Department of Town and Regional Planning, University of Sheffield
John Finney, Director of Planning, Leeds City Council, and a past president of the Royal Town Planning Institute
Paul Foley, Lecturer in the Department of Town and Regional Planning, University of Sheffield
Howard Green, Senior Lecturer in the Brunswick School of the Environment, Leeds Polytechnic
Malcolm Harrison, Lecturer in the Department of Social Policy and Health Services Studies, University of Leeds
Jeffrey Jowell, Professor of Public Law at University College London
Eamonn Judge, Principal Lecturer in the Brunswick School of the Environment, Leeds Polytechnic
Denzil Millichap, formerly Associate Research Assistant, Department of Law, University College London
Richard Mordey, Planning Consultant in private practice
Barry Pearce, Lecturer in the Department of Land Economy, University of Cambridge
Michael Purdue, Senior Lecturer in Law at the University of East Anglia
Jeremy Rowan-Robinson, Senior Lecturer in Law at the University of Aberdeen
Ian Simpson, Planning Officer with East Kilbride Development Corporation
Eric Young, Senior Lecturer in Law at the University of Strathclyde

NOTE: The opinions expressed by the contributors are personal ones, and do not necessarily represent the views of their employers.

PREFACE

John Finney

Development control is a critical stage at which our land use planning system determines the form and content of our future built environment. It is the 'sharp end' of the very considerable effort which goes into the formulation of development plans and policies by local planning authorities and indeed the work of land assembly and scheme preparation carried out by the development industry. Thus it is the area where planners are in the closest contact with the communities they serve, and with the many different types of development agency and the architects, surveyors and builders carrying out their work.
     The importance of this activity has been reflected in the creation of the National Development Control Forum, with membership drawn from both central and local government, concerned to consider with other interested parties - including the professions and the development industries - practical problems in the operation of development control and allied functions under Town and Country Planning legislation. The Forum has been instrumental in putting the views of those involved in development control at the 'coal face' to central government on many contemporary issues and proposals for changes and modifications to the system. It has also taken a major initiative with its 'Time for Design' experiment, which seeks to show how close co-operation between those involved in planning and the design of new building can bring a better quality of built environment to our urban communities. There are also Local Development Control Forums with similar membership looking at the way the process operates within our geographic County areas.
     There have also been a number of national

Preface

reports covering various aspects of development control in recent years, including the Royal Town Planning Institute's own <u>Development Control into the 1980s</u> (RTPI, London, 1979) which recognised that there was a need to disseminate information on good practice and improved management techniques, and that planning education should ensure an understanding of the development control process. The Institute's Working Party expressed particular anxiety that the roles and rights of those participants in the planning process - the applicant, the public and the Planning Authority - should be recognised and reflected in the way they interact with each other. I hope and trust that this volume will help to extend this understanding more widely.

Despite all this work there has been a notable gap in the literature available to both practitioners and students dealing with the many complex issues involved in the development control process. Malcolm Harrison and Richard Mordey, having recognised the importance of this omission have, together with their colleague authors, produced a volume that I welcome and commend to all those involved in any aspect of the planning process. Indeed I hope that it will do much to develop a better understanding of our development control framework and the opportunities it offers to ensure a good living and working environment in our towns, cities and villages for today's communities and as a heritage for future generations.

ACKNOWLEDGEMENTS

We would like to thank all those who have given advice on individual chapters, and Gill Harrison for detecting errors in the text. As editors we are grateful to our fellow contributors for their hard work and co-operation, and for their tolerance of our suggestions for cuts and amendments. Finally, we wish to thank Jane Welsh for her excellent work in preparing the manuscript for publication.

Malcolm Harrison
Richard Mordey

Part One

SETTING THE SCENE

Chapter 1

INTRODUCTION

Malcolm L. Harrison

AIMS AND SCOPE

Although there is an extensive literature concerned with land use planning in Britain, planning control itself remains a relatively neglected topic. Many of the most detailed and instructive publications on the subject have been designed primarily for legal audiences, or relate to highly specific research projects. This is not to suggest that academic planners and social scientists have ignored planning control as a general topic, for a number of books and reports in recent years have dealt with it directly or indirectly.[1] There have also been important central government enquiries into aspects of planning control.[2] Nonetheless, there is at present no text or reader wide-ranging enough to be of broad interest, which at the same time could offer some insights into the concrete concerns of current law, administration and practice. The aim for the present volume is to help fill this gap, with newly-written essays covering a wide range of topics. It is especially important to have such material in an easily-accessible form now, because there is so much political debate taking place about this field. We hope the collection will be helpful for students of planning, land economy, surveying, architecture, law, geography, and politics. It will also find a wider audience among people who practise in related areas.
 The book is in three sections. Part One sets the scene, Part Two covers several specific topics, and Part Three provides a brief concluding comment. Our scene-setting begins in the present chapter, with an overview of development control in the period since 1947. This is designed particularly for readers new to the subject. Pearce follows this

Introduction

with a review of the British literature, constructing his analysis around a series of issues that have long been prominent in debates about planning. The third chapter is an essay on property rights, giving a philosophical background for the volume. This is the only 'theory' essay in the collection, and some undergraduates may find it complex, but its purpose is simple: to deflate some of planning's more pretentious critics! Two more specific pieces follow. First, Purdue examines some current legal developments, with particular reference to judicial review processes. Then, in Chapter 5, Young and Rowan-Robinson explain the situation in Scotland, making clear the distinctive features of development control there.

Part Two is inevitably selective, for no book on planning control could hope to be comprehensive as far as individual topics are concerned. Indeed, for this reason we very much hope to be able to edit a second volume, with a stronger 'practice' emphasis, at some time in the future.[3] Nonetheless, the contributions cover a great deal of ground. We begin with two very contentious issues. First, Simpson writes about 'planning gain', considering the case for and against. Secondly, Booth reviews the history, basis and practice of design control. This is followed by an analysis of some problems related to industrial development control: Green and Foley include case study material in this chapter. Chapter 9, by Judge, then discusses computer analysis in relation to planning control and planning-related research. In Chapter 10 Jowell and Millichap focus on the issue of enforcement, dealing with a number of problems and reform possibilities. Finally, Mordey concludes this section of the book with an essay on planning aid. Part Three then rounds off the volume with some observations about development control's future, and about planning education in this sphere.

What is offered here is a collection of essays, but not the work of 'a collective'. The views of contributors are varied, and the editors have not imposed any common style or political orientation. We hope that this variety will ensure vitality, and give every reader things both to agree and disagree with. Even so, there are some general lessons to be learned from the volume as a whole. Readers will see that land planning is a complex matter, and in present circumstances sometimes necessarily so. Development control issues deserve detailed study,

Introduction

and little is to be gained by imagining that the system can suddenly be swept away 'at a stroke', without many adverse consequences. At a time when town and country planning's future seems less certain politically than in the 1960s and 1970s, what is required is a 'taking stock' exercise, not a resort to political rhetoric. There is scope for improvements, but this does not imply that the present system is without merits.

DEVELOPMENT CONTROL AND ITS SIGNIFICANCE

The public control of development and land use change lies at the heart of town and country planning operations in Britain. A large part of day-to-day planning has always revolved around decision-making related to the processing of planning applications by local planning authorities. Negotiations may take place, and judgements are made on these applications, which are submitted by developers varying from individual householders to large companies. The term development control has been used for many years to describe the activities whereby applications for permission to develop or change the use of land and buildings are considered by planning department staff, and other persons, and decisions issued. The definition of the field referred to generally as development control, 'D.C.', or 'control', has normally also extended to include certain central government activity, and in particular the consideration of planning appeals.

In making decisions planners and elected representatives have needed to have regard to development plans, and to other relevant documents and policies, but there has always been an element of administrative or political discretion. Plans have by no means been all-important. In some ways, indeed, perhaps the planning system developed less around the preparation and implementation of approved plans, than around the need to take development control decisions. The real basis of the 1947 system was the application for planning permission which was necessary before development, and permission was required equally before and after a plan had been approved.[4] Of course the position was always complicated by exceptions, by the legal precision required in defining terms like 'development' and 'change of use', and by the ability of central government to vary the incidence of the far-reaching control powers by regulation or

Introduction

order within limitations defined by statute. Nevertheless, the need to obtain permission applied for a vast range of development activities. In some spheres special legal and administrative arrangements were made to supplement ordinary development control, as in the cases of advertisements, or buildings of historical or architectural interest. As a whole the system can be characterised as a regulatory one of a fairly comprehensive kind, with a degree of flexibility built into it. As far as central government was concerned there was scope for overseeing or varying major policies, and some possibility of restricting or channelling local administrative discretions when desired. The adaptability of the system has proved considerable, since regulatory control has remained a persistent element in land planning throughout the post-war period. The nature of planning control work may well have widened in scope and deepened in sophistication since 1947, but the basic tasks have retained a large measure of continuity. The decisions issued have had consequences for rural conservation, for physical change in towns, for the character of developments, and for property values and economic returns.

PLANNING CONTROL 1947-1986: CONTINUITY AND TENSIONS

From the earliest years British land use planning relied upon moderating development forces more than on generating or directing them. There has been closer political agreement about regulation than over more direct forms of intervention (through compulsory purchase, municipalisation, New Towns, etc.). As the keystone of land development regulation, therefore, development control has attracted continuing support, at least as a general idea.

The regulatory approach had its basis well before the 1947 Town and Country Planning Act, since the development control arrangements of the 1940s were built upon inter-war experiences. In effect some established ideas of regulatory planning were fed into the wider notions that gained acceptance immediately after the war. At this time there was a broadening of the concept of town and country planning from regulative 'schemes' to a more positive instrument of purposive action.[5] Land planning was to operate in a context of considerable direct state involvement with development, so that

Introduction

development control perhaps appeared relatively unimportant.[6]

In later years, with directive state intervention apparently in decline, the regulatory aspects of planning assumed more prominence. It became clear that whatever degree of political consensus might exist at the level of general statements, there were potentially deep differences over the purposes, outcomes and processes of control. The distributional consequences, the power wielded by local authorities, and the environmental results, all gradually came to be seen as significant matters.[7] Certainly there was evidence of difficulties for some of the participants. McAuslan notes, for instance, a process of increased judicialisation in the years before 1965, leading to increasing delay and slowness in the planning machine.[8]

By the mid-1960s there were pressures for changes in the land planning system, and the advent of a Labour government led to significant legislation. Nonetheless, development control itself remained relatively undisturbed. Some of the changes in this period deserve mention. Particularly for conservation, countryside planning, and public participation, important alterations occurred. The changes in the development plans system, moreover, were substantial. At local level an influential feature of evolving professional thinking was the idea of 'environmental area' planning, and there also seemed to be more interest in positive long-term environmental management. For control itself, legislation at the end of the decade altered the appeals system to enable the minister to delegate some responsibilities for decisions to inspectors. Arrangements for buildings of special architectural or historic interest were changed, provision was made for formal delegation to officers by councillors, a time limit was introduced for permissions, and changes were made in control over statutory undertakers and office development. In addition a new inquiry procedure, involving Planning Inquiry Commissions, was introduced, to be used when development raised considerations of national or regional importance or presented unfamiliar technical or scientific aspects which merited a special inquiry.[9] Despite all this, however, the basic control system remained much as it had been since 1947.

During the 1970s politicians still did not differ markedly over the necessity for development

Introduction

control as such (by contrast Labour's policies for interventions via ownership of development land met strong opposition). Local government reorganisation was important, however, as was the arrival of the ombudsman on the planning scene.[10] Government also made efforts to relax controls over detail, towards and after the end of the decade.[11] Nevertheless, none of these changes were fundamental. Even the Conservative government of 1979, with its concern to reduce restrictions on private firms, did not initially move very far from the traditional system. In the present period new Acts have been passed,[12] 'together with a host of new subordinate legislation and administrative circulars'.[13] Yet even with enterprise zones, freeports, urban development corporations, simplified planning zones and other radical ideas, development control remains intact, although modified. Its future, however, is not as secure as it once seemed.

Despite the continuity of the regulatory system, there have been frequent disagreements about how it should run, and over its adaptation to varying ends. Questions have been raised about the extent to which socio-economic goals should be sought, about bargaining for 'planning gain', about third party rights and about exemptions from control. Conflicts have arisen over the balance between professional power, public participation, private capital interests, and political representation. There has also been tension between the idea of planning control as a set of once-for-all decisions related to applications, and as a longer-term managerial activity. Even the application of physical standards has not been entirely uncontentious, particularly as regards requirements which have appeared expensive or subjective. A favourite target for critics has been aesthetic control. Finally it is worth mentioning enforcement, where there have long been difficulties.

Some of the chapters later in this book touch upon specific issues mentioned above. It should be said, however, that many of the day-to-day problems experienced by officers, amenity groups and developers relate in reality to rather deep-seated conflicts of interest inherent in the regulatory approach or the way it has been shaped by governments and lawyers. The intensity of some conflicts results partly from the distributional consequences of decisions, which indirectly confer,

Introduction

maintain or remove financial benefits and power over the environment. Perhaps it is because of the significance of its results that development control's history has been characterised both by continuity and by tensions.[14]

NOTES

1. See J.B. McLoughlin, Control and Urban Planning (Faber and Faber, London, 1973); P. Hall, H. Gracey, R. Drewett and R. Thomas, The Containment of Urban England, Volume 2, The Planning System: objectives, operations, impacts (Political and Economic Planning, George Allen and Unwin, Sage, London, 1973); J. Simmie, Power, Property and Corporatism (Macmillan, London, 1981); J. Underwood, 'Development control: a review of research and current issues', Progress in Planning, 16, 3 (1981), pp. 179-242; M.L. Harrison, Land Planning and Development Control, Research Monograph (Department of Social Policy and Administration, University of Leeds, 1979). See also footnote 14, below.
2. G. Dobry, Review of the Development Control System, Final Report (Department of the Environment and Welsh Office, HMSO, London, 1975); Department of the Environment, Scottish Development Department and Welsh Office, Planning Control over Mineral Working (HMSO, London, 1976); see also House of Commons Expenditure Committee, Eighth Report, Planning Procedures, Volume 1, Report, Session 1976-77 (HMSO, London, 1977).
3. Ideally the present collection would be followed by companion volumes covering further topics: buildings conservation, development and ethnic minorities, rural control, office development, mineral workings, etc.
4. See Ministry of Town and Country Planning, Town and Country Planning Act, 1947, Explanatory Memorandum (MTCP, HMSO, London, 1947), Part I, para. 15.
5. J.B. Cullingworth, Environmental Planning 1939 - 1969, Volume 1, Reconstruction and land use planning 1939-1947 (HMSO, London, 1975), p. xi.
6. See comments in Hall, et al., op. cit., p. 390.
7. One of the earliest critical comments on the system is R. Glass, 'Planning in practice: an inquiry into the control of "development"', The Times (13th January 1954), p. 7.
8. J.P.W.B. McAuslan, 'The Plan, the

9

Planners and the Lawyers', *Public Law* (Winter 1971), pp. 253, 257. See also M. Grant, *Urban Planning Law* (Sweet and Maxwell, London, 1982), pp. 610-11, etc.

    9. D. Heap, *The New Town Planning Procedures* (Sweet and Maxwell, London, 1968), p. 85. For recent history see Grant, op. cit., pp. 601-7.

    10. Grant, op. cit., pp. 197, 254-6: R. Williams, 'Local planning and the Ombudsman', *The Planner*, 63, 3 (May 1977), pp. 78-80; R. Hammersley, 'The Local Ombudsman and his Impact on Planning', *The Planner*, 66, 1 (January/February 1980), pp. 10-11, 27.

    11. See discussion in Grant, op. cit., pp. 145-8.

    12. Local Government, Planning and Land Act, 1980; Town and Country Planning (Minerals) Act, 1981; Local Government and Planning (Amendment) Act, 1981; Wildlife and Countryside Act, 1981; see also Minister without Portfolio, *Lifting the Burden*, Cmnd. 9571 (HMSO, London, 1985).

    13. Grant, op. cit., p. 1.

    14. In June 1986 (after completion of the final draft for the present volume) a new publication was announced which deserves noting. Oxford Polytechnic and the Royal Town Planning Institute are publishing a set of study units under the title *Development Control. A Manual*. Their package is aimed particularly at 'continuing professional development', but it will also help meet the more general need for study material on development control. We hope that practitioners using the units will find that our book complements the manual.

Chapter 2

DEVELOPMENT CONTROL AND THE DEVELOPMENT PROCESS: AN INTRODUCTORY REVIEW

Barry J. Pearce

INTRODUCTION

This chapter offers a brief introduction to the British literature on the effects development control has on the private sector. As development control is now very much under attack as an instrument of government activity, many of the recent contributions either question its usefulness, or else have been stimulated to provide some defence against this attack.[1] The private-sector orientation of the government, perceived failures of past planning control, and the 'democratisation' of planning have all added weight to the challenge being made. One group of critics claims that the basic structure of development control is at fault, whilst another argues that the system is fundamentally sound but needs to be adapted to fit contemporary problems and opportunities. The government itself, and Parliament, have both played a major part in the process of re-appraisal. The Dobry review was followed by an investigation stemming from a Parliamentary Expenditure Committee, and then by a series of initiatives, policy statements and reforms, especially after 1979.[2] Now that the emphasis is on reducing disincentive effects on private entrepreneurship, attacks on development control present it particularly as a constraint on property development and, in consequence, economic advance. Despite all the interest, however, little rigorous research has been carried out on the consequences of development control. The sections below will consider how far the available literature makes possible an evaluation of the kinds of arguments and counter-claims that are prominent in current debates.

An Introductory Review

THE QUESTION OF DELAY

Some especially important assertions concern delay. Development control procedures are held to be so inefficient, inflexible and sluggish that they cause unjustifiable and damaging delays, by local authorities and by the inspectorate on appeal. Developers argue that delays are costly to their industry, producing extra 'holding' costs and a wastage of capital, and hence costly for the economy as a whole (through delayed production and postponed employment, income, rates and taxes). Various reasons are offered to explain this situation.[3] The machinery is said to be 'clogged up' with large numbers of small-scale or unimportant applications (such as those concerning householder developments like extensions). The development plan framework is thought to be incomplete and often out-of-date, and thus incapable of providing immediate guidance. Excessive consideration is believed to be given to trivial or subjective aspects (especially aesthetics). Planning authorities are said to be poorly managed (perhaps with infrequent committee meetings, inadequate delegation to sub-committees and officers, and inefficient clerical procedures). There is supposedly a lack of appreciation that to a developer time is money. There is thought to be an excessive concern to involve the general public. Local authorities are seen as frequently insisting on lengthy negotiations, before and after an application is made, sometimes changing their views during this process. Authorities are said to engage in unnecessary consultations with other public and semi-official bodies. Staff may be incompetent. Finally, delay is thought to be used as a means of applying pressure to encourage applicants to agree to changes they otherwise might resist.

In response to such claims the Dobry report was sympathetic, the Expenditure Committee was positive, and the present government has been supportive. For almost every assertion about delays, however, can be found some kind of rebuttal, especially from local authorities and their associations. Development control is seen as a relatively unimportant source of costly delay, and when it does hold things up there is said to be good reason. Authorities are said to have worked hard to improve management of their caseloads over recent years. It is held that comprehensiveness is important: often the fine detail can be the obstacle to achieving an overall public interest in the pattern of development. On

An Introductory Review

public participation, the defence is made that where public as well as private interests are involved, participation is now unavoidable in a democratic society. Indeed, it is noted that the scope for participation is not all that broad. In some countries (by contrast), third parties may have rights of objection to the grant of planning permission (see Chapter 11). On consultations, the argument is put that delay reflects the complexity and sensitivity of many proposals. Schemes in areas of heritage landscape or affecting listed buildings, and proposals that are departures from approved plans, are bound to take time to assess. In many instances it is in any case the consultees who are slow to provide their comments or give positive advice. Lastly, blame may be placed on applicants themselves. The Association of District Councils (ADC), for example, has suggested that between 40% and 60% of proposals are characterised by inept, invalid and incomplete applications, an ignorance of well-publicised policies and requirements, and changes of mind by developers. Moreover, delays frequently occur which have little to do with planning authorities, and are often far more important than the effects of planning control. Downturns in demand, problems in getting development land released by landowners, in financing completion of development, and in construction, and changes of ownership, can and all do lengthen the process of development.[4]

Only recently has much independent research begun to tackle these issues,[5] and quite often more information has only stimulated new unanswered questions. Sometimes evidence is apparently contradictory: thus one study of design guidance[6] notes that clear design standards and policies do not necessarily reduce the amount of time-consuming local authority/developer negotiation or lead to a pattern of clearly-conforming approvals and contrary refusals that may expedite proceedings, whilst another study has suggested that clearer development plan policies would reduce the time taken up by informal contacts and unacceptable applications.[7] On other occasions antagonists and supporters of planning control can both take cheer from the same findings, depending on how the facts are interpreted. On delegation to officers, for example, it is difficult to say exactly what importance should be placed on the findings of one ADC survey that 58% of officers were able to clear over 80% of their delegated applications within

13

eight weeks, but in the same period only 28% could determine 90% of their caseload.[8] Likewise, many of the findings on delays caused by applicants might equally be interpreted as a failure on behalf of local authorities to produce satisfactory guidance and information.

There are indeed difficulties in interpreting the evidence. First, there is the problem of defining exactly what is meant by an 'over-long' period for making a decision. Most of the literature concentrates on the time from when the application is received to when the applicant is informed of the decision. But delay can take place before an application (in pre-application negotiations) and after a decision (on appeal).

Second, there are difficulties in measuring the extent of 'delay' caused by inefficient control procedures when other 'causes' are occurring at the same time. It is possible that administrative inefficiency does not have a determining effect at all: that even substantial improvements to planning control procedures would make no noticeable difference to the time taken for a development proposal to go from inception to completion, because of other factors. The ADC has attempted to quantify causes of delay by noting the proportions of applications affected by various possible factors (for example in their 1978-9 survey they found 24% of applications were affected - 'delayed' - by committee cycles and member site visits).[9] But this does not allow any measure of the lag caused by each factor: a particular reason may occur in several cases but only lead to very small overall delays, and 'planning delay' may occur at exactly the same time as another source of delay.

Third, there may be 'planning delays' that are justifiable. Delay whilst the authority negotiates to improve an application may be an alternative to a refusal, and result in less wasted time for the developer. Some studies, also,[10] have supported the view that apparently excessive assessment periods are associated with genuinely controversial and complex development proposals (where consultations and advertising are needed and where objections are likely and need to be paid due regard). Whether delay is an important problem depends partly on the perspective chosen. Some have argued that a most important role for development control is to provide a neighbour protection or environmental policing service, adjudicating between private interests (and not just attempting to secure

An Introductory Review

a wider 'public interest'). Certainly, minor and small-scale developments can prove controversial, as witnessed by the findings of many appeal inquiries and ombudsman hearings. Some 33% of ombudsman findings of maladministration over the period 1976-7 to 1978-9 related to planning, and 36% of these came in the category of failing to consult third parties.[11] Whilst involvement of the public may add to delay, it can be interpreted as a benefit in making decision-making more democratic (and there is some evidence to support the view that even where the 'public' are involved it is not all that comprehensive an involvement[12]). In short, performance cannot be measured in time alone.

A final point is that only a limited amount of work has been done on the way developers themselves react to problems of delay in order to lessen their extent.[13] Even less is known on the costs to developers of adopting such preventative tactics. Studies have been made of the extent to which developers accumulate 'land banks', and whether these represent speculative/investment purchases or attempts to plan continuity of operation.[14] Thus between 1977-80 housebuilders held a minimum of approximately 1.7 years supply of land with planning permission[15] (with only larger developers being able to afford to maintain any sort of land bank of this kind). But really these studies have only been made with regard to residential developers, and no-one seems to have looked very closely at whether or not developers make multiple applications or utilise options and conditional contracts.[16] Some data are also available on the time taken with outline planning applications, indicating that little is to be gained by their use to reduce the costs associated with delay.[17] But only one or two studies have asked if some developers manage their overall direct relationships with the development control machine better than others; though Short et al.[18], after some empirical research, have produced a simple classification of developers (in this case housebuilders) based on success rates in securing planning permission and the degree to which they probe and explore the limits of planning.

An overall conclusion to be drawn on delays is that the issue is more complex than many people realise or are prepared to admit. In certain cases costly delays are caused by avoidable administrative inefficiency. Anecdotal but nevertheless real instances in support of this finding are readily available.[19] It is questionable, however, to assume that this reflects a general problem. Individual complaints should not be taken as conclusive evidence, since developers' perceptions of difficulties may rest on unrealistic expectations about time-scales, consultations, etc. To speed up the process, the Dobry approach, of setting up an expeditious appraisal route for small-scale and uncontroversial applications (probably combined with deemed approval after a specified time-period if no alternative action is taken) seems preferable to excluding developments from control altogether.[20] More delegation to officers also might be justifiable: an Audit Inspectorate study has established that more effective delegation can have a role in speeding up decisions.[21] There seems room for improvement, too, in consultation procedures with statutory authorities[22] (although progress may have been made here: for instance the National Development Control Forum's code of practice, introduced in 1980): a recent Scottish study has shown that consultations treated in series rather than concurrently are a particular problem.[23] There also appears to be scope for improvement through simpler and clearer forms and planning documents, progress-chasing mechanisms, etc. The Audit Inspectorate's work emphasised the importance of good management practices and clerical procedures.[24] There is little direct evidence on the likely effects the award of costs might have, as a means of persuading local authorities to act more swiftly.

One relevant idea attracting attention at the moment is that of making control decisions on the basis of plans alone. The Simplified Planning Zone idea is the latest variant (see below).

UNCERTAINTY AND DEVELOPMENT CONTROL

A second focus for criticism is the uncertainty faced by developers as a result of development control. This creates difficulties for their long-term planning, and increases risks of waste and failure. Discretionary powers are seen as crucial. Development control decisions inevitably often rest on informal (unpublished) documents and 'other material considerations', rather than on published plans, and as local authorities favour vague policy statements (to maximise flexibility and keep open opportunities for public participation), developers cannot easily predict whether a particular proposal

An Introductory Review

is likely to be approved. Effort has to be wasted in unsuccessful applications, or in lengthy discussions with officers (who often do not in any case make the final decision). Added to this, some have argued, is the problem of pluralistic decision-taking. Control officials may see things differently from plan-makers, and from councillors, and those deciding appeals see things differently again. Thus advice, and even the decisions made in development control, quite often do not seem 'authoritative' or final for quite a while: developers are left not knowing where they stand until and unless their applications are actually approved.

Research has thrown some light on uncertainty problems, although sometimes only indirectly. Some studies have shown that a large proportion of decisions made on applications are not covered by policies in development plans - Pountney and Kingsbury found the proportion varying between 24% and 51% in six case studies they conducted[25] - so that presumably developers have an inadequate policy framework within which to predict responses. Research by Bruton and Nicholson[26] has shown how the use of non-statutory plans and forms of development guidance has been growing, with the consequent danger of increased confusion as to what plans are in force. The literature suggests that development controllers are rarely in a position to ensure certainty, plans never become a really firm constraint, and all parties tend to collude to find ways of by-passing plan requirements.[27] The study of design guidance by Llewelyn Davies et al.[28] found that clear policies and standards (in this case related to design) do not necessarily reduce the amount of negotiation with developers, a finding seemingly confirmed by observation of the implementation of Enterprise Zone plans.[29] A study by Blacksell and Gilg of the implementation of an AONB established that even where the local authority had clear policies they often allowed developments that were not in line with their prescriptions.[30]

The picture is not clear-cut, however, for research on the implementation of an AONB by Anderson, and on National Park policies by Brotherton,[31] have noted instances where firm plans _have_ been adhered to. Moreover, a few studies have interpreted the absence of a speculative market in land (especially by contrast with the United States) as a reasonably good indicator of 'the

17

certainty created by the planning system'.[32]
Drawing conclusions from available research,[33] we may note a number of planning-related variables which influence the degree to which plans provide a context of reasonable 'certainty'. Firstly, whether or not plans and policies are well thought out and relevant to current issues. Secondly, the existence (or not) of a firm political will to implement plans. Thirdly, the extent to which plans are realistic in terms of what the power to control can achieve. Fourthly, the degree to which authorities seek negotiation. Fifthly, the division of power to control development, amongst different participants. Sixthly, vagueness of policy statements. Seventhly, the degree to which decisions are (or can be) enforced. Lastly, the rapidity of changes in the law 'backing up' control. It is however one thing knowing what the relevant factors are, but of course quite another establishing their importance in varying circumstances. On the fifth point, for instance, the significance of variations should not be over-stated: Fleming and Short have found in a case study a large measure of consistency between planners and politicians on control decisions, with only a very small proportion of officer recommendations being reversed.[34]

Whatever reservations might be suggested by the data, critics nonetheless readily come forward with proposals for 'reforms'. Perhaps the most controversial here is for a shift away from administrative discretion to an approach characterised by developers assessing for themselves whether permission is granted by 'development order', without the need for planning consent via an application. The regimes in Enterprise Zones (EZ) and in the proposed Simplified Planning Zones are along these lines. Although it is early days with respect to the EZ model, some difficulties and 'unforeseen' consequences have already been noted. The EZ approach may not reduce the extent of negotiations with developers. It denies the opportunity for public participation at the plan implementation stage (and at plan formulation stage since there is no need for a survey or local inquiry). It does not appear to reduce staffing requirements, for it decreases the caseload but increases the number of advice/informal contacts officers have to engage in. In the long run, it has been asserted, it is likely to reduce the ability of local authorities to tailor conditions and planning

An Introductory Review

standards to the new kinds of development that will inevitably arise (because local authorities will always have to change the planning scheme after some developments have gone through, and yet changing the scheme itself may prove difficult). It will also reduce the leverage that discretion allows to extract planning gains (planning agreements depending on the ability to say 'no').[35] Some of the problems have been exaggerated: there is provision for example in the EZ 'planning scheme' to define exceptions to the 'blanket' planning permission, and by all accounts this has been used quite readily by local authorities involved.[36] Only a few of the problems, moreover, have much to do with what is intrinsic in the 'zoning' approach. Most of the force of the criticisms could be dissipated if there was provision for frequently reviewing and where necessary revising the planning scheme, if designation was based on a survey and/or some kind of an inquiry, and if automatically-permitted developments could be linked with planning gain requirements. One possibility along the same lines as this, though perhaps limited in its application, has been put forward: that of allowing local authorities themselves to make (and thus approve) planning applications on land which is not under their ownership.[37]

STANDARDS, CONDITIONS, AND AGREEMENTS

Critics also argue that development control leads, through imposition of various 'standards', to extra direct costs for approved schemes. Control can for instance alter layouts or materials used, and can even mean additional building work. Through planning agreements open space can be dedicated to public use, extra community benefits and public infrastructure can be provided, and use of a building can be more tightly controlled.[38] All this is said to raise development costs, thus reducing profits and the capacity of the industry to meet both need and demand: the extra costs may even put at risk development going ahead.[39] One particular part of this argument relates to aesthetic control; that is dealt with at length in Chapter 7.

One noticeable gap in the literature relates to the quantitative assessment of the use of conditions and planning agreements. Jowell[40] completed a survey of 28% of development control authorities in

1977, and found that about half had achieved from developers certain planning 'gains' (gains which were not in the original applications), via the use of conditions and various forms of agreement. But that figure says little about the extent of their use, and is now out of date. There is little evidence on the proportion of developments that are subjected to such 'impositions'. There have been small-scale and local studies - for example, Henry's study[41] in a Berkshire district (where 'agreements' applied to less than 2% of full applications) - but several questions remain unanswered. For instance, is their use mainly on the more major developments, in the South-East? Also, how far do conditions and agreements actually make developers alter their schemes substantially? (On this point there is some evidence to suggest that local authorities use standard lists of conditions irrespective of whether or not the application already conforms to them[42].) Certainly no research has been conducted on the number of cases in which conditions and agreements have meant that development does not proceed: presumably if it does, the developer must still feel it is profitable. Indeed the presumption that a planning agreement always imposes a cost on the developer is open to doubt. Henry's study found that developers often obtain some benefit out of the exchange - for example phasing of the scheme in with other projects - which would have been difficult to achieve otherwise.

Another research question which has been largely ignored, concerning cases where a cost *is* involved, is its actual value and economic incidence.[43] Conventional economic theory would probably suggest that in the long run, although developers are the ones who directly meet the extra costs, they effectively pass them on, especially backwards to the landowner in the form of lower land prices. Others would suggest, however, that developers pass them forwards, in increased prices to the consumer (such as the owner-occupier in the case of housing).[44]

RESTRICTIONS ON THE ABILITY TO MEET NEEDS AND DEMANDS

Further claims about development control focus on its power actually to refuse applications, and its inflexible procedures which have a similar effect.

An Introductory Review

It is held to refuse too many desirable developments for trivial or suspect reasons. It resists hypermarket schemes which really pose little threat to established retail centres. It releases insufficient 'green-field' housing land in areas of development demand, thus intensifying pressures where development is allowed, and increasing house prices. The land it does release is inappropriate, or not actually available (perhaps because landowners do not wish to see it developed).[45] In addition, through tightly-demarcated land use categories, permission is only given for development capable of being assigned to very specific (dominant) use classes, so that multi-use developments are held up. The supply of premises for 'high-tech' firms, for instance, has been inhibited, apparently, because such schemes feature a combination of uses which vary over time and which the Use Classes Order cannot handle[46] (see Chapter 8). Critics vary in their views of causation with these various problems. To some, planning and markets are simply incompatible.[47]

Once more, however, responses may be found in the literature. With regard to insufficient land release, perhaps the most usual defence is that tight control in some areas (and of certain developments) is necessary to protect vulnerable environments and to ensure that everyone has reasonable physical access to the kind of location being protected. The point is also often made (though not very often explicitly in the literature) that control does not normally place a total ban on development, but shifts its location, so that usually (and especially where development demand is not highly locationally-specific) the demand for development is still being met. Thus even where green belts are in use, development just 'across the border' is allowed, and the slight disadvantages caused by increased commuting costs and house prices are outweighed by the gains of environmental protection. Indeed there can be benefits if development is channelled into areas or forms where it would not normally occur (inner cities, rehabilitation etc.). Furthermore, not everyone accepts that somehow commercial schemes mean desirable economic development. Property developments can lead to over-supply of some facilities (for instance offices), yet under-supply of others (for example leisure facilities), even in the strictest of efficiency terms.[48] Schemes have social as well as private costs and benefits.

21

Outcomes can include pollution, congestion, and sometimes consumer frustration.[49]
 Quite often the argument is put that development control is flexible enough to ensure that it does not refuse proposals which will lead to economic benefits. Indeed, it is suggested, it would be folly today to turn away economic activity, even in the most prosperous of areas.[50] Be that as it may, in one study Sillince found that refusal rates for industrial applications were not significantly associated with local unemployment levels.[51] On the inhibiting effect of tightly-demarcated land use categories the most usual defence is that control rarely goes to such an extreme. In the majority of cases the control of development is in terms of the principal use, allowing for uses which are incidental to the main purpose. Even with 'high-tech' developments the principal use on most sites is likely to be industry, and so storage, office, and research uses (no matter what proportion of the building they occupy) are likely to be subservient in function and hence ancillary uses which do not need to be specifically permitted.[52]
 On the more general issue that development control is negative and restrictive, one response is that it is actually quite positive, including identification of latent development opportunities, however apparently-depressed the area concerned.[53] Control prevents the best development opportunities being pre-empted or ruined by poor-quality schemes, enables easier land assembly, and so forth. Quite often partnerships with private enterprise have been worked out.[54] Furthermore, there is a view that the private sector needs the planning system. As one commentator has put it recently, private developers and investors need 'the assurance of a regulated land system, involving the allocation of development rights'.[55] Certainly on the issue of housing land availability it has been claimed that the volume builders want some but not too much land released, and they want it for themselves; for too much competition would cut into profit margins.[56]
 Nonetheless, studies have revealed that planning authorities are often poor at anticipating fluctuations in market demand. They 'respond to pressure but inevitably this is constrained by manpower and by the difficulty of coping with a higher proportion of non-conforming applications'[57] when pressure exerts itself. A West Midlands study of land released for housing

developments between 1968 and 1973 found that 38% of the land area released was not allocated for residential development in development plans prior to the submission of planning applications.[58] But even here there are problems. Is this last finding to be interpreted as showing how out of touch plans are, or how flexible control is in dealing with changed circumstances?

It is important to appreciate, also, that a number of 'obstacles' to development initiatives lie outside development control altogether. One relates to reasons for landholding, and especially the 'recalcitrance' of landowners in releasing development land. Various non-commercial motives and procedures on the part of landowners have been identified as helping to 'stall' the development process: 'control' and 'succession' motives, where the principal reason for owning land is to influence its use for the benefit of other land held by the same owner or for the benefit of the owner's family; lack of awareness of the real (opportunity) costs of holding land, exacerbated by poor techniques of land valuation; neglectful attitudes to investment management; and practices which encourage landowners to react not to opportunity costs of landownership but merely to its strict 'accounting' costs (such that low historic costs of purchase are taken as holding costs). In addition, landowners may wish to hold onto land in order to expand their premises at some time in the future, or so that they can conduct preferred activities on it (as with farming). And they may not want to release land because of the costs of regaining full control over sites let out to various users, because the proceeds of sale would not immediately benefit themselves, or because they feel the land they possess has a chance of being developed in the future, and yet this is not reflected in current market value.

Financial problems have been noted too, for example constraints on availability of credit from building societies for house purchases, and fluctuations in availability of institutional funds for commercial schemes.[59] Site preparation and construction problems have also been mentioned, especially with regard to small sites.[60]

Research on the inner city has found planning control to be a factor in the development process, but not an over-riding constraint. More important have been other influences, especially those relating to public sector land ownership.[61] On 'green-field' sites the planning machine has been considered more important, but even here other factors intervene. As well as those already mentioned there may be poor availability of infrastructure (some arguing that Water Authorities have been especially important). When a large number of these 'other' factors apply, developers can lack the experience necessary to tackle what have been previously-doubtful development opportunities, when the objective constraints become less important: although, at least in relation to inner city development, writers have also questioned the existence of a strong enough pattern of demand to maintain developers' interest.[62]

CONCLUDING COMMENTS

One underlying message of this chapter has been that many criticisms of development control may be unjustified, often because the development process is more complicated than critics assume. Of course some reforms could improve development control's operation and results, and this is so even though different people clearly want differing things from land use planning. These conclusions, however, do not tell us whether the system merits support <u>in principle</u>. To know that, one would need also to evaluate feasible alternatives. Only a few authors have explored seriously the merits of genuine alternative options.[63]

To conclude, a comment is required on the politics of development control, for the system does not operate in a vacuum. Several writings have touched on the influences upon it of 'sectional interests', including specific class groupings, local government professions, businesses and so forth.[64] This has not been the focus for the present review, but it is worth noting that actors involved in development may themselves influence control outputs. It has been suggested, for instance, that developers might use land banks, and the power to withhold development, to extort concessions from planners (particularly in depressed areas). Or developers can simply batter authorities with numerous applications in hopes that they will give way. The JURUE study noted earlier found that developers submit a considerable number of applications for housing on land not allocated by local authorities for that purpose, and a proportion of land eventually released for housing is not marked out for that use in development plans.[65]

The threat of appeal may also be used as a lever to obtain a permission. Another study has suggested that land and buildings may be left vacant, and property allowed to deteriorate, in order effectively to 'blackmail' planning authorities into giving permissions.[66] In addition property interests may be directly represented on planning committees, and may also be able to lobby governments directly.

Such findings need to be set in a wider political context, in which various interest groups compete for influence. Rydin's study (related to housing land), for example, has identified a number of organised lobby groups - large and small housebuilders, rural and suburban landowners, local government, the professions, promotional groups and the environmental lobby - showing how these were involved.[67] Some writers emphasise class, others note a range of types of organised interests. In some instances participants have secured the 'right' to be involved in decision-making: indeed, rather than conflict, there may even be tendencies for officer/developer convergence.[68] A full evaluation of development control of course would need to take account of such possibilities, as well as appraising the more 'technical' aspects of performance upon which the present review has concentrated.

NOTES

1. An exception is a small body of literature arguing for development control's extension: for example M. Shoard, The Theft of the Countryside (Temple Smith, London, 1980).
2. See G. Dobry, Review of the Development Control System, Final Report (HMSO, London, 1975); House of Commons, Expenditure Committee, Eighth Report, Session 1976-77, Planning Procedures, Volumes I-III (HMSO, London, 1977); Minister without Portfolio, Lifting the Burden, Cmnd. 9571 (HMSO, London, 1985); etc.
3. See evidence from British Property Federation, House Builders Federation, Royal Institute of British Architects (RIBA), and Royal Institute of Chartered Surveyors (RICS), in House of Commons, op. cit.; also Dobry, op. cit.
4. See House of Commons, op. cit., especially evidence from the local authority associations, St. Albans and Herts District Council, and the Town and

Country Planning Association; Royal Town Planning Institute, Memorandum of Observations on Development Control; Policy and Practice (RTPI, London, 1980); Association of District Councils, Survey of Development Control Performance 1977-8 and 1978-9 (ADC, London, 1978, 1979).

5. See National Building Agency, Town Planning Procedures for industrial development (NBA, London, 1977); Audit Inspectorate, Local Planning: The Development Control Function (HMSO, London, 1983); Building Research Establishment, The operation of Development Control (Department of the Environment, London, 1978); Scottish Development Department, Development Control Performance in Scotland (MVA Consultants, SDD, Edinburgh, 1985).

6. Llewelyn Davies, Forestier Weekes, and Bor, Design Guidance Survey (Department of the Environment/Housing Research Foundation, London, 1976).

7. National Economic Development Office, Industrial Development: a case study in factory building (Slough Estates, London, 1976).

8. Association of District Councils, op. cit., 1979.

9. Ibid.

10. See Building Research Establishment, op. cit. and Scottish Development Department, op. cit.

11. R. Hammersley, 'The Local Ombudsman and his Impact on Planning' and 'The Ombudsman and Planning', The Planner, 66, 1 (January/February 1980), pp. 10-11, 27, and 2 (March/April 1980), p. 56.

12. See E.S. Marcroft, 'Public involvement in development control', unpublished dissertation (Leeds Polytechnic, 1978), cited in J. Underwood, 'Development Control: A Review of Research and Current Issues', Progress in Planning, 16, 3 (1981), pp. 179-242.

13. For comments see J. Henneberry, 'Planning Delay in Perspective', The Planner, 68, 3 (May/June 1982), p. 72.

14. See P. Hall, H. Gracey, R. Drewett and R. Thomas, The Containment of Urban England, Volume Two, The Planning System (PEP, George Allen and Unwin, and Sage, London, 1973), pp. 163-245; Shankland Cox Partnership, Land availability for residential development (SCP, London, 1972); Federation of Master Builders, Future of house building: a national survey on land availability, production, planning and other restrictions (FMB, London, 1981); D.C. Nicholls, D.M. Turner, R. Kirby-

An Introductory Review

Smith and J.D. Cullen, *The private sector housing development process in inner city areas* (Department of Land Economy, University of Cambridge, 1980); H. Smyth, *Land Banking, land availability and planning for private housebuilding*, Working Paper 23, and *Land Supply, housebuilders and government policies*, Working Paper 42 (School for Advanced Urban Studies, University of Bristol, 1982 and 1984).

15. See R. Goodchild and R. Munton, *Development and the Landowner* (Allen and Unwin, London, 1985).

16. Although see Department of the Environment, *Housing land availability in the South East* (HMSO, London, 1975) and Goodchild and Munton, op. cit., chapter 7.

17. See M.T. Pountney and P.W. Kingsbury, 'Aspects of Development Control, Part 1: The relationship with Local Plans', and 'Part 2: The Applicant's View', *Town Planning Review*, **54**, 2 (April 1983), pp. 139-54 and **54**, 3 (July 1983), pp. 285-303.

18. J.R. Short, S. Witt and S. Fleming, *Land, Housing and Conflict in an area of growth* (forthcoming).

19. See for example trade magazines; Building, Building Trades Journal, etc.

20. Dobry, op. cit. See also M. Bligh, 'The Leeds householder application system', unpublished dissertation (Leeds Polytechnic, 1978), cited in Underwood, op. cit.

21. Audit Inspectorate, op. cit.

22. See Scottish Development Department, op. cit.

23. National Development Control Forum, *A code of practice in respect of statutory consultations on applications for planning permission* (Association of District Councils, London, 1980); Scottish Development Department, op. cit.

24. Audit Inspectorate, op. cit.

25. Op. cit.

26. See for example M. Bruton and A. Nicholson, 'Local plans and planning in England', *Planning Outlook*, **27**, 1 (1984), pp. 1-11.

27. A relevant study is H.D. Thomas, J.M. Minett, S. Hopkins, S.L. Hamnett, A. Faludi and D. Barrell, *Flexibility and commitment in planning* (Martinus Nijhoff, The Hague, 1983).

28. Op. cit.

29. R. Johnson, 'The Local Authority Planner's Role', *The Planner*, **69**, 6 (November/December 1983) pp. 193-5.

30. M. Blacksell and A. Gilg, 'Planning control in an Area of Outstanding Natural Beauty', Social and Economic Administration, 11, 3 (Autumn 1977) pp. 206-15.
31. M. Anderson, 'Planning policies and Development Control in the Sussex Downs AONB', Town Planning Review, 52, 1 (January 1981), pp 5-25; I. Brotherton, 'Development pressures and Control in the National Parks, 1966-1981', Town Planning Review, 53, 4 (October 1982), pp. 439-59.
32. Goodchild and Munton, op. cit.
33. For example, Blacksell and Gilg, op. cit.; P. Healey and M. Elson, 'The Role of Development Plans in Implementing Planning Policies', The Planner, 68, 6 (November/December 1982), pp. 173-6; Pountney and Kingsbury, op. cit.; I. Gault, Green Belt Policies in Development Plans, Working Paper 41, (Department of Town and Country Planning, Oxford Polytechnic, 1981); Anderson, op. cit.; M. Elson, Land release and development in areas of restraint: an investigation of local needs policies (Department of Town and Country Planning, Oxford Polytechnic, 1982); J. Jowell, 'Bargaining in Development Control', Journal of Planning and Environment Law, 1977, pp. 414-33; S.C. Fleming and J.R. Short, 'Committee rules O.K.? An examination of planning committee action on officer recommendations', Environment and Planning A, 16, 7 (July 1984), pp. 965-73.
34. Op. cit.
35. For relevant studies see R. Tym and Partners, Monitoring Enterprise Zones, Year One - Year Three reports (Department of the Environment, London, 1982, 1983, 1984); G. Hadley, 'Enterprise Zones in Britain: The Form and Consequences of the Planning Scheme Approach', Planning Outlook, 27, 1 (1984), pp. 34-8; M.G. Lloyd and R. Botham, 'The ideology and implementation of Enterprise Zones', Urban Law and Policy, 7, 1 (1985), pp. 33-55; Minister without Portfolio, op. cit.; M.G. Lloyd, 'Privatisation, liberalisation and simplification of Statutory Land Use Planning', Planning Outlook, 28, 1 (1985), pp. 46-9; S. Taylor, 'The Politics of Enterprise Zones', Public Administration, 59, 4 (Winter 1981), pp. 421-39; P. Purton and C. Douglas, 'Enterprise Zones in the U.K.', Journal of Planning and Environment Law, 1982, pp. 412-22; D. Massey, 'Enterprise Zones: a political issue', International Journal of Urban and Regional Research, 6, 3 (September 1982), pp. 429-34.
36. Perhaps the main local authority fear is

that Simplified Planning Zones would be imposed upon them.
37. Royal Town Planning Institute, Simplified Planning Zones: comments to the DoE (RTPI, London, 1984).
38. See Jowell, op. cit., and J.N. Hawke, 'Planning agreements in practice I and II', Journal of Planning and Environment Law, 1981, pp. 5-14 and 86-97, for comprehensive coverage of possible 'planning gains' that may be obtained.
39. See various arguments in evidence from developer interests, in House of Commons, op. cit.
40. J. Jowell, 'The limits to law in urban planning', Current Legal Problems, 30, (1977), pp. 63-83.
41. D. Henry, Planning by agreement in a Berkshire District, Working Paper 69 (Department of Town and Country Planning, Oxford Polytechnic, 1982), and 'Planning by agreement: a local survey', Journal of Planning and Environment Law, 1984, pp. 395-400.
42. P. Booth, 'Development Control and Design Quality, Part 1: Conditions: A Useful Way of Controlling Design?', Town Planning Review, 54, 3 (July 1983), pp. 265-84.
43. Although see K. Willis, 'Planning agreements and planning gain', Planning Outlook, 24, 2 (1982), pp. 55-60.
44. For discussion see M. Ball, Housing policy and economic power: the political economy of owner occupation (Methuen, London, 1983).
45. N. Mobbs and R. Langton, Planning for new homes (House Builders Federation, London, 1977). On hypermarkets see R. Schiller, 'Superstore Impact', The Planner, 67, 2 (March/April 1981), pp. 38-40.
46. See Herring, Son and Daw, Property and technology: the needs of modern industry (HSD, London, 1982); Debenham, Tewson and Chinnocks, High-tech: myths and realities (DTC, London, 1983); Royal Institute of Chartered Surveyors, Amending the Use Classes Order to deal with high-tech developments, Discussion Paper 28 (RICS, London, 1984).
47. For example see Adam Smith Institute, Local government, planning and housing, The Omega Report (ASI, London, 1983); R. Jones, Town and Country Chaos (ASI, London, 1982).
48. See for instance P. Ambrose and B. Colenutt, The property machine (Penguin, Harmondsworth, 1975); R. Barras, 'The office development cycle in London', Land Development Studies, 1, 1 (January 1984), pp. 35-50.

49. See for example, F. Hirsch, Social limits to growth (Routledge and Kegan Paul, London, 1977).
50. For example, Royal Town Planning Institute, Submission of evidence to the Nuffield Foundation's Committee of Inquiry into the British Town and Country Planning System (RTPI, London, 1984).
51. J. Sillince, 'Development Control Standards and Industrial Applications', Planning Outlook, 27, 1 (1984), pp. 41-2.
52. J. Henneberry, 'The Use Classes Order and High Technology Developments', The Planner, 71, 9 (September 1985), pp. 23-5.
53. See Johnson, op. cit.; M. Howell, 'Swansea:a case study of working together', The Planner, 69, 6 (November/December 1983), p. 196; I. Stuart, 'Gloucester: a case study of working together', The Planner, 69, 6 (November/December 1983), p. 197; S. Byrne, 'Positive Control: the Nottingham Approach to Development', The Planner, 69, 4 (July/August 1983), pp. 124-6.
54. For example, see M. Boddy, 'Practice Review', The Planner, 69, 5 (September/October 1983), pp. 175-6, and K. Young and C. Mason (eds.), Urban Economic Development (Macmillan, London, 1983).
55. D. Cadman, 'Planning - Who Needs It?', The Planner, 69, 6 (November/December 1983), pp. 207-8.
56. Ball, op. cit.
57. S. Barrett, M. Stewart and J. Underwood, The Land Market and the Development Process, Occasional Paper 2 (School for Advanced Urban Studies, University of Bristol, 1978).
58. Joint Unit for Research on the Urban Environment (JURUE), Planning and land availability (University of Aston, Birmingham, 1977).
59. See M. Boddy, The Building Societies (Macmillan, London, 1980); J. Plender, That's the way the money goes: the financial institutions and the nation's saving (Andre Deutsch, London, 1982); D. Cadman, 'Property finance in the U.K. in the post-war period', Land Development Studies, 1, 1 (January 1984), pp. 61-82.
60. Nicholls et al., op. cit.; see also School of Land and Building Studies (SLABS) Research Unit, Housing land in urban areas, Working Papers 1-4 (Leicester Polytechnic, 1984).
61. See Nicholls et al., op. cit.; also S. Markowski, Study of vacant land in urban areas (Centre for Environmental Studies, London, 1978);

M.J. Bruton and A. Gore, 'Vacant Urban Land in South Wales', The Planner, 67, 2 (March/April 1981), pp. 34-5.
  62. For various relevant points see Nicholls et al., op. cit.; D.C. Nicholls, D.M. Turner, R. Kirby-Smith, and J.D. Cullen, 'The Risk Business: Developers' Perceptions and Prospects for Housebuilding in the Inner City', Urban Studies, 19, 4 (November 1982), pp. 331-41; Department of the Environment and House Builders Federation, Study of the availability of private house building land in Greater Manchester (DoE, London, 1979).
  63. See for example B.J. Pearce, 'Instruments for Land Policy: a classification', Urban Law and Policy, 3, 2 (1980), pp. 115-55.
  64. For instance J. Simmie, Power, property and corporatism (Macmillan, London, 1981); Ball, op. cit.; C. Hague, The Development of Planning Thought (Hutchinson, London, 1984).
  65. Joint Unit for Research on the Urban Environment, op. cit.
  66. Goodchild and Munton, op. cit.
  67. Y. Rydin, 'Residential Development and the Planning System', Progress in Planning, 24, 1 (1985), pp. 1-69, and 'The Struggle for Housing Land: A case of confused interests', Policy and Politics, 12, 4 (October 1984), pp. 431-46.
  68. See for example E. Reade, 'Town and country planning', in M.L. Harrison (ed.), Corporatism and the Welfare State (Gower, Aldershot, 1984), pp. 92-110.

Chapter 3

PROPERTY RIGHTS, PHILOSOPHIES, AND THE
JUSTIFICATION OF PLANNING CONTROL

Malcolm L. Harrison

INTRODUCTION[1]

An understanding of modern property rights concepts and conflicts is crucial to any attempt to analyse land use planning, and to explore justifications or criticisms of development control. It is essential, therefore, that our book should contain an early chapter focussed upon this topic, to provide a philosophical backcloth to the material that will follow. The chapter is concerned with questions of ownership and power, and particularly with some of the criticisms that are made of town planning, apparently from a 'property-rights perspective'. In order to understand the case against planning, and potential replies to that case, it is necessary to come to terms with political and philosophical assumptions that underpin differing views. Property is a more complex matter than has been supposed by some of the critics of planning control. Given differing sets of assumptions, property rights claims may provide support for planning, as easily as for its opponents. Although advocates for the private developer have been quick to invoke notions of property, arguments from the rights of property stand on contested territory, and cannot be monopolised by any one interest group.
 The present essay will concentrate on presenting a sketch of key issues only (consequently the elements of literature review included must be severely limited). The chapter rests on the assertion that there are competing notions of 'ownership' and property rights, which hold differing implications for the practice of planning. The discussion is arranged in seven parts. Firstly, general comments are made about rights and property.

Property Rights

Secondly, attention is given to a current
conventional wisdom or dominant view about property,
permeating much development and planning literature,
and also pervading some of the writings of
economists and philosophers which are often claimed
to be relevant. To follow up this discussion, a
separate section is then devoted to the ways in
which this conventional approach has been elaborated
and re-interpreted by 'anti-collectivist' economists
and their academic and political associates.
Fourthly, examples are given of the implications of
these ideas for planning policy. Then some
alternatives to the conventional view are
introduced very briefly, and the point is made that
planning control might be justifiable from the
perspective of one or more of these alternative
conceptions. Sixthly, the place of various
competing notions is dealt with in terms of
politics, attention being drawn to the central
conflict between economic liberalism and
participatory democracy. This leads to the
conclusion that any particular notion of a property
rights system must seek its defence in a normative
theory of political and economic life. This in turn
will usually reflect one or other of a range of
alternative conceptions of how society and economy
actually *are* arranged. Finally, the chapter ends by
arguing that land planning's critics face
difficulties in the property debate. Indeed,
private rights claims and theories cannot be used
easily to rebut the case for planning control,
unless democracy itself is to be rejected. Although
rights, cannot exist outside a political and socio-
economic context, and the abstract notion of a right
can always be challenged, planners might easily seek
to provide theoretical support for the activities of
planning authorities by reference to rights, or to
claims for rights.

RIGHTS AND PROPERTY: DEFINITIONS AND PROBLEMS

It is as well to begin with the word 'property'.
Everyday usages imply obvious physical possessions,
but there are problems here. Firstly, many non-
physical things are dealt with in terms of property
rights. A historical review would reveal a broad
range of potential items, including not only things
like land or buildings, but also people (slaves),
mental constructs such as honour or reputation, and
even emotions (as with 'conjugal affections'). All

33

might be seen as amenable to property rights claims. More conventionally, one might cite the right to an income, the right to control the use of a scientific discovery, copyright, and the notion of property rights in jobs (or 'offices'). Kruse notes that rights to 'intellectual property' may go further than rights in respect of material items.[2] A second problem in focussing directly on material objects is the historical and geographical variation in meanings attached to the term 'property', reflecting religious, political and cultural environments. Bound up with notions of property are concepts of the person, and what person and property mean depend upon specific socio-economic settings. Looking at physical items, which someone seems to possess, may tell us very little. In any case, insofar as property means more than mere temporary physical possession, access to, or use of an item, the notion requires recognition <u>by others</u> of an individual's claims to continued shared or exclusive enjoyment. Thus property rights are relationships of power, obligation, kinship, custom or convention. Inasmuch as the concept involves enforceable claims, property cannot exist without sanction by state institutions or some powerful intermediary or economic 'interest'. Of course, in return the property system at any given moment itself conditions possibilities of political, social and economic interaction, at least in the short term: property is 'a man-made institution which creates and maintains certain relations between people'.[3] For analytical purposes, therefore, it is safer to approach property in terms of relationships, and a range of rights, claims and powers, rather than focussing in the first instance on specific physical items.

The argument so far is that 'property' should not necessarily be assumed to be a quality inherent in items themselves. Nonetheless, in Western societies the term usually implies identification of items on which obligations and claims focus, and around which relationships between people appear to revolve. In 'advanced' economies the word property often implies clear separation of individuals (or 'legal subjects') one from another, and from items ('legal objects').[4] Things exist in which people have separable property, as individuals (or acting with other individuals). These items are generally resources, frequently interpreted as commodities to which rights of property give access (via quantification, equivalence and exchange).

This implied distinction between legal subject and object which lies at the heart of Western concepts of property is not a universal one, and a clear disjunction between persons and things may be inappropriate for interpreting systems of exchange in other settings.[5] A rights-based approach itself is grounded in specific cultures and views of the material (and mental) world. There may be a degree of ethnocentrism about applying current Western property (and behavioural) notions to other cultures.[6] Nevertheless, the present chapter will concentrate on property primarily in the Western form; that is to say in terms of rights and relationships connected with use of items which have been <u>specified</u> as separate from people and (in some degree) from social relations. Even though economic activity is nowadays often organised within or by corporate institutions (which have distinctive legal characteristics, and complex consequences for property politics), this does not necessarily erode the legal subject/object distinction. Much dispute centres today not around the separateness of objects, their saleability, and so forth, but on who shall exercise rights over them, and on how rights are divided. This brings us to the issue of ownership, and to the conventional wisdom (and alternative ideas) discussed below. Nonetheless, perhaps resonances persist from earlier days, when separation was less firm. Even in current property politics, notions of 'stewardship' survive, and these may imply <u>recognition</u> of relationships between people rather than merely with objects.

The term 'ownership' may now be introduced formally, in its modern conventional Western sense, as primarily an expression of a recognised powerful legal subject/object connection. Property rights systems are seen as defining the legitimacy and extent of claims and relationships for those individuals, groups or administrative agents who seek to defend or establish powers or obligations in relation to specific items or resources. Within such systems, ownership tends to denote recognition of priority for a particular actor in relation to an object. Ownership varies as a concept, referring to varying degrees of control and measures of obligation in differing contexts. For this reason legal specification of its meaning often needs to be precise. Its bounds are determined by politics and state sanction, it is always conditional, is often shared, and may involve duties as well as powers. Even so, ownership is typically seen as having to do with the right to use, to transfer, and to exclude other people from the thing owned.[7] Property rights, however, should not simply be seen as the 'rights of ownership'. Someone who holds a right is not necessarily the owner of the object to which it relates, even though we might choose to refer to that right as a 'property right'. In the literature generally, it is frequently argued that ownership is best seen as a bundle of rights, and that an owner will be that person who has an acknowledged priority, through possession of a specified broad range of rights in relation to some object.[8] Thus, although several persons may have rights relating to a single item, one may have an especially large share. All have property rights in the object, but one is the owner. This opens the possibility of divided ownership, where no individual has a dominant collection of powers. More generally, it means that property ownership involves an aggregation of several distinct rights.

Efforts have been made to classify the elements which together usually amount to 'full ownership'. The classic discussion is by Honoré.[9] His list of 'standard incidents' of ownership includes the right to possess, the right to use, the right to manage, the right to the income of the thing, the right to the capital, the right to security, the rights or incidents of transmissibility and absence of term, the prohibition of harmful use, liability to execution, and the incident of residuarity.[10] Honoré is including characteristic prohibitions and limitations, as well as rights, even though what he is dealing with is the 'liberal concept' of ownership. Thus he makes clear that the kinds of ownership found in Western societies never confer uninhibited and absolute powers: ownership itself <u>implies</u> limitations. Nonetheless, the present essay will use the term 'the liberal concept of full ownership' below, as an expression of the most unrestricted notions of ownership based on a set of rights.

Some reservations need to be emphasised concerning ownership generally. Clearly, ownership may imply duties, and it has seldom meant unconditional or complete control of all the rights of property in the bundle. From earliest times there have been limitations on individuals' property rights.[11] Persons have rarely had unrestricted control over objects. As property rights for one usually mean a deprivation or exclusion for somebody else, economic and cultural forces, and the distribution of power among political and economic actors, have determined how the rights have been shared out, and sanctioned. This might be interpreted in terms of class. In any event, patterns of rights have changed with socio-economic pressures and conflicts, and from time to time there have been complex sharings.[12] Often, for example, management and day-to-day use have been separated from other rights. It is sometimes held that the advance of capitalism curtailed many customary, common or traditional rights, reduced the importance of duties, and emphasised possessive individualism.[13] More generally, it may be asserted that notions of ownership resting on the legal subject/object distinction relate to the 'needs' of capitalism. Thus, historically, commodity exchange might be held to have furnished the idea of a subject as the abstract bearer of all possible legal claims.[14] It may be wrong, of course, to assume a sharp transition from an imperturbable feudalism to capitalism, or uninhibited possessive individualism.[15] Even today, many notions of ownership co-exist although the liberal concept of full ownership is widespread. Furthermore, however popular the liberal concept may be, we cannot argue that this notion is a fixed and necessary one, unless we assume that the economic and political relationships it embodies represent some kind of superior societal model.

The term 'rights' also deserves separate comment. It is possible to argue that there are no such things as rights in any abstract sense, and that questions concerning them are reducible to issues of power, its distribution and its justification. Thus rights have no independent meaning outside specific socio-political and cultural contexts (unless some metaphysical reasoning is applied).[16] Indeed, property rights could be treated purely in material terms, as recognised relationships (of power, obligation or influence) between persons or organisations, legitimating or making enforceable individuals' or groups' claims to a share of control which excludes other people or agencies. In effect a claim could be said to be a right when acknowledged in some way (especially through the political system). Thus, depending upon the shifting sands of recognition, property 'rights' would come and go. Of course this is what happens in practice, emergent claims being placed on the agenda of current politics. At any time, however, there are degrees of recognition of

37

rights claims. Some are backed fully by law, others by administrative custom, and others only by assertions about morality. Even the most formally-recognised rights may clash, for legal frameworks are rarely fixed or absolutely clear. Furthermore, some claims are not often expressed formally, yet seem implicit in widespread material conflicts of interest, as 'submerged' rights claims to which parts of the political system may be under pressure to respond. Other rights might be read off from the form of the political process itself. For instance, participatory rights in relation to property could be held to follow from citizen rights in the electoral system. Analysts thus face a difficulty. If rights depend upon recognition, what constitutes that recognition?

    A simple practical approach is adopted for this essay (as there is no space to discuss the recognition issue). The unqualified term 'rights' will be understood to apply in situations where a large measure of legal or administrative recognition is currently given in Britain, or where recognition appears a necessary condition for the exercise of other (acknowledged) rights or to follow logically from them. Discussion, however, will also refer to certain rights claims, which currently have less formal status, but might appear 'just' to many people.

THE CONVENTIONAL WISDOM AND ITS CONSEQUENCES FOR LAND PLANNING

Some critics of planning claim to be pragmatic, concerned primarily with achieving better outcomes, and thus sceptical of the capacities of collective decision-making. Others openly take the side of particular private interests. Whatever the line of argument, however, and despite frequent references to improved outcomes, assumptions about power and property underpin many of the writings.

    The ownership notion employed most frequently in literature dealing with land planning, and especially in attacks on planning powers, is probably a modified form of the liberal concept of full ownership. This implies that one person (or organisation) does or should possess most or all of the rights in the property bundle. A second tier of rights-holders may also be identified, with subsidiary or postponed legal claims (perhaps neighbouring owner-occupiers, or people with residuary rights). Writers vary, however, in how far they acknowledge the qualifications or restrictions noted by scholars (duties, penalties, etc.). Certainly few stress what the more perceptive of modern right-wing theorists might concede: that established holdings are conditional on the popular franchise.[17] Thus property is usually conceived of, by critics of planning, in terms of existing legally-sanctioned distributions among identifiable individuals: private individuals' rights are taken properly to constitute almost the *entire* rights landscape, to the exclusion of customary obligations, widespread 'community' rights claims, political interactions, claims about common resources, etc. Where community or politics are mentioned in British planning literature, it is rarely in terms of property rights (or rights claims), but rather as outside factors that might have to be taken into account in reducing individual freedoms.[18]

One reason for the style of contributions is that the liberal concept of full ownership seems deeply entrenched in popular consciousness (although variables of class and culture need to be noted). For planning literature the consequence is that references to property inevitably deal mainly with the rights of private individuals or organisations who happen at present to have the chief powers of ownership, or who have some other lesser but clearly-identifiable legal rights. Talk is of landowners and developers, and occasionally of nuisance to neighbours, with perhaps just a few fleeting thoughts about 'third parties'. Not surprisingly, therefore, there is a conventional wisdom that property problems concern mainly the extent and limitations of public authority power over private owners, supplemented by issues that arise when one acknowledged owner acts to the detriment of another. Politics is portrayed as something *external* to the system of property rights, a force that 'interferes' (rather than being intimately linked with rights distributions and transfers). In effect, ' full ownership' has become so accepted that governments face great difficulties if they seek to challenge it, and alterations are presented as deviations from a norm. Changes thus appear 'political', and the legal status quo 'natural'.[19] In the popular press this leads to crude assertions about such matters as the infringement of liberty or the owner's 'natural rights' to develop.[20] The same themes are found,

39

however, in more scholarly contributions. Individual owners need to be 'freed' from state hegemony. As one writer puts it:

> The time has now come for a fundamental change in the direction of town planning and a retrenchment in the scale of its activities, away from collectivism .... towards liberalism and individualism in which each man is responsible for his own affairs and planning assumes the role of a caretaker and umpire.[21]

References may be made to ways in which public power weakens the 'natural order' of the market. Legal changes (such as the introduction of planning controls) are interpreted as 'interferences'.[22]

It is clear that ownership is often being conceived of here essentially in terms of a 'snapshot' taken of formal private legal entitlements which are supposed to have existed at a particular moment, and which, it is thought, should still exist in as complete a form as possible. This line of argument has a long history, and connects with views that are applied to a wide range of governmental activities. In the early post-war period, for instance, several developments in English law might be described as restricting or taking away the unhindered power of (individual) utilisation of property.[23] To critics, such developments have been seen as unjustifiable invasions of (supposedly) 'non-political' market arenas, that are essential for freedom and 'economic efficiency'.[24] The 'anti-collectivist' writers prefer systems of decision-making where the individual makes most of the managerial decisions for 'his' or (occasionally) 'her' property, within a set of rules or regulations of a minimal kind.[25] Such rules may build certain external cost factors into the decision-making considerations of the individual owner, although this must not be carried too far. Thus, wherever possible, rules reflect the requirements of other private owners with identifiable property holdings, rather than vague notions of the 'public interest',[26] 'community', or welfare.

Because such views are important, further comments will be made on the academic tradition involved, and its assumptions. First, however, a reservation must be noted in respect of land. Writers on property may treat land and natural resources as special cases, because of exhaustibility, 'externalities', concepts of stewardship, or the need for co-operation or co-ordination.[27] Some advocates of economic individualism, therefore, may accept planning at the margins, either to co-ordinate developments or occasionally to veto or modify them. Whether landed property is a special type, however, is open to debate. Some writers distinguish between forms of property held for differing reasons. For example: for personal consumption, as a means to the acquisition of revenues, to establish relations of power and dependence between their holders and others, or for the exercising of authority over labour.[28] It is doubtful, however, whether land can be separated off via a classification of this (or a similar) type. Property in land involves rights both to benefit directly and to control. It is not always a distinctive form of property, even though land itself may differ from shares or movable goods. When natural resources are cited as exceptions by some 'anti-collectivists', the reason probably lies not so much in distinctive qualities of the rights involved. Rather, the cause may be found in doubts about the results of unrestrained exploitation, and in recognition that such visible resources cannot be taken too freely without political opposition.

ECONOMISTIC DEVELOPMENTS OF PROPERTY THEORIES

Certain economists and other academics favouring possessive individualism, growth maximisation, and incentives, have built up an extensive literature dealing with property rights. While a full liberal notion is generally employed (consciously or unconsciously) to buttress these approaches, attention is given to so-called 'externalities', and to possibilities for bargaining that could be created by more elaborated systems of private rights. Such ideas are associated especially with particular American writers, who are often invoked by British disciples. Bracewell-Milnes, for instance, states:

> The creation of wealth through ownership is closely related to the concept of solving or mitigating economic problems through the extension of property rights. This applies especially to problems of 'externalities'

41

(uncompensated effects of economic activity on outsiders) ... Modern theory on the subject originates in an article by Professor R. H. Coase.[29]

This kind of work needs to be placed alongside other developments in economics. It reflects not merely predispositions against collective solutions, but also the desire to extend a narrow type of economic analysis into spheres of public administration, social policy, social anthropology, and political behaviour. Its more extreme products are therefore a species of 'disciplinary ethnocentrism'. They can be challenged on the grounds that they involve an 'economistic simplification' which assumes that 'all protagonists are individually rationalistic maximisers', and because they claim that the 'model of economism, individual choice in a condition of scarcity, can handle the whole of human behaviour'.[30] Nevertheless, some of the American work is sophisticated, _if_ one is prepared to accept its assumptions. It is attractive to interest groups that fear the unrestricted play of pluralistic politics in bringing about redistributions of property rights. It offers apparently 'technical' (although certainly not neutral) solutions to political disagreements. Everything, it appears, has its price, and can be bought and sold, and there is supposedly always an 'optimum' outcome to be sought. Many rights can themselves be 'owned', and therefore bought and sold. So acceptable have these approaches been, that in the USA the term 'property rights literature' is sometimes seen as _synonymous_ with economistic approaches based on 'rational' behaviour by individual 'owners' of rights.[31]

Crucial to the political acceptability of these ideas has been the prospect they offer for providing justification for a pattern of ownership which rests primarily on a liberal (rather than a socialistic, paternalistic, or communitarian) concept of managerial prerogatives. Thus the function of these intellectual manoeuvres appears to be to leave intact as far as possible the _managerial_ powers of the individual chief owner. He or she supposedly possesses power for 'efficient free market' reasons, quite independently of politics, and political challenges over control must be converted into simple monetary obligations or purchasable rights.[32] One view is that commonly-held rights weaken incentives to 'conserve' resources or to maximise productivity. Numerous studies have been undertaken to prove this kind of thesis, and advocates argue that the evidence for their case is overwhelming.[33] By applying such ideas, justifications can be found for ignoring political relationships implicit in existing rights distributions, and concentrating instead on the marginal changes in legal rights needed to ensure an 'efficient' market. One attraction of the approach (for its supporters) thus lies in the legitimacy it confers on attempts to depoliticise decision-making. The basic intention is to confine the role of politics (or to limit its range of participants to a select circle). Indeed in some of the writings one could fairly easily substitute the phrase 'day-to-day politics' for 'negotiating costs'.[34] Elsewhere the attack on politics (or its pluralistic or 'mass' forms) is more direct.[35] Denman and Prodano, for example, are clear that a 'community cannot make decisions ... Decisions can only be taken by a single will'.[36]

At a practical level, however, economists run into problems once they try to answer questions about social and environmental costs falling outside the concern of the chief property-holder. As indicated above, the usual response is to argue for the establishing of more individual claims, particularly to payments in respect of 'externalities'. Unfortunately for this approach, there is no obvious limit to the recognition of 'externalities', since human actions influence other people in so many ways. Furthermore, it would be difficult to reduce all shared rights, customary claims, or 'externalities' to meaningful financial figures. Attempts to do so through law would probably bring land development to a halt, because charges borne by chief owners could be immense if related to the value external actors placed on pollution-free air, liberty of access, and so forth.[37] Perhaps this is one reason why economistic arguments are rarely carried to their logical conclusions, and why a measure of political control is usually accepted as an inexpensive concession, providing common security for chief owners.

Such difficulties have not prevented critics of planning from proposing alternatives to planning control by public authorities. Ideally, an alternative for such critics would be composed of private rights put into the form of legal codes for nuisance, compensation, and so forth. As Pearce

43

explains, in a useful paper, the aim of such changes 'would be to privatise what are currently state-held real property rights, to expand the bundle of *private* rights and obligations associated with land and thus capable of "ownership", so that landholders would have recourse to more direct legal remedies against any external harms or environmental damage that might arise'.[38] The thrust of such approaches is towards a system in which owners of property can protect themselves, individually, from being caused uncompensated harm by other owners. It is sometimes claimed that an elaborate structure of rules would allow 'trade-offs' between neighbours, which would be more 'efficient' than the impositions of absolute restrictions implied in planning standards set by a local authority. At the heart of the arguments lies fear of a broad-based political discussion (which could imply a range of 'non-owners' trying to 'interfere' in estate management).

SOME IMPLICATIONS FOR PLANNING POLICY

Many limitations of British land planning can be traced to liberal full ownership, and the power of those economic interests that depend upon it. Very direct interventions via compulsory purchase have always been resisted, except where servicing, reconstruction, development, or 'land assembly' tasks were clearly far beyond the scope of private organisations. By contrast, there has been a measure of consensus about development control, partly because it leaves development initiatives in private hands. The astonishing feature of this system, however, is not its over-concern with small details, but the extraordinary modesty of its means for influencing social and economic change in explicit and constructive ways. At the same time, planners have had considerable difficulties in achieving even physical objectives, on matters such as on-going maintenance, restoration after mineral extraction, and preservation of popular physical landmarks. Furthermore, some developments have escaped control: farming, for instance, has produced major countryside changes without much constraint.
Underlying some law and much central government guidance on development control is the idea that chief owners must be allowed maximum freedom in land use and development, subject only to restraints designed to protect other people from certain

Property Rights

limited types of immediate adverse effects, and to restrictions meant to safeguard particular physical features of the environment.[39] Planning control has remained largely a matter of once-for-all veto, rather than a power to intervene actively in the management of property,[40] despite the efforts of some local authorities to act more positively. Planning conditions which seek to inhibit (or share) managerial power may be resisted especially fiercely. For instance, if planning authorities wish to influence occupancy they face difficulties. A restriction designed to give local people protection in a housing market, through requiring that new houses should be for local needs only, runs up against the liberal notion of full ownership. Controls (over which purchasers the owner may sell to) reduce the value of the land, but, even more important, conflict with the right to sell freely, and (apparently) with the ability to raise loans of capital on the land (for a typical government comment see H. of C. Debates, 6th series, volume 53, session 1983-4, Written Answers, Mr. Macfarlane, 8th February 1984, col. 657: see also DoE Circular 1/85[41]). A dual housing market would be a severe threat to liberal notions.[42] No wonder then, that central government's response to the issue of second homes in Wales has been minimal, or that residents with a different view of property rights have begun to take matters into their own hands.[43] Experiences in the post-war period suggest that planning is a very limited tool for managing socio-economic and physical changes when control takes the form merely of a power to veto, or to apply simple physical standards. Yet this form is the one generally most acceptable within a system dominated by the full liberal notion.

Planners have often been criticised, as far as physical goals are concerned, for trying to apply fixed standards and requirements. Quite often such standards are difficult to defend, but the reasons for their use may be overlooked. Standards partly represent a response to pressures to portray planning as neutral and technical, rather than as inherently partly political (and redistributive in its outcomes). Fears that local planning authorities might discriminate between developers on welfare grounds, or introduce obviously political criteria into decision-making, have encouraged restricted views as to the proper scope of planning powers. If planning controls can be taken to mean merely the imposition of a few more standards

45

alongside building regulations, then there is less scope for interference with the developer's managerial prerogatives, and the separation of property use from political discussion can be maintained.

Despite the limitations of development control, even the power of veto or the right to set general physical standards may be challenged by some advocates of economic individualism, or be allowed only grudgingly.[44] Some of the alternatives envisaged have already been mentioned above, but it is worth re-emphasising the implicit central goal. This is to circumvent pluralistic political discussion, a concern which the rise of amenity pressure groups and public participation has made appear more and more pressing to developer interests. Not only has planning control been very much restricted by the strength of support for 'full liberal' ideas, but the very existence of an extensive system of control run by local authorities is frequently challenged from liberal and economistic standpoints. Advocates of land use planning, therefore, must turn to other ideas about ownership in seeking to justify forms of planning control which are to influence social, economic and physical outcomes seriously. This is especially so if they wish to conceive of planning as a matter of shared management of resources, operating partly in response to local community preferences. It is now time to glance briefly at some possible alternative starting-points.

SOME ALTERNATIVE NOTIONS OF OWNERSHIP AND RIGHTS IN LAND PLANNING

The liberal concept of full individual ownership is not the only property rights notion that exists in Britain. Other ideas surface in debate. Potential opponents of the liberal concept range from conservative traditionalists to socialists, so that varied claims arise. Furthermore, there is the 'Marxian stream', with its distinctive critical perspectives on existing property arrangements, and its capacity to offer a basis for alternative claims. The present essay cannot cover fully all these diverse ideas (or the social forces they might reflect), and it will not discuss Marxian analyses. Its aim is more modest: simply to introduce some notions bearing on rights claims that are especially relevant to town planning in its present-day

political context.
For convenience the ideas are grouped into three categories. Firstly, those linked to <u>duties, obligations, established customs and traditions</u> that have few connections with economic individualism.[45] Some of these relate to 'pre-capitalist' (or more modern) concepts about responsibilities implied by rights or ownership.[46] Others concern claims based on custom or religion, or ideas about stewardship on behalf of future generations.[47] Secondly, <u>centralised management concepts.</u> Such views may imply separation of the right to an income from the right to manage or direct the use of a thing. Private institutions may embody a division of this kind. Our present interest, however, is in claims on behalf of state agencies seeking powers of guidance (while leaving part of the bundle of rights elsewhere). Strong national planning directives could be defended in this light, the claim being that the state has a share of the property rights in the enterprises it seeks to guide. Nationalisation depends on the right to take control still more fully (albeit with compensation), but it may set up a variant of centralised management, with a new division of powers between levels of authority. Our third group concerns <u>co-operative and community concepts.</u> Examples may be found in the idea of 'local community' control over development, or the idea of local work-forces claiming a right to influence the use of industrial capital in the firms for which they work. Some community rights can be deduced logically from rights of participation implicit in local electoral representation: consequently they have more status than mere moral rights <u>claims</u>.
Having sketched some alternative ideas, it will be worth commenting on potential implications for land planning, before going on to consider political meanings. Some rights claims founded on one or other of these notions could not be dealt with by the economist's conception of 'externalities' or the lawyer's ideas of 'nuisance'. There can be claims for the elimination of which a chief owner might be unable to compensate financially. Furthermore, the ideas embody varied notions of efficient or rational behaviour as regards management, exploitation or exchange. With the first category conformity to planning control might be seen as part of a network of obligations implicit in ownership itself. With the second notion, implying partitioned ownership, decision-taking power may also be shared. Land use

47

planning could be justified straightforwardly by the view that certain rights of property reside in hands other than those of the local owners. This might be confined to powers to prescribe physical standards, or it might go further to involve claims about determining estate management strategies, the distribution of benefits, a range of potential purchasers for the assets, and so forth. In the case of co-operative and community concepts, there are again potential justifications for planning control, this time via the local authority as an electoral forum. In practice this represents one of the most serious current political challenges to the liberal notion of full individual ownership. British central government can be relied upon to accommodate powerful private economic interests but local politics is less predictable! Frequently, local people and local authorities have sought to oppose the unfettered activities of major owners. Over the years there have gradually emerged rights for people to participate, to be informed about local development applications, to have access to information, and to have representations noted. In effect there is now a set of well-recognised property rights here, mediated by local authorities in accordance with established administrative rules, and partly acknowledged in legislation. Quite often, perhaps, this unfortunately has led to actions of a negative kind against rather trivial changes, while large developments have escaped unhindered. Furthermore, the rights have been largely of a veto kind as far as control of private sector developers has been concerned. There is no reason, however, why more positive managerial planning could not be legitimated through the notion of shared community property rights. We have only to reconsider questions about controlling occupancy of second homes in Wales to see the idea's relevance: local people are advancing property rights claims that go well beyond powers over the appearance of buildings or land-use allocations. Indeed, public inquiry processes already embody an element of recognition of participatory claims bearing on positive land management.

POLITICAL PHILOSOPHIES AND PROPERTY RIGHTS

Readers already will have perceived connections between specific concepts about rights and ownership on the one hand, and perspectives on political, legal and economic arrangements on the other. It is now necessary to be more specific. There are two closely-connected starting points. Firstly, the apparent separation of the legal, the political, and the economic provides an essential foundation for numerous 'anti-collectivist' theorisations of liberty, property and economic activity. The liberal concept of full ownership connects in the last resort with a belief that individual property-use decisions should be unhindered by day-to-day 'community' politics, and determined in 'free market' conditions, under rules 'appropriate' to markets (and laid down in fairly fixed legal formulations). Secondly, some liberal notions of economic life imply severe limitations on democratic and participatory processes.[48] The term liberal democracy is misleading, since democratic control is not compatible with free markets. Democratic participation inevitably involves limitations on freedom of management, exchange and transfer, on the right to exploit assets, and so forth. This incompatibility partly explains the development lobby's longstanding resistance to 'public participation',[49] and central government's equivocal attitude to the activities of local environmental groups. In effect, participatory involvement may threaten the individual's or organisation's private power (inherent in the existing pattern of formal property rights distributions).[50] Politics, therefore, is only accepted by advocates of economic individualism insofar as there is acknowledgement that political interactions at national level *may* be allowed to have a modifying or developmental effect upon legal codes within which markets operate. General regulatory laws which are relatively stable, or change only incrementally, are preferred to the play of competitive and open politics. We should not forget, of course, that a system based on formal law may tend to give supremacy of representation in decision-making to people with financial resources and firm property-holdings, rather than to 'non-owners' or the poor.[51]

One argument for 'anti-collectivist' positions rests on incentives, and the view that individual control ensures maximum growth through exploitation of resources. A second argument relies on themes of bureaucratic incompetence, the dangers of public sector professional power, and so forth. In situations where economic growth is not universally accepted as having primacy, the first argument is difficult to maintain (even leaving aside the endless questions of 'externalities'). The second argument has great force, but not as a defence against participatory claims. Indeed it is a paradox of public affairs that attempts to confine the role of politics often lead to the growth of institutional mechanisms of the very kinds that some 'libertarian' theorists claim to dislike! As the present writer has argued elsewhere, corporatist decision-making structures can reflect attempts to avoid the open play of electoral politics.[52] In land use planning some aspects of professional power and administrative discretion arise precisely because of the desire of governments, lawyers and businessmen to confine planning to 'technical' rather than socio-political questions.[53] An appeal to fears of bureaucracy is not therefore a very helpful support for the full liberal notion. Nor, of course, can liberty be appealed to easily, since the property rights of one person represent power to exclude others, and to restrict their actions.

None of this is to suggest that the liberal notion of full ownership has no merits. Rather, the writer wishes to show that in the end its extreme forms depend upon a belief not in liberty as such and certainly not in democracy, but on an assertion that the role of political interactions should be confined severely, and that the liberty that is crucial is the freedom for existing possessors to do as they wish. By contrast, other views of property conjure up very different concepts about political and economic life. Paternalism, or ideas of local, religious, class or family obligations, may underpin views based on stewardship, duty or tradition. Here people are not perceived as solely economic actors, nor necessarily as political ones. Centralised management may connect with views about the nation state and its institutions, and the proper functions of governments. Co-operative and community concepts depend on the claim that decisions about resource-use should be made through discussion, persuasion, and voting. Some of these varied views may convey feelings about the importance of kinship, solidarity, altruism and mutual dependencies. Theorists of economic individualism bent on defending the liberal notion of full ownership must always reject these, even when tolerating some measure of centralised management for the sake of security and certainty.[54]

As a final comment on political implications of

these alternative perspectives, it must be said that
each implies not only a view of what should be, but
also an interpretation of what is. To underwrite
the liberal notion it is probably necessary to
assume that existing distributions are neither
inherently very rigid nor unjust, nor set within
societies where class, ethnic and gender divisions
strongly influence opportunity-patterns (or where
inheritance is of great importance and social
mobility slight). Furthermore, 'free markets' must
be assumed to be present or feasible in most
contexts, and to operate without large elements of
corruption, illegality or the inter-penetration of
public and private sector decision-making. The
other normative conceptions make quite different
assumptions about how Western societies are
arranged. Before normative alternatives can be
evaluated properly, therefore, analyses of the
characteristics of modern states are required.[55]

CONCLUSIONS

The aim of this essay has been to open up new
perspectives on town planning. The arguments have
been tentative, yet the conclusion is clear.
Extensive land planning powers might be justified by
reference to property rights claims, just as easily
as they might be challenged from a property-rights
perspective. Indeed, those who advocate a
significant reduction in planning controls, on
grounds of property, put themselves in a difficult
position. They must deny not only that share of
power which central government requires in return
for sanctioning an existing distribution of assets,
but also local participatory claims to be consulted
and to influence outcomes.[56]
    The field of property rights has been neglected
too long by academics in town planning. If a
theoretical basis for planning is to be presented,
it must find its foundations in political, social
and economic theory. One route of exploration will
be through analyses of property rights and rights
claims. At a practical level any planning system
will achieve distributions of powers between
individuals, local communities, interest groups, and
central state agencies. To refer continuously to a
single (liberal) notion of ownership, as a way of
resisting this, merely debases the debate. For
anyone who favours local democratic participatory
processes, development control powers rest on just

claims for a right of property. How that right should be exercised, and its scope, remain open political questions.

NOTES

1. Thanks are due to David Beetham, Peter Craig, Tim Dant, Owen Hartley, Alan Hooper, Ray Mailly, Kirk Mann, Eric Reade, Margaret Southwell and Ken Willis for helpful comments on earlier drafts of this chapter.
2. V. Kruse, The Right of Property, translated by P.T. Federspiel (Oxford University Press, London, 1939), p. 76.
3. C.B. Macpherson (ed.), Property: Mainstream and Critical Positions (Basil Blackwell, Oxford, 1978), p. 1. 'Man-made' is appropriate, since property systems have reflected the disproportionate share of power enjoyed by men rather than women. Property illuminates important dimensions of gender relations: see R. Hirschon (ed.), Women and Property - Women as Property (Croom Helm, London, 1984), p. 1, etc. Legal and ideological practices may 'construct men's and women's ability to act as fully independent subjects in relation to property quite differently': see A. Whitehead, 'Women and Men; Kinship and Property: Some General Issues', in Hirschon, pp. 176, 189-90.
4. For Marxists this connects with commodity relationships upon which capitalism depends. For a relevant discussion see E.B. Pashukanis, Law and Marxism: a general theory, translated by B. Einhorn and edited by C. Arthur (Ink Links, London, 1978).
5. See Whitehead, op. cit., and M. Strathern, 'Subject or Object? Women and the Circulation of Valuables in Highlands New Guinea', in Hirschon, op. cit., pp. 158-75.
6. For contrasting perspectives see for instance J.B. Callicott, 'Traditional American Indian and Traditional Western European Attitudes towards Nature: An Overview', in R. Elliot and A. Gare, Environmental Philosophy (Open University Press, Milton Keynes, 1983). For an example of an economistic and deterministic interpretation of behaviour in a 'foreign' culture, see H. Demsetz, 'Toward a theory of property rights', The American Economic Review, LVII, 2 (May 1967), pp. 347-59. This frequently-cited paper effectively ignores the social system and power structure!
7. L.C. Becker, Property Rights: Philosophic

Foundations (Routledge and Kegan Paul, London, 1977), p. 18.

8. Some writers imply the possibility of ownership of a right: a bundle of rights (ownership) might be held to relate to a single right (or a number of rights). For example, the 'owner' might have the power to pass on the right, to use it exclusively, and so forth. A good example in planning literature is in B.J. Pearce, 'Instruments for land policy: a classification', Urban Law and Policy, 3 (1980), pp. 118-9. See also discussions in D.R. Denman, The Place of Property (Geographical Publications Ltd., Berkhamsted, 1978), pp. 26-8, and A.M. Honoré, 'Ownership', in A.G. Guest, Oxford Essays in Jurisprudence (Oxford University Press, Oxford, 1961), pp. 107-47 (especially 133-4).

9. Ibid.; cf Kruse, op. cit. pp. 105-18.

10. The right to the capital consists of the power to alienate the thing and the liberty to consume, waste or destroy the whole or part of it, although not necessarily without restriction. The incident of transmissibility means that the interest can be transmitted to successors and so on, ad infinitum. Honoré refrains from calling this a 'right', in deference to the view that the exercise of a right might depend on the choice of the holder. Absence of term means that the interest is not certain to determine at a future date (although there are limits here). Liability to execution means that the owner's interest may be taken away, as in the case of debt, or perhaps through expropriation by the state (although Honoré is cautious here). The incident of residuarity covers the point that it is characteristic that when an interest less than ownership terminates, legal systems provide for corresponding rights to vest in another (the owner).

11. See M. Cohen, 'Property and Sovereignty', in C.B. Macpherson, op. cit., pp. 167-71; Kruse, op. cit.; Honoré, op. cit., pp. 144-5.

12. For a fascinating discussion of some of the history of English property rights see R.S. Neale, 'The Bourgeoisie, Historically, Has Played a Most Revolutionary Part', in E. Kamenka and R.S. Neale (eds.), Feudalism, Capitalism and Beyond (Edward Arnold, London, 1975), pp. 84-102. A valuable historical study related to planning is M. McMahon, 'The Law of the Land: Property Rights and Town Planning in Modern Britain', in M. Ball, V. Bentivegna, M. Edwards and M. Folin (eds.), Land Rent, Housing and Urban Planning (Croom Helm,

London, 1985), pp. 87-106.
  13. For relevant comments see C.B. Macpherson, 'Capitalism and the Changing Concept of Property', in Kamenka and Neale, op. cit., pp. 104-24.
  14. See Pashukanis, op. cit., but also P. Hirst, On Law and Ideology (Macmillan, London, 1979), and C. Sumner, 'The Rule of Law and Civil Rights in Contemporary Marxist Theory', Kapitalistate, Working Papers on the Capitalist State, 9, Political Practice and the State (1981), pp. 63-91.
  15. See, for instance, H.E. Hallam, 'The Medieval Social Picture', and F.J. West, 'On the Ruins of Feudalism - Capitalism?', both in Kamenka and Neale, op. cit.: pp. 28-49 and pp. 50-60.
  16. A feasible counter-argument may be noted here, purporting to provide a basis for claims that individually-held property rights are founded in universal human needs, independently of cultural settings. It might be claimed that there are psychological needs which must always be met through particular kinds of personal property. This is difficult to substantiate: as Trasler points out, in an authoritative piece on the psychology of ownership, 'possessions' are invested with social meanings. Actions relating to ownership and possessiveness can only be explained in terms which reflect the particular meanings which possessions have in specific social settings. See G. Trasler, 'The Psychology of Ownership and Possessiveness', in P.G. Hollowell (ed.), Property and Social Relations (Heinemann, London, 1982), p. 46. The form of property institutions, of course, cannot be explained simply by reference to the means of satisfaction of the desire for physical objects. See also Cohen, op. cit., pp. 164-5. For a possible justification of notions of property rights in terms of 'species characteristics', see Becker, op. cit., pp. 102-3, where reference is made to studies of animal behaviour. As Becker comments on his own discussion, it would be 'presumptuous to call these considerations arguments'.
  17. See J.M. Buchanan, 'The Political Economy of Franchise in the Welfare State', in R.T. Selden (ed.), Capitalism and Freedom. Problems and Prospects (University Press of Virginia, Charlottesville, 1975), pp. 69-70. Since even a theorist as admired as Nozick appears to deploy a simple model of property, without many reservations, it is hardly surprising that lesser authors do so too. See R. Nozick, Anarchy, State, and Utopia

(Basil Blackwell, Oxford, 1974); J. Paul (ed.) Reading Nozick (Basil Blackwell, Oxford, 1982), chapters 16, 18, etc.; and A.M. Honoré, 'Property, Title and Redistribution', in V. Held, Property, Profits, and Economic Justice (Wadsworth Publishing Company, Belmont, California, 1980), pp. 84-92.
18. A possible exception may be Denman (op. cit.) whose views are complex.
19. The writer is grateful to David Beetham and Margaret Southwell for observations on this point.
20. An excellent example is a letter from A. Henney and H. Rose in The Times, Wednesday 9th July 1980.
21. K.G. Willis, The Economics of Town and Country Planning (Granada, London, 1980), p. 261.
22. For instance, B. Bracewell-Milnes, Land and Heritage: the public interest in personal ownership, Hobart Paper 93 (Institute of Economic Affairs, London, 1982), pp. 29-30.
23. W. Friedmann, Law and Social Change in Contemporary Britain (Stevens and Sons, London, 1951), pp. 22-8.
24. A major figure relevant to this tradition is F.A. Hayek: see his The Constitution of Liberty (Routledge and Kegan Paul, London, 1960), and The Road to Serfdom (George Routledge and Sons, London, 1944). In reality, of course, no concept of efficiency or rational resource use has meaning without the prior specification of property rights forms.
25. Such views may differ from those of conservatives: see R. Scruton, The Meaning of Conservatism (Macmillan, London, 2nd edition, 1984), chapter 5.
26. Nonetheless, 'public interest' ideas may be implicit in the general line of argument; see below, footnote 33.
27. For instance, see issues noted by Hayek, 1960, op. cit., pp. 229, 341, 349, 368-9; and Becker, op. cit., pp. 109-10.
28. G. Causer, 'Some Aspects of Property Distribution and Class Structure', in Hollowell, op. cit., p. 131.
29. Bracewell-Milnes, op. cit., p. 48.
30. B. Schaffer and G. Lamb, Can Equity be Organized? (Gower, Farnborough, and UNESCO, Paris, 1981), pp. 17, 20, etc. (This contains a powerful commentary covering the 'public choice' school).
31. For summaries see B. Ward, The Ideal Worlds of Economics (Macmillan, London, 1979), p.

325, etc.; E.G. Furubotn and S. Pejovich, 'Property Rights and Economic Theory: A Survey of Recent Literature', The Journal of Economic Literature, 10, 4 (December 1972), pp. 1137-62.

32. These themes are not pursued consistently: some British writers favour 'free markets', yet urge close co-operation of public agencies with private developers. They are really seeking a restricted politics which privileges certain interests.

33. See, for example, L. De Alessi, 'The Economics of Property Rights: A Review of the Evidence', in R.O. Zerbe (Jr.), (ed.), Research in Law and Economics, 2 (JAI Press Inc., Greenwich, Connecticut, 1980), pp. 40-2, etc. Such exercises suggest that economic liberals feel a need for a defence in terms of the 'public interest', both in respect of allocation of property rights and appropriate forms of intervention. The approaches purport to offer this. Results supposedly will be 'better for society' if there is only minimal intervention. If intervention becomes essential, then 'superior' outcomes will be achieved through incentives rather than removal of an owner's managerial powers. The present essay is not concerned with outcomes as such, but with claims which might be argued for. The writer is not convinced, however, of the desirability of according priority to economists' ideas about social benefits.

34. For instance, see Demsetz, op. cit., pp. 356, 358.

35. Denman, op. cit., p. 40, etc.; Willis, op. cit., pp. 257-8; D.R. Denman and S. Prodano, Land Use (George Allen and Unwin, London, 1972), pp. 125-6.

36. Ibid., p. 126.

37. A simple example is a general right to use a footpath over 'privately-owned' land. If it was necessary to 'buy out' all potential users before developing land, the cost could be enormous.

38. B.J. Pearce, 'Development Control: A "Neighbour Protection Service"?', The Planner, 70, 5 (May 1984), p. 9.

39. For comments on individualistic conceptions in legal interpretations see M. Loughlin, 'Private Property, Public Regulation and the Role of the Courts', unpublished paper for Third Urban Law Conference; Law, Market and Plan (University of Warwick, September 1981).

40. See M.L. Harrison, Land Planning and Development Control, Research Monograph (Department

of Social Policy and Administration, University of Leeds, 1979).
41. Department of the Environment, Circular 1/85, The use of conditions in planning permissions (HMSO, London, 1985), paras. 72-81.
42. For the issue in the Lake District context see Willis, op. cit., pp. 86-8. For a relevant general analysis see M. Loughlin, Local needs policies and development control strategies, School for Advanced Urban Studies, Working Paper 42 (University of Bristol, 1984).
43. See A. Grosskurth, 'North Wales: the fire next time', Roof, 8, 5 (September/October 1983), pp. 19-22. Also speech by Mr. D. Wigley in H. of C. Debates, 6th series, volume 2, session 1980-81, on Town and Country Planning Act 1971 (Amendment) Bill, (31st March 1981), cols. 162-6.
44. In British planning journals, for instance, see A. Sorensen and R. Day, 'Libertarian Planning', Town Planning Review, 52, 4 (October 1981), pp. 390-402; A. Sorensen, 'Planning Comes of Age: A Liberal Perspective', The Planner, 68, 6 (November/December 1982), pp. 184-5, 188; 'Towards a Market Theory of Planning', The Planner, 69, 3 (May/June 1983), pp. 78-80.
45. For relevant comments see Scruton, op. cit. For a general history of property rights ideas see R. Schlatter, Private Property (George Allen and Unwin, London, 1951).
46. Honoré notes that ownership is not merely a bundle of rights; 1961, op. cit., pp. 134, 113, etc.
47. See H. Newby, C. Bell, D. Rose and P. Saunders, Property, Paternalism and Power (Hutchinson, London, 1978), pp. 332-4.
48. See A. Wolfe, The Limits of Legitimacy (The Free Press, New York, 1977); also A. Arblaster, The Rise and Decline of Western Liberalism (Basil Blackwell, Oxford, 1984), pp. 264-83, 326-32, etc.
49. Consultation causes delay for developers, so they have an additional practical financial concern.
50. For economic liberals, localism (and the needs of clan, village, or town to which people belong) must take second place. 'Tribal sentiments' must give way for the sake of the 'Great Society': F.A. Hayek, Law, Legislation and Liberty, volume 2, The Mirage of Social Justice (Routledge and Kegan Paul, London, 1976), pp. 134, 143-4, etc. For American evidence of pressures against localism see G.L. Clark and M. Dear, State Apparatus (Allen and

Unwin, Boston, 1984), pp. 125-30.

51. For some problems of relying on legal codes of nuisance, etc. in planning, see Pearce (1984), op. cit., pp. 10-11.

52. M.L. Harrison (ed.), <u>Corporatism and the Welfare State</u> (Gower, Aldershot, 1984); M.L. Harrison, 'The Coming Welfare Corporatism', <u>New Society</u>, 67, 1110 (1st March 1984), pp. 321-3.

53. See Harrison, 1979, op. cit.

54. Some right-wing writers weld together quite incompatible elements: for instance Bracewell-Milnes (op. cit.) unites markets with paternalism.

55. See, for instance, Wolfe, op. cit.; C. Lindblom, <u>Politics and Markets</u> (Basic Books, New York, 1977); B. Jessop, <u>The Capitalist State</u> (Martin Robertson, Oxford, 1982).

56. One argument they may use is that local government does not respond to democratic processes, but to sectional interests or party pressures. This is a weak approach, for it may mean conceding the case for participation and democracy, abandoning the full liberal notion, and effectively debating the issues on their opponents' ground. This does not invalidate the point, however, that the local authority case for control rests partly on <u>effective</u> mediation on behalf of residents. See Chapter 11 for some relevant issues.

Chapter 4

SOME CURRENT ISSUES IN THE LAW ON DEVELOPMENT CONTROL IN ENGLAND AND WALES, WITH PARTICULAR REFERENCE TO THE ROLE OF THE COURTS AND JUDICIAL REVIEW

Michael Purdue

INTRODUCTION

Development control from a legal viewpoint is essentially the creation of statute and subordinate legislation. This sets up the broad framework with its network of public authorities with their various powers and duties. The wording of that legislation, and the extent to which certain rights and interests are protected, necessarily both legitimates and restricts the actual operation of the planning machinery. A distinctive feature of the system is the extent and degree to which the High Court serves to supervise the decision-making of the planning authorities. Grant in his book Urban Planning Law remarks, 'Town and country planning is not a function which Parliament has vested in judges. Theirs is a supervisory and not an executive role, concerned with issues not of policy but of law'.[1] Yet, although the courts can only overturn decisions of local planning authorities and the Secretary of State on the grounds of errors of law (and cannot substitute their own decisions), the elasticity of the judicial concept of an error of law gives the courts an important power to influence development control. This chapter concentrates on this aspect of the system, and discusses the current issues which are being brought before the courts.

THE ROLE AND SIGNIFICANCE OF JUDICIAL REVIEW IN RELATION TO DEVELOPMENT CONTROL

Until recently the term 'judicial review' was

relatively unknown to the general public, but today it seems that every week newspapers report that some person or other is challenging the validity of actions by one public body or another through this process. The increasing resort to judicial review probably reflects the development of the subject itself, and a new awareness of its availability and potential. It also coincides with the intense debate and disagreement over the role of public bodies in the United Kingdom.

In the context of development control a distinction must be made between the statutory right of challenge provided by S.245 of the Town and Country Planning Act 1971, and the inherent jurisdiction of the High Court to review the decisions of inferior courts, tribunals and other public bodies; a procedure which has now been put on a statutory basis by the Supreme Court Act 1981. The main difference lies not in the grounds of challenge, which are broadly similar - though there are fine distinctions which can be made - but in the body whose decision is being challenged. S.245 is almost solely concerned with decisions of the Secretary of State, and so cannot be used to challenge the decision of a local planning authority.[2] It is now settled law, however, that in the right circumstances the legality of a determination of a planning application by a local planning authority can be challenged by an application for judicial review under S.31 of the Supreme Court Act 1981. This process is known as an application by way of Order 53, which is the number of the particular rule of the Supreme Court which sets out in detail how the application is to be made.

An application for judicial review of a planning decision can be made by a person who has a statutory right of appeal to the Secretary of State, if the court considers this to be appropriate,[3] but its main importance is that it sets up a remedy for objectors and other third parties, where redress is not provided for directly by the legislation. In this regard, the courts have been generous in their view as to who has the right of access to the court. S.31 lays down that the person seeking leave of the court to proceed with an application for judicial review must have 'sufficient interest' in the matter to which the application relates. This has been taken to include local residents,[4] and in one case Comyn J. accepted that a person might have a legitimate bona fide interest in places far removed

Some Legal Issues

from where he lived.[5] As to the statutory right to challenge decisions of the Secretary of State, this is restricted to 'persons aggrieved'; but again this has been interpreted to include not only persons who have appeared at any public inquiry, which may have been held, but also local residents generally[6] (see also Chapter 11). This all suggests that the High Court sees itself as a mechanism by which the general public, as well as the main participants, can insist that development control is operated legally.

While the easing of the rules of access or standing means that third parties can and do challenge development control decisions in the courts, the costs of litigation and the limited chances of success ensure that the main protagonists in the courts are developers and local planning authorities who are attacking the validity of a decision of the Secretary of State on appeal. The chances of successfully challenging the legality of a decision of a local planning authority are narrowed not only by the inherent limitations of judicial review, but by the nature of decision-making at that level. Because of the broad way that the powers of deciding planning applications are drafted, the local authorities rarely act obviously without jurisdiction: so their decisions are normally more likely to be held to be invalid because of the way they have exercised their powers. In the terminology of judicial review, their decisions may be invalid because they have **abused their powers** by using them for the wrong purposes or for the wrong reasons, or because they are **flawed** by some procedural irregularity. In the case of decisions by the Secretary of State on appeal against a planning determination, the likelihood of the court finding such an error is increased by the existence of a written decision. This, especially in the case where there has been a local public inquiry, means that there exists what the Americans would describe as a 'record', by which to check the legality of the decision-making process. The two main grounds of review come together in the duty imposed upon the Secretary of State to give reasons for his decision,[7] as the courts will check to see whether such reasons are adequate and intelligible. A judgement by the courts that the reasons are inadequate or unintelligible will result in the decision being overturned unless it is clear that the applicant has not been prejudiced. This is so even if otherwise no error of law has been

committed.
　　The result is that the courts fulfill two main functions. First they supply an authoritative statement as to the range of factors that can be properly taken into account in operating the development control powers, and the purposes to which these powers can be put. Second, they provide a means of imposing a check on the quality of decision-making itself by requiring the reasoning process to be spelt out and justified. The basis for the first function can be traced to the doctrines of the Rule of Law and the Separation of Powers, the courts being constitutionally the proper body definitively to interpret statutory powers. As to the second function, this can be defended not only on the grounds that justice or fairness requires a decision-maker to explain the basis of his or her decision, but also because it improves the quality of decision-making generally. The main doubts turn on the ability, expertise and impartiality of the judiciary to carry out these tasks.[8]
　　It is also very hard to judge the practical consequences of judicial intervention. On the one hand the number of decisions overturned by the courts is still relatively small compared with the total number of planning decisions, and in many cases the resulting decision (which follows on the review) will be the same as to outome even if the reasoning is different. On the other hand, if the court's views on the scope of development control are faithfully followed, then judicial review can have an important impact. Again, fear of having decisions quashed for lack of reasons may result in an improvement generally in the standard of decisions or at least the quality of the writing. Neither of these claims, however, can be tested fully without empirical research.
　　The discussions below look at two specific areas which have been the subject of judicial scrutiny; the question of policy and the way that policies are applied. Some general conclusions will then be drawn.

THE SOURCES, STATUS AND SCOPE OF POLICY

When the present system of development control was instituted in 1947, the expectation was that in the long-term the predominant source of policy would be the development plans. In fact these have always

Some Legal Issues

had to be supplemented by non-statutory plans and policies, and today the statutory documents are in danger of being submerged under a mass of less formal ones; development control notes, circulars, ministerial decisions, and even after-dinner speeches by ministers. The key is S.29 of the Town and Country Planning Act 1971, which provides that the local planning authority shall have regard to 'any other material considerations' as well as the development plan. In a recent decision of the House of Lords (Great Portland Estates v Westminster City Council [9]), Lord Scarman put the position as follows:

> Development plans are no inflexible blueprint establishing a rigid pattern for future planning control. Though very important, they do not preclude a local planning authority in its administration of planning control from considering other material considerations.[10]

This would be unexceptional if it simply meant that the policies in the plans did not have to be applied rigidly, but had to give way to special circumstances. What has happened is rather that the courts have accepted that in determining a planning application or appeal, the relevant decision-maker is not precluded from considering - and indeed may be bound to have regard to - the policies contained in non-statutory documents.

Thus 'material considerations' can be stretched to cover the policies in draft plans,[11] government circulars,[12] ministerial decisions,[13] a speech by the Secretary of State for the Environment,[14] and the report of a working party set up by that Secretary of State.[15] The obvious practical consequences are a general downgrading of the importance of the formal development plans, and a corresponding avoidance of the rights of public participation in policy formulation. This is particularly so at the appeal level, where government circulars appear to be becoming increasingly influential.

At the same time, the exact legal status of the various sources of policy is uncertain. While the legislation indicates the relationship between the structure plans and local plans, it does not indicate any clear hierarchy between the plans and other material considerations. It would seem, therefore, that it is entirely up to the relevant planning authority what weight it places on a particular policy. In a recent circular the Department of the Environment has emphasised that the policies in the plans may have to give way to other policies, and it is stated here that 'They [the plans] should not be regarded as overriding other material considerations ...'.[16] It is worth noting, though, that S.86(3) of the Local Government Planning and Land Act 1980 imposes a duty on a local planning authority, when determining a planning application, to seek the achievement of the general objectives of the structure plan. This must undoubtedly underwrite the structure plan as the dominant planning instrument; but as commentators have pointed out the duty is couched in such vague terms as to be almost meaningless, especially when the objectives of structure plans are often expressed in extremely broad and utopian terms themselves.[17]

Equally problematic is the question of whether the determining authority has to explain why it has decided not to apply particular policies. In the case of policy in the development plan, it has been held that where that policy is relevant it must be considered and reasons be given for not following it;[18] though failure here will not matter if it clearly did not affect the outcome.[19] As to the policies or arguments which come under the heading of material considerations, if the policy is put to the determining authority and it is relevant, it equally must be dealt with in the reasons for the decision. In one case Sir Douglas Franks Q.C. seemed to suggest that all material considerations had to be regarded by the decision-makers, even if the arguments were not specifically put to them,[20] but he went out of his way to repudiate this suggestion on a later occasion.[21] It does however seem that with circulars, where a particular policy directly bears on an application it must be discussed, even if it has not been raised by the parties.[22] Where a circular is not directly or specially applicable, it seems that it can be assumed that it has been taken into account as part of the general planning background even if it was not directly referred to by the decision-maker.[23]

The decisions of inspectors on planning appeals fall into a rather special category. The courts have emphasised that they do not amount to binding precedents, and that the inspectors themselves have no power to make policy.[24]

Yet where a previous inspector has made a decision on a particular point and this decision is

Some Legal Issues

referred to by another inspector, the latter must either distinguish it or give reasons for not following his or her colleague.[25]
As to the meaning of the policies being applied, the final arbiter is not the original draftsman of the policies, but the courts themselves. In this way the interpretation of a particular provision in a circular or a structure plan becomes a matter of law.[26]
Finally, there is the well-known problem of the scope of planning policies, the questions being for what purposes can decisions be made and for what reasons? Here the courts have cautiously accepted that the planning legislation is not just concerned with the protection of the environment and physical amenities, but also with social and economic issues. In this regard, the recent decision in <u>Great Portland Estates</u> v <u>Westminster City Council</u> (cited above) is important as it gives the highest judicial authority to the principle that particular activities may be protected if they contribute to the activities of a city as a whole. Lord Scarman endorsed the policy in the Westminster Local Plan of protecting 'specific industrial activities' as a 'powerful piece of positive thinking within a planning context'.[27] Economic or financial aspects of planning have always caused judges difficulties, but it is now accepted that the financial viability of a proposed development can have implications which are clearly planning considerations. Also, although this has never been authoritatively stated, it would appear clear that the development control powers can be used to promote employment, otherwise most of the present government policies would be ultra vires.
This means then, that planning authorities have a fairly free hand as to their planning objectives or goals (although of course central government may seek to constrain them). Where the courts are more likely to intervene is when the powers are being used to try to force a private individual to take on a function given by statute to a public authority: for instance, by refusing permission because of a failure to provide public car parking.[28]

THE PROCESS BY WHICH POLICIES ARE APPLIED

The Act and the regulations made under it lay down detailed requirements as to the way the development control powers are to be exercised. Apart from these statutory procedures the courts will insist on what they consider to be fair dealing. These rules, traditionally known as the rules of Natural Justice, must be observed even if there has been scrupulous adherence to the statutory procedures. It has recently been held that there is no question of it being harder to prove a breach of natural justice merely because the statutory rules have been followed.[29] In requiring fair dealing the courts are essentially concerned that the decision-maker should not be biased in any way, and that the parties who are going to be affected by the decision are given every opportunity to make their case. With respect to the statutory procedures, the main task of the judge is one of statutory interpretation, and the main difficulties arise once it has been decided that there has been a failure to abide by the rules. This is because it by no means necessarily follows that a breach will result in the decision being held to be invalid. The courts may decide that the particular provision is not of great consequence, and thus that the failure does not invalidate. More importantly, they may exercise their discretion to refuse a remedy. This applies whether the decision is being challenged by way of application for judicial review or by statutory appeal. So in Main v Swansea City Council[30] the Court of Appeal held that although the failure to observe the notification procedures, set out in S.27, would be a ground on which to invalidate the subsequent decision, the delay in bringing the action meant that they would refuse to do this. In theory an extremely important breach will mean that the decision never existed, and is in effect so much waste paper, but in the vast majority of cases the courts always retain a residual discretion. The result is that it is hard to lay down hard and fast rules as to the consequences of a breach. It has been held recently that failures to observe the Town and Country Planning (Development Plans) (England) Direction 1981 can be disregarded as being merely directory,[31] while The Town and Country Planning General Regulations 1976 (S.I. 1976/1419) (governing applications by or on land owned by local planning authorities) must be strictly followed.[32] Various fine distinctions and sub-rules can be attempted but basically it depends on the view the court takes as to the importance of the provision and the seriousness of the breach and its consequences.

The rules of fair dealing which the law imposes on the development control system originate from

Some Legal Issues

procedures devised for judicial adjudication. Although now prepared to impose a duty to act fairly on a person carrying out an administrative function, the judiciary attempt to tailor or modify the procedures to the particular function. So we find that different rules apply at different stages of the processing of a planning application. As regards the stage where the application is being determined by the local planning authority, that authority has not yet been required to give the applicant or other interested parties a right to a hearing. At the most, a practice of allowing such a hearing might be held to give rise to a 'legitimate expectation' to be heard, so that the local planning authority could not go back on that practice.[33] It has been held that the council members making the decision must not have any financial interest in the application, and the participation of such a member will render the decision void.[34] The case of the local planning authority having a corporate interest in the application is far less clear-cut (where the authority is making the application or when it has some financial interest in the site). In *Steeples* v *Derbyshire County Council*[35] Webster J. held that the decision would be void if a reasonable man would have thought that there was a real likelihood that the interest had a material and significant effect on the decision. However, since then, two other judges have gone back on that strict test and it would seem that it does not matter what the reasonable man would have thought, provided the local planning authority was not in fact biased.[36] What is still unclear is what is meant by bias. It may be that even if the members making the decision try not to be influenced by the council's interest, there may be circumstances where their decision just cannot be made properly.[37]

In contrast, where the Secretary of State is deciding an appeal or has called in an application, the rules are much stricter. The legislation of course provides a right to a hearing, but even where this is waived and the decision is made through the written representations procedure, it has been held that the rules of natural justice must be followed. A decision will be quashed if it is based on arguments or evidence which have not been put to both sides.[38] Where a hearing *is* held, the inspector is expected to keep to an extremely high standard of procedure. At this stage the test is not whether the breach in fact affected the final decision, but a more subjective one. Thus in

67

<u>Performance Cars Ltd</u> v <u>Secretary of State for the Environment</u>,[39] where during an inquiry the applicant was not given adequate time to look at new documents, Lord Denning in quashing the decision emphasised that people should not go away from any inquiry thinking they have not had a fair deal. Again, in <u>Simmonds</u> v <u>Secretary of State for the Environment</u>,[40] where it might have seemed at the end of the inquiry that the inspector was allowing one side further argument, Forbes J. said that it was sufficient if the circumstances gave the impression that some impropriety had taken place, even if the evidence showed that this was totally untrue.

Finally, there are signs that the courts are developing a more substantive approach to fairness. In particular Mr. Justice Woolf (now Lord Justice Woolf) has shown an awareness of the need for local planning authorities to conform to principles of good administration.[41] It is conceivable that in future years we may see judges making an even closer scrutiny of planning decisions, and adopting a role that is nearer to that of an ombudsman.

CONCLUSIONS

As a weapon judicial review is expensive and unpredictable, but it will continue to be used by developers, local authorities and third parties as the final card to be played in development control battles. If the High Court did not exist, some other body would have to be created. The Secretary of State is too closely involved in the process to be left with the final word on the scope and procedure of the operation of the system. On the whole, it is submitted that especially since there is now more continuity and specialisation of the judges who perform the function,[42] judicial review does not do a bad job. It provides some protection against irrational and high-handed decision-making. The main criticisms to be made are that the guidance it gives on matters of scope and procedure is too uncertain and ambiguous, and that the power to quash for error of law can sometimes be used to impose the judges' own views as to the merits of the issue. However, the first fault stems mainly from the open-ended nature of the statutory system itself, and the second is endemic to any system of review. To the present writer the main needs in the future are for the judiciary to become more expert in the

Some Legal Issues

intricacies of planning, and - more importantly - to encourage a wider representation of interests in the weighing of decisions. In respect of the second need, the courts will have to develop further the concept of third party rights, and move away from an obsession with formal private property rights as the only rights worthy of protection.

NOTES

1. M. Grant, Urban Planning Law (Sweet and Maxwell, London, 1982), p. 631.
2. But see the exception of Tree Preservation Orders made by the local planning authority; S.242(2) and S.60.
3. See R v Hillingdon London Borough, ex parte Royco Homes Ltd [1974], Q.B. 720.
4. See Covent Garden Community Association Ltd v Greater London Council, Journal of Planning and Environment Law, 1981, p. 183.
5. See R v Hammersmith and Fulham Borough Council, ex parte People Before Profit Ltd, Journal of Planning and Environment Law, 1981, p. 869.
6. See Turner v Secretary of State for the Environment (1973) 28 P. & C.R. 123, and Hollis v Secretary of State for the Environment, Journal of Planning and Environment Law, 1983, p. 164.
7. There is only an express duty to give reasons in the case of decisions following a public inquiry - sec Rule 13 of The Town and Country Planning (Inquiries Procedure) Rules 1974 (S.I. 1974/419) - but it seems that reasons must still be given, at least if requested, for decisions made following written representations: see Westminster City Council v Secretary of State for the Environment and City Commercial Real Estates Investments Ltd, Journal of Planning and Environment Law, 1984, p. 27, and Sir George Grenfell - Baines v Secretary of State for the Environment, Journal of Planning and Environment Law, 1985, p. 256.
8. See P. McAuslan, The Ideologies of Planning Law (Pergamon Press, Oxford, 1981).
9. (1984) 3 W.L.R. 1035.
10. p. 1045.
11. R v City of London Corporation, ex parte Allen (1980) 79 L.G.R. 223; Davies v London Borough of Hammersmith and Fulham, Journal of Planning and Environment Law, 1981, p. 682.
12. See J.A. Pye (Oxford) Estates Ltd v West Oxfordshire District Council, Journal of Planning

69

and Environment Law, 1982, p. 577.

13. See Rockhold Ltd v Secretary of State for the Environment and South Oxfordshire District Council, Journal of Planning and Environment Law, 1986, p. 130.

14. See Dimsdale Development (South East) Ltd v Secretary of State for the Environment and Hounslow London Borough Council, Journal of Planning and Environment Law, 1986, p. 276.

15. See Westminster City Council v Secretary of State for the Environment and City Commercial Real Estates Investments Ltd, op. cit., footnote 7 above.

16. Department of the Environment, Circular 14/85, Development and Employment (HMSO, London, 1985).

17. See R v Royal County of Berkshire, ex parte Mangnall, Journal of Planning and Environment Law, 1985, p. 258.

18. See Ynystawe v Secretary of State for Wales, Journal of Planning and Environment Law, 1981, p. 874.

19. See R v Sevenoaks District Council, ex parte W.J. Terry, Journal of Planning and Environment Law, 1984, p. 420.

20. See Bradwell Industrial Aggregates v Secretary of State for the Environment, Journal of Planning and Environment Law, 1981, p. 276.

21. See Francis Joseph Tierney v Secretary of State for the Environment, Journal of Planning and Environment Law, 1983, p. 799.

22. See London Borough of Newham v Secretary of State for the Environment and East London Housing Association Ltd (decided 17th February 1986 but not yet reported at time of writing).

23. See Hatfield Construction Ltd v Secretary of State for the Environment and the London Borough of Redbridge, Journal of Planning and Environment Law, 1983, p. 605.

24. See Chelmsford Borough Council v Secretary of State for the Environment and E.R. Alexander Ltd, Journal of Planning and Environment Law, 1985, p. 316, and Rockhold Ltd v Secretary of State for the Environment and South Oxfordshire District Council, op. cit.

25. See Rockhold Ltd v Secretary of State for the Environment, op. cit.

26. See Rockhold Ltd v Secretary of State for the Environment, op. cit. and Stephenson v Secretary of State for the Environment, Journal of Planning and Environment Law, 1986, p. 357.

27. Great Portland Estates v Westminster City Council, op. cit., pp. 1042 and 1043.
28. Westminster Renslade Ltd v Secretary of State for the Environment, Journal of Planning and Environment Law, 1983, p. 454.
29. See Reading Borough Council v Secretary of State for the Environment and Commercial Union Properties (Investments) Ltd, Journal of Planning and Environment Law, 1986, p. 115.
30. (1985) 49 P. & C.R. 26.
31. See R v St. Edmundsbury Borough Council, ex parte Investors in Industry Commercial Properties Ltd (1985) 1 W.L.R. 1168 and R v Carlisle City Council and the Secretary of State for the Environment, ex parte Cumbrian Co-operative Society Ltd, Journal of Planning and Environment Law, 1986, p. 206.
32. See Steeples v Derbyshire County Council (1985) 1 W.L.R. 256, and R v Lambeth London Borough Council, Journal of Planning and Environment Law, 1986, p. 201.
33. See R v Liverpool Corporation, ex parte Liverpool Taxi Fleet Operators' Association [1972] 2 Q.B. 299, and Council for the Civil Service Unions v Minister for the Civil Service [1984] 3 All E.R. 935.
34. See R v Hendon Borough Council, ex parte Chorley [1933] 2 K.B. 696.
35. (1985) 1 W.L.R. 256.
36. See respectively Glidewell J. in R v Sevenoaks District Council, ex parte W.J. Terry, op. cit., and Stocker J. in R v St. Edmundsbury Council, ex parte Investors in Industry Commercial Properties Ltd, op. cit.
37. See on this Glidewell J. in R v Sevenoaks District Council, ex parte W.J. Terry, op. cit.
38. See Lewis Thirkwell Ltd v Secretary of State for the Environment, Journal of Planning and Environment Law, 1978, p. 844.
39. (1977) 34 P. & C.R. 92.
40. Journal of Planning and Environment Law, 1985, p. 253.
41. See Ynys Mon Isle of Anglesey Borough Council v Secretary of State for Wales and Parry Brothers (Builders) Co. Ltd, Journal of Planning and Environment Law, 1984, p. 646, and R v Torfaen Borough Council, ex parte Jones (decided 2nd September 1985 but not yet reported at time of writing).
42. See L. Blom-Cooper, 'The New Face of Judicial Review: Administrative Changes in Order

53', Public Law (Summer 1982), pp. 250-61.

Chapter 5

DEVELOPMENT CONTROL IN SCOTLAND

Eric Young and Jeremy Rowan-Robinson

INTRODUCTION

The purpose of this chapter is to provide some idea of the way in which the development control process operates in Scotland. Our concern is less with describing the legal framework, since a practitioner from England or Wales would find a great deal that is familiar in the Scottish legislation, than with the way in which the process operates within that framework. In seeking to do this we have had to be very selective, concentrating on those aspects of the process which provide a distinctive Scottish dimension.

This dimension owes much to the different context within which development control is carried on in Scotland. Control operates within a different administrative structure and, to an extent, within a distinctive policy framework.[1] It also operates against the background of a very different legal system and under separate, though broadly similar, legislation. All in all, the differences in development control amount to much more than the mere appearance of the word 'Scotland' in the titles of most of the relevant statutes. The main implications of the different administrative, policy and legal contexts within which development control operates in Scotland will be considered in turn.

THE ADMINISTRATIVE FRAMEWORK

The Secretary of State for Scotland
Overall responsibility for development control in Scotland rests with the Secretary of State for Scotland, this responsibility being discharged in the main through the Scottish Development Department

(SDD). The fact that the Secretary of State is also responsible for many other governmental functions concerned with land, such as roads, housing and agriculture, may well assist co-ordination in Scottish land use policies. As in England and Wales, the Secretary of State's role is primarily of a supervisory and advisory nature. Although he has wide statutory powers in relation to development control, and though it is to him that appeals against the decisions of planning authorities are made, the minister has sought in recent times to reduce his involvement in detailed development control.[2] This process of 'disengagement' has continued, with the result that today only a very small proportion of planning applications, involving proposals in which there may be a clear national interest, need to be notified to the minister in order that he may consider whether to exercise his power to 'call in' a particular application for decision by himself.[3]

Effective supervision calls for good liaison, and the scale on which the planning system operates in Scotland allows the SDD to gain a fuller knowledge of the working of the system at local level and to establish closer working relationships (many of those involved in the planning process at national and local level being personally known to one another) than is perhaps possible in England.

Local Planning Authorities
The arrangements for the discharge of planning functions at local level are to be found in the Local Government (Scotland) Act 1973[4] ('the 1973 Act'). The 1973 Act implemented a thoroughgoing reform of the local government structure, replacing a piecemeal pattern of 430 local authorities with a more uniform two-tier structure of regional and district councils, except that in Orkney, Shetland and the Western Isles all local government functions were allocated to the islands area councils.

Planning functions differ from other functions, however, in that they do not fit into the two-tier structure in a uniform way. In the three most sparsely-populated regions - Borders, Dumfries and Galloway, and Highland - district councils were thought not to have adequate resources to carry out planning functions, and in these three regions the regional councils, referred to for planning purposes as 'general planning authorities', are responsible for all planning functions in their

Development Control in Scotland

areas. Also termed 'general planning authorities' are the three all-purpose islands area councils. Elsewhere, planning functions are split between regional and district councils, referred to respectively in the legislation as 'regional planning authorities' and 'district planning authorities'. The principal regional planning function is the preparation of the structure plan. The preparation of local plans and the carrying out of development control functions are primarily the responsibility of district planning authorities.

For most local government services the two-tier structure does not involve division of functions between the tiers, or the subordination of one tier to another. However, planning is different in that the structure plan is intended to set out the strategy within which other planning functions are to be carried out, and if the integrity of the structure plan is to be preserved, the content of local plans and the operation of development control must, to some extent, be subordinated to it. Legislation therefore provides that local plans must generally conform to the structure plan,[5] that regional planning authorities have certain reserve powers in relation to local plans,[6] and - the most important aspect of the two-tier system so far as development control is concerned - that the regional authority may, in specified circumstances, direct that an application for planning permission is to be determined by the region instead of, as would normally be the case, by the appropriate district authority.[7]

Under S.179 of the 1973 Act, as originally enacted, a planning application might be 'called in' by the region where a proposed development either (i) did not conform to a structure plan approved by the minister; or (ii) raised a 'new' planning issue of general regional significance. Cullingworth suggests that the division of planning functions in Scotland was made on a 'much better basis' than in England and Wales,[8] but the broad terms of S.179 of the 1973 Act left scope for disagreement between region and district; almost any type of development might, in appropriate circumstances, satisfy the criteria for call in. However, a study in 1979 concluded that although regions might not have been as restrained in the use of their powers as the Secretary of State had recommended,[9] they did not 'on the whole appear to have shown an excessive inclination to interfere in the development control process'.[10] Even so, the study noted some

variations in practice between regions.
    The distribution of planning functions between regional and district planning authorities was one of the matters examined by the Committee of Inquiry into Local Government in Scotland (the Stodart Committee). The committee concluded that 'call in' powers should remain available to regions;[11] only thus could their strategic policies be safeguarded against the possibility that districts might, in the exercise of their development control powers, undermine those strategies. More precise definition of the power was, however, recommended, and the word 'major' was substituted for 'new' in the second branch of S.179 of the 1973 Act (above).[12] According to SDD Circular 6/1984[13]: 'a major planning issue arises where a proposed development is not covered by established policies or where a proposed development, if approved, would significantly prejudice the continued effectiveness of established policies.'. In the exercise of his powers to determine an appeal by a district planning authority against a regional call in, the Secretary of State will, states the circular, be guided by these principles.

POLICY AND OPERATIONAL ISSUES

Policy Guidance for Development Control
The development control process is intended, as in England and Wales, to operate within a framework of policy guidance. SDD Circular 32/1983, Structure and Local Plans, states, for example, that local plans should provide 'the essential basis for sound development control decisions and for providing clear guidance to potential developers ...'. The Scottish legislation (differing from the English) provides that there should be complete coverage of Scotland with local plans as soon as possible.[14] Progress with plans has been slow; by May 1985 only 51 per cent of Scotland was covered by adopted local plans. However, despite the perceived importance of local plans for development control, a research report, An Evaluation of Local Plan Production and Performance,[15] tentatively concludes that there is little evidence to suggest that delay in their preparation is prejudicing local planning.
    There is no obligation on the Secretary of State to prepare policy guidance on land use allocation at the national level, and until fairly recently he only did so where it was clear that some

Development Control in Scotland

indication of national policy was necessary in the interests of co-ordination or consistency in development control.[16] However, in 1972 the report of the Select Committee on Scottish Affairs, Land Resource Use in Scotland,[17] recommended the preparation of an indicative national plan for Scotland. In its response,[18] the government acknowledged the desirability of more central government guidance but baulked at the idea of a rigid 'national structure plan'. Instead, they agreed to build up a set of guidelines on those aspects of land use planning which required all-Scotland examination. The result is a series of National Planning Guidelines which have been published at intervals since 1974 and which deal with such diverse topics as 'Coastal Planning', 'Major Shopping Developments' and 'High Technology Industry'. As with local plans, the guidelines are intended to provide important support for development control.[19]

The guidelines are unique to Scotland. Although, like the Development Control Policy Notes in England and Wales, they seek to draw together central government policy on certain areas of development control, the guidelines go a good deal further and in some cases actually designate areas where particular types of development should be encouraged or discouraged. (The guidelines do not, however, constitute a comprehensive framework for regional and district planning; there are, for example, no guidelines for resources which are not natural, nor for power generation purposes, and financial resources for urban renewal and change are not covered.[20]) Though the guidelines represent a constraint on planning authorities' discretion, they do not appear to have been received as unwelcome dictation from central government. This may be because drafting of the guidelines has been undertaken in consultation with the planning authorities, and because, as Wannop observes, they are 'largely apolitical'[21] (in the sense that they are almost entirely concerned with locational issues and do not deal with expenditure or social priorities).

With the notable exception of the guidelines, national policy guidance has tended to emerge in an unsystematic way in circulars[22] or Planning Advice Notes.[23]

There is a further aspect of policy guidance for development control which is unique to Scotland. The Local Government (Scotland) Act 1973 confers powers on regional and general planning authorities to prepare regional reports. Although they do not form part of the statutory development plan, such reports must be taken into account in the exercise of development control powers (1973 Act, S.173). Regional reports are simply statements of planning policy proposals. When such a report is prepared, it must be submitted to the Secretary of State but is not subject to his approval. The minister is, however, required to make observations on the report. Regional reports were seen by some as providing a vehicle for the sort of corporate policy plan advocated by the Paterson Committee.[24] However, the reports suffer from the same sort of ambiguities that bedevilled the first generation of English structure plans;[25] it is not clear whether they are essentially intended to be no more than land use documents or whether they may serve a broader purpose. Although the first round of regional reports, prepared under a direction issued by the Secretary of State in 1975, provided a useful basis for the preparation of the original structure plans in Scotland,[26] their subsequent impact on the planning process and, in particular, their effects so far as development control is concerned, though varying from authority to authority, have been fairly limited.

'Operational' Issues
The present government appears to have some fairly definite ideas about the way in which planning control in Scotland should operate on a day-to-day basis. The last five years have seen a steady stream of advice and exhortation on such matters as the attitude to and the management of development control. This advice has been similar in philosophy, though perhaps less abrasive in tone, to that in England and Wales.
    The underlying theme of this 'operational' advice has been the need 'to release the spirit of enterprise' and to ensure that decisions are taken more quickly.[27] This theme was translated into official advice in SDD Circular 24/1981 (<u>Development Control</u>),[28] which stated that: 'The Secretary of State considers that swift and sound decision taking should continue to be the main development control priority' and that 'it is of vital importance that development proposals that will generate jobs and wealth should be considered quickly and sympathetically'.

The advice has been supported by amending legislation, regulations and circulars designed to simplify the procedures for keeping development plans up to date,[29] extending the scope of some categories of development for which permission is automatically granted,[30] and reducing delays in the processing of appeals.[31]

As a further step, the SDD commissioned research to identify the factors which affect the pace of decision-making by planning authorities on planning applications. The report, Development Control Performance in Scotland,[32] identified certain shortcomings in administrative practice, but concluded that, in general, development control performance, measured in terms of speed of decision-making, was already relatively good.[33] The report went on to point out that the speed of the development control process is often dictated by factors such as defective applications, delays by consultees and the level of objections to proposals, all of which are beyond the control of the planning authority.

The report also emphasised that as a measure of performance, speed of decision-making has serious limitations. It ignores the quality of the decision and also the fact that many authorities seek to negotiate amendments to applications to make them acceptable; as the report observes, most applicants would prefer a delayed approval to a quick refusal.

A subsequent report[34] (due to be published shortly) examines the factors affecting the performance of planning authorities in submitting their observations to the Secretary of State on planning appeals. The research was prompted by the fact that in 1983 only 20 per cent of observations were submitted within the statutory two month period, whereas in England and Wales 85 per cent of planning authority observations were received by the Department of the Environment (DoE) within a similar period. The report found that protracted delays were often due to slack office procedures and failure to accord a high priority to the preparation of observations. Significantly, however, it was also found that there are, in proportion to population, far fewer town planners employed by Scottish planning authorities than is the case in England and Wales - in relative terms probably only two-thirds as many, and as few as one-third as many engaged on development control. The report makes a large number of recommendations for improving performance in the submission of

Development Control in Scotland

observations.

LAW AND PROCEDURES

Although the Scottish and English legal systems 'remain separate and - a unique constitutional phenomenon within a unitary state - stand to this day in the same juridical relationship to one another as they do individually to the system of any other foreign country',[35] the very substantial differences between the two systems do not result in nearly as many differences in the law on development control as might perhaps be expected. The reason is, of course, that it is only in a few respects that Scots common law impinges on the operation of the planning legislation. And although Scottish planning law is largely contained in separate statutes and delegated legislation, and differs in many matters of detail, it is broadly similar to that which applies in England and Wales. Some of the more important legal and procedural differences are outlined below.[36]

The Courts
In planning matters in Scotland the Court of Session's function is very similar to that of the High Court in England. There is a right of appeal from the Court of Session to the House of Lords.

Far fewer town planning cases, relative to the countries' respective populations, have come before the Scottish courts than the English. There are probably two reasons for this. First, until comparatively recently the Scottish courts appeared to afford little encouragement to those seeking to challenge the decisions of administrative authorities.[37] Secondly, the fact that development pressures are generally less strong in Scotland than in many parts of England probably means that there is often less of a financial incentive to challenge Scottish authorities' decisions.

However, in recent years the number and variety of town planning cases coming before the Scottish courts have increased significantly. Nonetheless, decisions of the English courts are very important in Scotland. They are far more numerous and therefore provide more substantial coverage of problem areas. In the interpretation of similarly-worded legislation the courts in one jurisdiction

generally pay great respect to decisions in the other.[38] English decisions are widely referred to in argument and are frequently relied on by the Scottish courts in arriving at their decisions.[39] There are, of course, cases in which the courts of the two countries have arrived at different conclusions on similar issues, but in most such cases the relevant cases in the other jurisdiction were not brought to the court's attention. In British Airports Authority v Secretary of State for Scotland,[40] for example, in which the court accepted the proposition that a condition which was unnecessary is ultra vires, the several cases in which the English courts have rejected that proposition were not brought out in argument before the court. An exception to the general rule that the courts will seek to interpret similarly-worded legislation in the same way is to be seen in the decision of the Court of Appeal in R v Greenwich London Borough Council, ex parte Patel[41] not to follow the Court of Session's decision in McDaid v Clydebank District Council[42] on the scope of the jurisdiction of the courts to question the validity of enforcement notices (see below).
    In general, however, the main difference to be discerned between the decisions of the courts of the two countries appears to be one of attitude.

A Private Rights Approach?

The principles of judicial review permit the courts a good deal of discretion, with the result that judicial attitudes can be very important. While judicial attitudes are not as homogeneous as is sometimes suggested, some Scottish judges (particularly the members of the First Division[43]) have shown themselves, we would suggest, particularly concerned to protect private rights - often to a greater extent than seems evident in England.
    Griffith's contention that in planning law the judges are 'sharp in their scrutiny of the way public authorities exercise their powers'[44] appears to be borne out by some of the views expressed by Scottish judges. In Wordie Property Co. Ltd v Secretary of State for Scotland,[45] for example, Lord Cameron said that 'as the Secretary of State's powers are concerned with interference with the private rights of property of the subject, I think that it is the duty, as well as the right, of the court to scrutinise anxiously the exercise of

these powers ...', while in <u>Lawrie</u> v <u>Edinburgh Corporation</u>[46] the Sheriff (K.W.B. Middleton) said (in the context of the scope of planning authorities' powers to require remedial action in respect of waste land): 'In a matter of this kind the public interest in preserving the amenity of the city must be balanced against the public interest in protecting individual liberty, and I cannot regard the former as being paramount'. One or two examples of the effect of this kind of approach may be mentioned.

A restrictive approach to the scope of the planning legislation and of the objectives which planning authorities may seek to achieve by way of conditions is, for example, to be seen in <u>David Lowe & Sons Ltd</u> v <u>Musselburgh Town Council</u>.[47] Taking the view that a planning permission for residential development could not competently be qualified by a condition providing that the site in question should be developed in the proportion of one private house to every four local authority houses, the Lord President and Lord Cameron said that planning was not concerned with questions of ownership or occupation, and that planning powers could not be used to restrict the freedom of landowners to dispose of their land as they chose.

A restrictive view of planning authorities' powers to impose conditions on a planning permission was also taken by the court in <u>British Airports Authority</u> v <u>Secretary of State for Scotland</u> (see above), in which the Court of Session held that a condition could only be legitimately imposed on a grant of planning permission if the condition in question was necessary, the court itself being prepared to judge the question of necessity.[48]

A strict approach to administrative decisions having an adverse effect on the rights of a property owner is to be seen in two cases involving enforcement action. In <u>McNaughton</u> v <u>Peter McIntyre (Clyde) Ltd</u>[49] an enforcement notice required landowners to remove rubble and other material they had dumped on land and to restore that land to its condition prior to the unauthorised development. The notice was held invalid for lack of specification; it did not tell the landowners 'precisely and unambiguously' what they had to do to comply with the notice. In England similarly-worded notices have been held sufficiently specific.[50] In <u>McDaid</u> v <u>Clydebank District Council</u>[51] the Court of Session had to consider the effect of S.85(10) of the Town and Country Planning (Scotland) Act 1972

Development Control in Scotland

('the 1972 Act'), which provides that the validity of an enforcement notice may not, except by way of appeal to the Secretary of State, be questioned in any legal proceedings whatsoever on various specified grounds. The terms of S.85(10) did not, however, prevent the court declaring an enforcement notice to be a nullity as not having been properly served (even though failure in service is one of the grounds specified in S.85(10)). As one commentator said of the decision: 'one is left to wonder what purpose S.85(10) is meant to serve'.[52] Though much will depend on the subsequent interpretation of this decision, as matters stand at present it is certainly difficult to envisage many situations in which S.85(10) will serve what clearly appears to be its intended purpose - the protection of an enforcement notice from challenge in the courts until appeal to the Secretary of State has first been made.

The First Division of the Court of Session has tended to insist upon the observance of a very 'judicialised' style of decision-making on the part of the Secretary of State following the holding of a public inquiry, stressing the importance to be attached to the evidence presented to the inquiry and insisting that there must be an adequate 'factual' basis for the inquiry decision.[53] The exercise of this degree of control over superficially procedural matters has the effect of restricting the discretion of the decision-maker and of downgrading the importance of the 'policy' element in inquiry decisions. The explanation for this attitude would seem to be that here (as in other areas of the law) the members of the First Division, favouring a strongly 'property oriented' approach to development control, have tended to interpret statutory procedural requirements affecting rights of private property in a very strict fashion. Demonstrating, perhaps, that judicial attitudes to such matters are by no means homogeneous, however, the members of the Second Division have sometimes adopted a less strict attitude to such requirements, an approach more favourable to the public authorities concerned with development control.[54]

Publicity for Planning Applications: 'bad neighbour' development and neighbour notification

Perhaps the most notable difference between development control procedures in Scotland and

England lies in the requirements to publicise planning applications, the Scottish requirements going far beyond those in the English legislation.

For long the lack of any statutory requirement to publicise planning applications, and the resultant absence of any opportunity for interested members of the public to make their views known, was defended by government on practical grounds - any change would, it was said, overload the development control machinery - and also on grounds of principle - the development control system, it was argued, was concerned to control development in the public interest and it was not the function of the system to seek to protect private interests.

A minor change of attitude occurred in 1959 when (as in England and Wales) it was provided that applications for 'bad neighbour' development - development such as refuse disposal facilities or places of public entertainment which might have a very adverse effect on a neighbourhood - had to be publicised. Initially, the statutory provisions were very narrow in their scope, being confined to a mere six categories of development.

Over the years, various bodies, including the Scottish Law Commission, the Scottish Committee of the Council on Tribunals, the Select Committee on Scottish Affairs and the Law Society of Scotland, urged extension of the publicity requirements, and the categories of 'bad neighbour' development were very considerably extended by the Town and Country Planning (General Development) (Scotland) Order 1975 ('the GDO').[55] Not only do the Scottish provisions designate all the classes of development which had been included in the English GDO of 1973,[56] they go a considerable way beyond the English order's provisions. The Scottish order specifies additional types of development such as licensed premises but, more importantly, also includes five types of development defined not by reference to development categories but by reference to the effect the development will have on a particular area. Thus it covers proposals which would alter the character of an area of established amenity, or introduce significant change into a homogeneous area, or affect residential property by noise, fumes, smoke, etc., or bring crowds into a generally quiet area, or cause noise or activity between 8.00 p.m. and 8.00 a.m.

A paper produced by the SDD in 1977, <u>Review of the Management of Planning</u>, which sought to stimulate discussion on possible changes in the land use planning system, spoke somewhat dismissively of the 'neighbour protection' service provided by the planning legislation. 'At this level', said the paper, 'planning is doing little more than providing a conciliation and arbitration service between neighbours', taking up staff time which could be employed on tasks 'which are arguably more important ...'. The paper suggested that development proposals should only be advertised when the planning authority considered such action would be worthwhile.

However, many responses to the paper not only favoured retention of the obligation to publicise 'bad neighbour' development but suggested a widening of the obligation. As a result, the legislation was amended to require that all planning applications should be publicised in some way.[57] The new arrangements thus enlarge the opportunity for neighbours (many of whom may, of course, be primarily concerned with protection of their own property 'rights'), and others interested in participating in the making of development control decisions, to influence the attitudes of the public authorities responsible for the control of development in the 'public interest'. Such influence may, of course, be viewed by a developer as extraneous interference with his or her development proposals.

In terms of the GDO it is, in general, the duty of the applicant to serve a copy of a planning application on owners, lessees and occupiers of neighbouring property. Government departments and local authorities are also to observe the procedure. Any person wishing to make representations to the planning authority has a period of 14 days within which to do so.

If neighbour notification proves impossible or would, in the opinion of the planning authority, be unduly onerous, the application must be advertised in a local newspaper. 'Bad neighbour' development is still subject to press advertisement. Advertisements are now placed by the planning authority, the cost being recovered from the applicant. 'Block' advertisements are therefore now possible and advertisements can be placed at regular intervals in the same newspaper so that members of the public become familiar with the pattern of their appearance.

Enforcement of Planning Control: the Law and the Courts

Individually the Scottish differences concerning the enforcement of planning control (some resulting from differences in the legislation, others a consequence of differences in the legal system generally) are relatively minor, but cumulatively they make effective enforcement even more difficult than in England and Wales.

Scotland has its own very distinctive system of criminal justice and procedure. This affects enforcement in two ways. First, in the Sheriff Court (in which a planning prosecution will invariably take place) decisions on prosecution are in all cases made by a public prosecutor (the procurator-fiscal). Even though the planning authority may consider that a particular case merits prosecution, it is for the fiscal not only to decide whether there is evidence sufficient to justify prosecution but also to determine, in the light of his very wide discretion, whether, taking account of factors such as pressures on prosecuting resources, the relative seriousness of the offence and alternative methods of disposal, criminal proceedings should be instituted.[58] Some planning authorities have suggested that procurators-fiscal are reluctant to prosecute in planning cases. However, a research report, The Enforcement of Planning Control in Scotland,[59] found that there was, in general, little evidence to substantiate this claim.

Secondly, obtaining the evidence necessary to justify a prosecution is likely to be much more expensive in staff time than in England and Wales. This is because, in Scotland, no one can be convicted of a crime unless there is evidence of at least two witnesses implicating him or her in the commission of the offence with which he or she is charged. Often, therefore, an enforcement officer will have to be accompanied by a colleague to provide the necessary corroboration.

Under S.270 of the 1972 Act a planning authority can, as a preliminary to enforcement action, require the provision of information as to interests in land. Although it is an offence not to provide the required information, such notices are widely disregarded, thus increasing the risk that an enforcement notice may fail as a result of some inaccuracy. However, because of the attitude of some sheriffs to what they may view as 'bureaucratic' prosecutions, some planning authorities see little point in reporting such offences. Scottish planning authorities are at something of a disadvantage compared with their English counterparts in obtaining information as to the planning history of a site, in that the Scottish Act does not allow for inquiry as to the time when activities on a site began.

In contrast to the position in England and Wales, failure to comply with an effective enforcement notice requiring the taking of steps other than the discontinuance of a use is not an offence in Scotland, and the only remedy available is for the planning authority themselves to take direct action: for example, to remove an unauthorised building. Few authorities have made use of these powers; private contractors may be reluctant to undertake such work and there is the risk that it may turn out to be impossible to recover the expense of direct action from the landowner.

In Scotland it is generally assumed that where penalties are prescribed for breach of a statute, the public body charged with the administration of the legislation must 'be content with the infliction of the statutory penalties upon offenders ...',[60] and that the common law remedy of interdict is therefore not generally available in respect of breaches of planning control. In England and Wales it seems that the equivalent remedy of injunction will be granted in some cases (see Chapter 10).

The Scottish courts have not shown a sympathetic attitude to planning authorities in cases in which the validity of enforcement notices has been in issue (see, for example, McNaughton and McDaid above). The general level of fines imposed on conviction for failure to comply with an enforcement notice - a level described by the Convention of Scottish Local Authorities (COSLA) in 1981 as 'derisory' - may also be indicative of a judicial lack of sympathy towards enforcement. The research report mentioned above (The Enforcement of Planning Control in Scotland) found that the average fine for a first offence was about £50; when second and subsequent convictions were taken into account the average rose to about £70.

Enforcement in Practice
In The Enforcement of Planning Control in Scotland, it was suggested that the measure of the effectiveness of the enforcement system should be

the extent to which it is capable of bringing a breach of control to a conclusion speedily and with economic use of resources, while still providing safeguards against arbitrary use of power. On this measure, the process might, at first sight, seem to be working satisfactorily. The great majority of breaches of planning control are resolved without recourse to formal procedures, in many cases quite quickly. However, in a minority of these cases negotiations drag on for months and even for years. In the 17 per cent or so of breaches in which recourse to formal procedures proves necessary, delay of that order is not uncommon. Thus, in quite a large minority of cases, the system fails in terms of speed of operation. And, as the report points out, it is often those living close to the unauthorised development who are the principal losers (see the example mentioned below).

One of the several explanations for this situation is the exploitation by developers of the opportunities for fending off a decision to take enforcement action, for suspending the operation of an enforcement notice - in particular, by lodging an appeal to the Secretary of State - and for postponing or even avoiding prosecution. The large proportion of enforcement appeals which are withdrawn at a late stage suggests, for example, that the appeal process is often simply being used to spin out the period for which a breach of planning control can be continued.

The real importance of the number of cases in which developers 'play the system' - of the order of 10 to 15 per cent - lies not so much in their number 'as in the disproportionate effect which they appear to have on the credibility of the enforcement process as a whole'.[61]

While the report identifies measures which might be adopted by planning authorities to improve effectiveness, it concludes that fundamental change in the system is desirable. There is at present scope for those familiar with the system to postpone the day of reckoning literally for years and, when that day finally comes, the reckoning often turns out to be little more than a token fine. The report concludes:

> So long as the ultimate sanction is weak, there will be repercussions along the chain of the enforcement process. Developers ... know that they can continue to breach planning control with relative impunity. Planning

Development Control in Scotland

authorities, for their part, knowing the
weakness of their position, will be forced back
upon negotiation and persuasion and may in the
end have to compromise on the planning merits
of the case.[62]

One example may serve to illustrate the weakness of
the system. The offender began, in breach of
planning control, to operate a substantial and
apparently profitable scrap business on agricultural
land. Not only was the site located in the green
belt, but access to it was unsatisfactory and the
operation of the business caused substantial
disturbance to the occupier of an adjoining house.
Over a period of twelve years convictions in respect
of the breach resulted in successive fines of £20,
£50, £50, £100 and £100, but the unauthorised use
continued. During this period the occupier of the
house felt obliged to move. The planning authority
appear to have come to the conclusion that further
action against the development was pointless. Other
planning authorities appear to have gone a
considerable way along the same path.

Planning by Agreement: the Law
A planning authority may enter into an agreement
with any person interested in land in their area,
'in so far as the interest of that person enables
him to bind the land', for the purpose of
restricting or regulating the development or use of
the land (1972 Act, S.50). Once recorded in the
public register of deeds relating to land (the
Register of Sasines or, in some areas, the Land
Register), such an agreement can be enforced by the
planning authority against successors in title of
the person with whom the agreement was made.
  The presence of the words 'in so far as the
interest of that person enables him to bind the
land' (for which there is no equivalent in S.52 of
the Town and Country Planning Act 1971, which
provides for the making of planning agreements in
England and Wales) suggests that in Scotland an
agreement will only 'run with the land' if entered
into with a person who has an interest in the land
in a strict conveyancing sense.[63] The position in
England and Wales appears to be different.[64]
  So far as Scotland is concerned, there is no
common law restriction (as south of the border) on
the enforceability of positive obligations relating
to land. The type of obligation that may be validly

89

included in an agreement under S.50 is therefore a matter of interpretation of the phrase 'restricting or regulating'. This suggests to us that although every obligation in an agreement need not be of a negative character, the agreement, taken as a whole, must have as its main purpose the essentially negative objective of restricting or regulating development or use of land. The legislative changes in England and Wales relating to positive obligations[65] would seem to mean that it is possible for an English planning authority to achieve wider purposes by means of an agreement than can a Scottish authority.

In England and Wales an application may be made to the Lands Tribunal for variation of a S.52 agreement. Though the Lands Tribunal for Scotland has power to vary certain land obligations, an obligation imposed by a S.50 agreement does not appear to be capable of variation under the relevant legislation.

The Use of Planning Agreements

The use of planning agreements in development control has given rise, south of the border, to controversy focussing on two main issues; the attempt by planning authorities to secure from an applicant for planning permission some benefit unrelated to the subject matter of the application, and the propriety of an essentially covert and unstructured bargaining process (see Chapter 6).

The use of agreements to secure certain types of gain has been categorised as unacceptable by the Secretary of State for Scotland. SDD Circular 22/1984, Section 50 Agreements, states that planning authorities should not treat 'an applicant's need for permission as an opportunity to obtain some extraneous benefit or advantage'. Research carried out in 1982 showed that it was only relatively recently that planning agreements had come to be made in any significant numbers in Scotland and that the great majority of agreements were concerned with perfectly normal development control matters.[66] SDD Circular 22/1984 is therefore primarily directed at obviating a problem which has yet to arise on any scale in Scotland.

Public Inquiries: Post-inquiry Procedure

Public inquiry procedures are virtually identical to those which operate south of the border, but there

Development Control in Scotland

is one notable exception. In line with a recommendation of the Franks Committee,[67] where the decision following an inquiry is to be made by the Secretary of State the inquiries procedure rules provide for the preparation of the inquiry report in two parts.[68] After the close of the inquiry the reporter (the counterpart of the English inspector) must, if asked, circulate Part I of his report, comprising a summary of the evidence and his findings of fact, to the parties. The parties have fourteen days to propose corrections or amendments of this factual part of the report and, in the light of any comments, the reporter may amend Part I. He then proceeds to prepare Part II of the report, which is to include any necessary reasoning and his recommendations, if any. Both parts are then submitted to the minister.

The procedure generally adds at least a month to the process, and the various difficulties inherent in preparation of the two-part report (which have led on occasion to court action) have resulted in suggestions by the SDD in 1977 and again in 1983 that the practice followed in England and Wales should be adopted instead. The proposals for change did not, however, draw support.

Development Control in National Scenic Areas

Though Scotland contains many of the remaining wilderness areas in the United Kingdom, there are, for various reasons, no national parks in Scotland.[69]

Prior to 1980 many areas of landscape value were subject to a variety of types of designation imposing restrictions on development. However, following a comprehensive survey by the Countryside Commission for Scotland (CCS), there was published a report, Scotland's Scenic Heritage,[70] which identified forty areas of outstanding landscape, comprising in total about one eighth of the area of Scotland, considered to be in need of special protection as part of Scotland's national heritage.

In 1980 there were introduced special arrangements for development control in these National Scenic Areas.[71] While control is still primarily the responsibility of the appropriate planning authority, supervisory functions are exercised by the CCS and by the SDD. Where a planning authority propose to grant planning permission for development (except for relatively minor proposals) in a National Scenic Area, they must consult the CCS. If, contrary to CCS advice, the planning authority still support a proposal, they must notify the Secretary of State who will then decide whether to 'call in' the application.

CONCLUSION

In 1980 Derek Lyddon, then chief planner with the SDD, stated that colleagues from the DoE had noted that Scottish planning 'is no longer an adaptation of English practice but a significantly different system ...'.[72] At the strategic level, and using the term 'planning' in its widest sense, there may be an element of truth in this statement, but it clearly cannot be justified in relation to development control.

The broad framework of development control in Scotland remains much the same as when it was introduced on a comprehensive basis in 1948. In view of the considerable scrutiny to which it has been subjected in the intervening years, this is perhaps suprising. There have, however, been many relatively minor changes; indeed, so numerous have these been of late that the report Development Control Performance in Scotland[73] made a plea for a period of stability.

To avoid undue confusion amongst those engaged in development a measure of conformity between the English and Scottish development control systems may be thought desirable. However, at the margins the Scottish system has tended to diverge from that operating in England and Wales, and as time has gone by the divergence has become more noticeable. It is not easy to unravel the reasons for this, but the main one would appear to be that matters subject to administrative decentralisation are usually now the subject of separate Scottish legislation, even where the substantive content is similar to legislative proposals for England and Wales. This allows the Scottish Office a degree of freedom to initiate independent proposals in some areas of law; an element of Scottish autonomy will be tolerated by central government so long as United Kingdom priorities are not infringed.[74] Such initiatives would seem to owe much to the formal and informal working relationships among members of the 'policy community' in Scotland, relationships which are more easily established and maintained in a small country. The existence, for example, since local government reorganisation in Scotland, of only one local authority association, a single society of directors of planning, and a relatively small number of planning authorities appears to mean that co-ordination and opportunities for communication, comment and influence on the part of such bodies (and other interest groups), not only on proposed statutes but also on subordinate legislation and on circulars and other guidance, is likely to be simpler and more effective than in England and Wales.

The most notable of the accumulation of minor differences between the Scottish and English systems of development control are the wider publicity requirements for development proposals in Scotland (which have been generally welcomed despite certain practical problems[75]), and the extent to which the SDD has been able, by means of national planning guidelines, to engage in an informal zoning exercise at national level. The DoE's commitment to streamlining development control would, we suspect, act as a disincentive to the adoption of more extensive statutory publicity requirements in England. Though the concept of national planning guidelines might have attractions for the DoE, we think it questionable whether, since the SDD's success in this field appears to owe much to the close working relationships mentioned above, the preparation of such documents is an exercise which could be successfully undertaken in the somewhat different conditions prevailing in England.

So far as the operation of planning control in Scotland is concerned, it is of particular interest in the context of the general working of the town planning legislation, and indicative perhaps of the strength of development control, that there is little evidence of major problems or dissatisfaction with development control decisions made during a long period when development plan guidance has been relatively slight. As regards the operation of development control within a two-tier system of planning authorities, a number of regional and district authorities are still finding co-operation difficult on some issues. However, planning is a political process, and, as with conflict between the Secretary of State and planning authorities, it is perhaps healthy that differences of view should be openly debated. The fact that development pressures are less strong in most of Scotland than in parts of England probably explains why 'planning gain' has not so far been an important issue in Scotland, and also why, in proportion to the respective countries' populations, there have, over the last ten years, been far fewer planning appeals in Scotland (though the number has increased significantly since 1975) than in England and Wales. That fact may also go some way towards explaining the relatively small number of planning cases which have come before the Scottish courts.

In view of the wide range of suggestions made in the SDD paper, Review of the Management of Planning,[76] it is interesting to speculate whether the present relatively minor differences between the English and Scottish systems would have been altogether much more substantial had the Scotland Act 1978, providing for devolution of most planning matters to a Scottish Assembly and a Scottish Executive, come into force.

NOTES

1. The administrative framework, the institutions of government, the network of policy-making, and the role of local government are discussed in M. Keating and A. Midwinter, The Government of Scotland (Mainstream Publishing, Edinburgh, 1983).
2. See, for example, the discussion paper, Review of the Management of Planning, issued by the Scottish Development Department in 1977.
3. See Scottish Development Department, Circular 24/1981, Development Control.
4. As amended by the Town and Country Planning (Scotland) Act 1977 ('the 1977 Act'), and the Local Government and Planning (Scotland) Act 1982 ('the 1982 Act').
5. Town and Country Planning (Scotland) Act 1972, S. 9.
6. See SS. 176 and 177 of the 1973 Act.
7. 1973 Act, S. 179, as amended by S. 3 of the 1977 Act and S. 66 of and Sched. 3 to the 1982 Act.
8. J.B. Cullingworth, Town and Country Planning in Britain (George Allen & Unwin, London, 9th edition, 1985), p. 50.
9. See Scottish Development Department, Circular 51/1975, Town and Country Planning under the New Local Government System. See also Scottish Development Department, Circular 28/1976, Development Plans.
10. E. Young, 'Call in of Planning Applications by Regional Planning Authorities', Journal of

Planning and Environment Law, 1979, p. 358.
11. Report of the Committee of Inquiry into Local Government in Scotland, Cmnd. 8115 (HMSO, Edinburgh, 1981), especially chapter 6. And see M. Keating, 'The Stodart Committee and Planning in Scotland', The Planner, 68, 1 (January 1982), p. 22.
12. 1982 Act, S. 66 and Sched. 3.
13. Local Government and Planning (Scotland) Act 1982.
14. 1973 Act, S. 176.
15. Scottish Development Department, 1984.
16. See, for example, Department of Health for Scotland, Circular 40/1960, Green Belts and New Houses in the Country; and Scottish Development Department, Circular 43/1971, Shopping Location Policy: Out of Town Shopping Centres.
17. House of Commons Paper 511-i, Session 1971-72 (HMSO, London, 1972).
18. Land Resource Use in Scotland: The Government's Observations on the Report of the Select Committee on Scottish Affairs, Cmnd. 5428 (HMSO, Edinburgh, 1973).
19. Speech by Mr. Malcolm Rifkind, then Minister for Home Affairs and the Environment at the Scottish Office, to the Royal Town Planning Institute (Scottish Branch) in January 1980.
20. See U.A. Wannop, 'Scottish Planning in Practice - 1: Four Distinctive Characteristics', The Planner, 66, 3 (May/June 1980), p. 64.
21. U.A. Wannop, 'National Planning Guidelines 1981: Priorities for Development Planning', Town Planning Review, 53, 2 (April 1982), p. 226 (review). See too D. Diamond, 'The Uses of Strategic Planning: The Example of the National Planning Guidelines in Scotland', Town Planning Review, 50, 1 (January, 1979), p. 18.
22. See, for example, Scottish Development Department, Circular 21/1983, Private House Building Land Supply: Joint Venture Schemes.
23. See, for example, Planning and Small Businesses, Planning Advice Note 29, (Scottish Development Department, 1982).
24. The Report of the Working Group on Scottish Local Government Management Structures (HMSO, Edinburgh, 1973). And see J. Friend, G. Lind and S. McDonald, Future Regional Reports: a Study of Form and Content (Institute for Operational Research, for Scottish Development Department, 1978).
25. See on this J.B. McLoughlin, The Evolution

of Strategic Planning in Scotland and the Origins of the Regional Report (SSRC Project HR/5639, Working Paper, 1978).
    26. See S.T. McDonald, 'The Regional Report in Scotland: A Study of Change in the Planning Process', Town Planning Review, 48, 3 (July 1977), p. 215.
    27. See note 19 above.
    28. See too Scottish Development Department, Circular 21/1983, op. cit.
    29. See the Town and Country Planning (Structure and Local Plans) (Scotland) Regulations 1983, S.I. 1983/1590; and Scottish Development Department, Circular 32/1983, Structure and Local Plans.
    30. See the Town and Country Planning (General Development) (Scotland) Order 1981, S.I. 1981/830 (as amended).
    31. See Scottish Development Department, Circular 26/1984, Planning Appeals; and the Town and Country Planning (Determination of Appeals by Appointed Persons) (Prescribed Classes) (Scotland) Regulations 1980, S.I. 1980/1675.
    32. MVA Consultancy (Scottish Development Department, 1985).
    33. The Scottish Development Department does not publish information about the time taken by individual authorities to determine planning applications but Scottish Development Department, Circular 24/1981, Development Control, stated that over 70 per cent of applications were dealt with within two months and 90 per cent within three months.
    34. J. Brand, R. Stevenson and U. Wannop, Factors Affecting the Performance of Planning Authorities in Submitting Observations on Planning Appeals (Scottish Development Department, forthcoming).
    35. Report of the Royal Commission on the Constitution, 1969-1973, Cmnd. 5460, (HMSO, London, 1974), Vol. 1, para. 76.
    36. For a detailed treatment of these matters see E. Young and J. Rowan-Robinson, Scottish Planning Law and Procedure (William Hodge & Co., Glasgow, 1985).
    37. In the context of town planning, see, for example, Peter Holmes and Son v Secretary of State for Scotland 1965 S.C. 1.
    38. See, for example, the comments of Lord Denning in W. & J.B. Eastwood Ltd v Herrod [1968] 2 Q.B. 923.

39. See, for example, Glasgow District Council v Secretary of State for Scotland 1980 S.C. 150 (whether partial demolition of building involved 'development'); and Lithgow v Secretary of State for Scotland 1973 S.C. 1 (whether decision of minister following public inquiry valid).
40. 1979 S.C. 200.
41. The Times, 5th July 1985.
42. 1984 S.L.T. 162.
43. The Court of Session is divided into an Inner House (broadly equivalent to the English Court of Appeal), consisting of two divisions, each of four judges, and an Outer House consisting of Lords Ordinary who sit singly.
44. J.A.G. Griffith, The Politics of the Judiciary (Fontana, Glasgow, 2nd edition, 1981), p. 132.
45. 1984 S.L.T. 345.
46. 1953 S.L.T. (Sh. Ct.) 17. Contrast the comments of Harman L.J. in Britt v Buckinghamshire County Council [1964] 1 Q.B. 77.
47. 1973 S.C. 130. And see E. Young, 'Planning Condition Apportioning Land Between Private and Local Authority Housing', Journal of Planning and Environment Law, 1975, p. 139.
48. See E. Young, 'Is an Unnecessary Condition Ultra Vires?', Journal of Planning and Environment Law, 1983, p. 139.
49. Unreported, but see Scottish Planning Law and Practice, 1981, 2, p. 15.
50. See, for example, Ormston v Horsham R.D.C (1965) 17 P. & C.R. 105.
51. 1984 S.L.T. 162.
52. C.T. Reid in Scottish Planning Law and Practice, 1984, 13, p. 74.
53. See, in particular, Wordie Property Co. Ltd (above); and Wilson v Secretary of State for Scotland (unreported, but see Scottish Planning Law and Practice, 1981, 2, p. 16).
54. For an example of a decision involving an espousal, in McAuslan's terminology (see P. McAuslan, The Ideologies of Planning Law, Pergamon Press, Oxford, 1981), of a more 'public interest' based ideology, see London and Clydeside Properties Ltd v City of Aberdeen District Council 1984 S.L.T. 50.
55. See now the GDO of 1981.
56. See now the GDO of 1977.
57. See S. 23 of the 1972 Act, as amended by the 1982 Act; and the GDO of 1981, as amended by the GDO of 1984. And see C.M. Brand and B. Thompson,

'Third Parties and Development Control - A Better Deal for Scottish Neighbours?', Journal of Planning and Environment Law, 1982, p. 743.
 58. See D. Batchelor, 'The Prosecution of Planning Offences', Scottish Planning Law and Practice, 1985, 15, p. 36.
 59. Report by J. Rowan-Robinson, E. Young and I. McLarty (Scottish Development Department, 1984).
 60. Magistrates of Buckhaven and Methil v Wemyss Coal Co 1932 S.C. 201, per Lord President Clyde. See, however, G. Jamieson, The Competency of Interdict in the Enforcement of Planning Control, Scottish Planning Law and Practice Occasional Paper (Planning Exchange, Glasgow, 1983).
 61. Rowan-Robinson, Young and McLarty, op. cit., para. 8.08.
 62. Ibid., paragraph 8.28.
 63. See Scottish Development Department, Circular 22/1984, Section 50 Agreements; and note by M. Deans in Scottish Planning Law and Practice, 1984, 13, p. 81.
 64. See Pennine Raceway Ltd v Kirklees Metropolitan Borough Council [1983] Q.B. 382.
 65. See the Local Government (Miscellaneous Provisions) Act 1982, S. 33.
 66. J. Rowan-Robinson and E. Young, Planning by Agreement in Scotland: the Law and Practice, Scottish Planning Law and Practice Occasional Paper (Planning Exchange, Glasgow, 1982).
 67. Report of the Committee on Tribunals and Enquiries, Cmnd. 218, (HMSO, London, 1957), para. 345.
 68. See the Town and Country Planning (Inquiries Procedure) (Scotland) Rules 1980.
 69. See G.E. Cherry, Environmental Planning, Vol. II, National Parks and Recreation in the Countryside (HMSO, London, 1975), chapters 4 and 8.
 70. Countryside Commission for Scotland (Redgorton, Perth, 1977).
 71. See Scottish Development Department, Circular 20/1980, Development Control in National Scenic Areas, and the directions issued with it.
 72. D. Lyddon, 'Scottish Planning in Practice - 2: Influences and Comparisons', The Planner, 66, 3 (May/June 1980), p. 66.
 73. Op. cit.
 74. See Keating and Midwinter, op. cit.
 75. See L.R. Guildford, 'Notification and Publication of Planning Applications', Scottish Planning Law and Practice, 1985, 14, p. 6.
 76. Op. cit.

Part Two

THE SYSTEM IN OPERATION: SOME SPECIFIC TOPICS

Chapter 6

PLANNING GAIN: AN AID TO POSITIVE PLANNING?

Ian Simpson

INTRODUCTION

This chapter examines planning gain, and its effects on the system which regulates development. The term 'planning gain' usually refers to the results of the practice by which local authorities persuade developers to provide facilities not required for their own schemes. Heap and Ward state that this 'involves the withholding by the local planning authority of planning permission for development until a section 52 agreement has been negotiated and completed'[1], but some authorities also seek planning gain through more general policies. This may be by defining categories of planning applications which require the provision of particular facilities; or a development plan could state where the authority is to seek community benefits from developers. Local authorities can also seek planning gain in their roles as landowners or as partners to developers. Its negotiation, however, normally coincides with the submission of a planning application. The benefits are usually negotiated in accordance with S.52 of the Town and Country Planning Act 1971 (S.50 of the 1972 Act in Scotland): but see also S.111 of the Local Government Act 1972, and S.33 of the Local Government (Miscellaneous Provisions) Act 1982. The chance to negotiate will be more common in areas where there is pressure for development, and where development values are likely to be high. The present 'official' view of such agreements is set out in DoE Circular 22/83, <u>Town and Country Planning Act 1971: Planning Gain</u>.
It seems that the negotiation of planning bargains has become common practice, particularly where major development is proposed. There are

several possible reasons for the increasing adoption of planning gain approaches.[2] Planning controls have a decided influence on land values. Where increases in values result from the granting of planning permission or the allocation of land in a development plan, then there may be concern over the high profits of developers (especially if some of the infrastructure costs fall externally, on public sector agencies). This may stimulate attempts to collect what might be seen, in one sense, as a form of local development 'tax', through planning gain. Given that at present there is no other suitable form of betterment 'recapture', planning gain may be seen as one means whereby local authorities recoup development values, or gain community benefits from the development process. Other reasons for the increasing incidence of planning bargaining include the absence of the need for ministerial consent for Section 52 agreements, and the financial pressures on local authorities (which increasingly have been deprived of funds for development). Additionally, the widening of planning considerations to include social and economic factors has not been favoured by the courts or government, so that for local authorities perhaps less may be hoped for through the imposition of conditions on a permission than through bargaining. Government encouragement for partnership schemes has also led to an increase in the number of planning agreements. Economic, administrative, and political factors have therefore contributed to the increase in numbers of attempts to achieve planning benefits by agreement.

The present chapter, however, is not concerned so much with tracing the rise in the use of planning agreements (nor with evaluating current official policies on the topic), as with exploring matters of principle, and the practical implications. The sections below review the major issues, considering both the case against planning gain and the arguments for it. A series of case studies follows, where the aim is to illustrate the results of this kind of bargaining. Finally, conclusions are drawn about the usefulness of planning gain, and about possibilities for the future.

THE ISSUES: CRITICISMS AND OBJECTIONS

Planning gain can be contentious, and various specific criticisms have been made. Many are covered in the Report of The Property Advisory

Planning Gain

Group (PAG), Planning Gain. Their main objection is that:

> as soon as a system of accepting public benefits is established which goes beyond the strict consideration of the planning merits of a proposed development, the entire system of development control becomes subtly distorted, and may fall into disrepute.[3]

Developers may feel that unless they offer planning gain then their application may receive less sympathetic or speedy consideration. They therefore negotiate with authorities, the grant of permission being dependent to some extent on the benefits offered as opposed to the merits of the application. The PAG Report states:

> If the grant of planning permission is regularly associated with a developer's providing some benefit or gain unrelated to his proposed development, doubts will be raised about the objectivity with which authorities operate the development control system.[4]

In this way planning gain is characterised as the 'selling' of planning permission, and a developer's chances of obtaining permission could depend on whether he or she could pay the local authority's price.

Heap and Ward[5] consider that bargaining means that local authorities are more interested in sharing the profits of development, and argue that authorities are acting outwith their powers by applying non-material considerations when determining applications. Thus local authorities appear more interested in profit control than in development control and good planning. Some critics take the view that planning authorities have no role relative to the taxation of development gains since this is a national function.

Another line of criticism concerns the private nature of negotiations. Planning bargaining is conducted in secret and there is often no opportunity for the public to participate or express their views (even though planning legislation allows for publicity for certain types of applications and the planning system allows for public participation and consultation in relation to development plans). There may be exceptions, when committees open to the public do discuss agreements (although perhaps not

103

the details), but frequently negotiations will be entirely private. Jowell has suggested that the 'dealing behind closed doors atmosphere of planning gain might not be a good thing for government or society'[6]. The Law Society also refers to secrecy when it recommends that 'no less publicity and opportunity for consultation should be accorded to a proposal for development which involves the making of a planning gain as is required for the application itself'[7].

Cowan refers to decisions where development was dependent on the amount of financial gain which would accrue to the council, and where massive office development was approved on the basis that the development would provide rates: 'times are hard and we must take everything we can get'[8]. Cowan argues that:

> planning should be constantly making apparent the difference between the mechanism of the planning system on the one hand and of the market on the other, but at present the two look inextricably confused. In such a situation planning is likely to be the eventual loser.[9]

Jowell too refers to finance colouring an authority's view more strongly than planning considerations, and to some developers being focussed on more than others.[10]

Efforts to obtain planning gain can also introduce delay into the development process. The longer an application is held up, the more the costs of a developer may increase prior to development being commenced.

Clearly then, there are some potentially serious problems in using a planning gain approach, and these have been acknowledged by some advocates as well as critics of land use planning. Planning decisions should conform with planning policies and authorities should not refuse permission for acceptable proposals because the developer does not offer planning gain, nor should they grant permission for unacceptable development simply because they are able to extract planning gain. The RTPI while accepting that 'The power to negotiate planning gain is an integral part of our planning legislation, and cannot be abandoned without reconsidering the whole system of planning', also indicates that the payment of planning gain should never lead to unacceptable development being given permission and that local authorities should not seek planning gain not mentioned in a development plan or brief.[11]

Summary of the Case Against Planning Gain
The main criticisms of planning gain are that it is of dubious legality, and it is site specific and thus may undermine comprehensive planning. It can cause delay, the trading process undermines professional practice, and if development is in accordance with the development plan then no extraneous benefits should be sought. As a result of planning gain final plans are the product of 'horse-trading' between developers and the local authority, hence the 'corruption' of planning by land values and market pressures. It is argued that bargaining is contrary to the ideal which sustains planning, namely the pursuit of the 'public interest' without concessions to private interests: through planning gain a developer may be allowed development that would not otherwise be permitted. This has led to planning authorities being 'bribed' by the possibility of achieving some planning gain, or developers being coerced into providing facilities which they would not normally provide and are not legally required to provide.

Almost all critics see planning gain as a means by which developers can buy themselves a planning permission or, on the other hand, as something used by local authorities to blackmail prospective developers. Such practices, it is argued, can only undermine the integrity of the development control system.

THE ISSUES: A RE-EXAMINATION

Before putting the case for planning gain, it is useful to look in a little more detail at four specific topics.

Planning Gain and Legality
In determining applications planning authorities are required to take account of the development plan and any other 'material considerations'. Underwood states, 'The question of material considerations is a crucial one for development control ... since it is through this concept that the limits to public intervention in the planning sphere are

defined'.[12] Since 'planning' is not defined in legislation, then it is difficult to determine what is relevant or 'material' to planning and 'it is really in the courts that the scope of the concept has been tested'.[13] Judicial decisions have sought to curtail what local authorities consider to be material through restrictions on planning conditions (while of course central government has also played an important role through circulars and appeal decisions). Local authorities have sought to by-pass this restraint on their powers through the use of planning agreements and 'bargains' over planning permission. Some local authorities continue to consider material considerations properly to include social, economic and other factors, and the increasing use of 'planning gain' could indicate that considerations outwith the 'normal' scope of planning control are considered 'material' by local authorities. Thus the ambiguities about the purposes of planning, and the vagueness of some terms in planning legislation, have led to planning by agreement. Given that authorities use agreement to secure gains which could not be framed as conditions (or if they were would be ultra vires), then presumably the morality of the community sharing increases in development land values is seen by planning authorities as being more important than the legal issue of the limits of planning control.

Planning Gain and Comprehensiveness
As noted above, the claim is sometimes made that site-specific bargains may undermine a more comprehensive approach. This criticism assumes a purity about the plan-making system, and does not recognise that planning authorities are subject to political pressures. Some authorities have abandoned the comprehensive form of planning and opted for an incremental type, based on the revision of selected planning policies. There has been frustration at the lack of finance to implement plans, particularly when social and economic problems are mounting. This has led to a rejection of strategic planning in favour of short-term policy initiatives which can offer speedier and more tangible results. Planning practice has until recently been concerned with the problems of controlling growth and regulating development. Now many local authorities are concentrating on ways in which planning can help to promote and initiate

development. Planners will refer to the development plan if one exists, but in many cases it may not, and decisions taken are influenced not only by a development plan but by developers, the public and politicians as well as planners. This has resulted in a more pragmatic style of planning. It is difficult to support a system of planning which does not recognise this, nor allow for political involvement.

Planning Gain and Time Delays
It is possible that planning gain can add to delay in the development process. Delay in decision-making and the time to negotiate a legally-binding document can add to the cost of development, but this ignores the fact that some permissions are never implemented, and that developers will have a bank of schemes in order to plan ahead. Given a positive attitude by a planning authority then the negotiation of planning gain may not contribute to delay in development control. Indeed it can make decision-making speedier, getting rid of the risk element for surety of permission. In any case, while agreements can add to delay, research in Scotland by Rowan-Robinson and Young has shown that their use affects only a small proportion of planning applications, and in turn planning gain is only likely to form a small proportion of these agreements.[14]

Planning Gain and Professional Practice
The most-voiced criticism of planning gain is that it is arbitrary, and the 'horse-trading' process undermines 'professional practice'. Such a view depends on the assumption that planning officers can abide by clear rules in determining applications. This may be possible, for example, where a development proposal encroaches on a green belt, but more often development control concerns making choices, weighing information and reaching a compromise. Grant explains that critics of planning gain see development control as 'a process of interpreting and applying clear-cut rules to planning applications, as if it were a narrow technical, judicial type of operation'.[15] Instead planning has to balance competing claims on land and to resolve tensions which arise from conflicting interests. In many instances the development proposed will not fit exactly to the

requirements of the development plan. In some instances other policies may be in conflict with the proposal, or government circulars may have asked authorities to take an alternative view. Decision-making is, therefore, fraught with difficulty.

Individual authorities will view similar applications differently, depending on local priorities and circumstances. How do planners determine what is a satisfactory location for development and what is not? Should land-uses be segregated, or should they be mixed? How and when should an authority consider national, regional, local or other interests in its decision-making? An authority in reaching a decision will give more weight to one input than to another. For instance, local objections might over-ride the policy as contained in a development plan. Another authority may decide to overlook objections in favour of some economic benefit or housing priority. Thus, different authorities will reach different decisions on similar applications, depending on local criteria and circumstances. The decision-taking of local authorities therefore allows for local judgements. In this context, bargaining over specific cases does not necessarily run counter to 'good planning practice', but rather may contribute to it.

The Case for Planning Gain

Planning gain offers the possibility of positive action. Development control is able to refuse developments inconsistent with the development plan, but planners cannot force development consistent with it. Planning bargains are increasingly seen as one way of carrying out more 'positive' planning, and achieving public benefits. Bargaining plays a positive role, and where an authority wishes to grant consent, then it can negotiate the provision of necessary facilities, thus enabling proposals to be implemented.

The power to negotiate planning gain is an integral part of planning legislation and to restrict planning gain could lead to lower standards of development. Planning gain is also accepted by developers; it is a way of getting permission faster, and the gains can enhance the development. To local authorities planning gain sometimes offers relief from otherwise expensive obligations, and to developers it avoids delay and uncertainty in achieving a permission. Both have an interest in planning gain remaining an accepted practice.

Planning Gain

Government has been trying to encourage better relationships between developers and local authorities, and this implies mutual adjustments through discussion. The negotiation of planning gain, despite its imperfections, has a role in returning to the community some of the benefits of development values. The pursuit of gain from profitable development is, therefore, a way for planning authorities to tap external finance at a time of strict expenditure control. Since the demise of the Community Land Act, there have been few ways in which a planning authority might secure community benefits from development. Planning gain offers a way for the community at large to share in increases in land values, rather than speculators retaining all the wealth created.

FOUR CASE STUDIES

Planning gain harnesses part of the profits from development for the benefit of the community and local authority, and can encourage authorities to take a positive view of proposals. On the other hand, they may be condemned for unethical 'selling' of planning permissions, being seen as too anxious to share expected profits from development (instead of applying appropriate planning policies). In general terms there is some justification for local authority participation in the land market, but if this is contrary to the needs of local communities then it is undesirable. Planning gain should not mean that unacceptable development is permitted: planning must be more than a form of 'accounting' which pays attention only to the financial rewards of schemes for local authorities. Relevance to local needs ought to be a principal criterion: the key question concerns the extent to which local communities may expect to benefit. On occasions, the gains sought may be contrary to the wishes of local people. If a local form of betterment 're-capture' does not satisfy local requirements, and if it is used to justify unwarranted development, then development control is not performing well. The case studies below illustrate possibilities for unimpressive outcomes, as well as the scope for positive achievements. In the first two illustrations, fictional local authority names have been inserted rather than the real ones.

Planning Gain

Office Development at 'South Wharf', 'Riverborough', London[16]

In 1980 six interrelated applications and two supporting listed building applications were submitted for the redevelopment of an important area on the south bank of the Thames. 'Riverborough' Council held a public meeting to discuss these proposals, and the meeting ended with residents voting overwhelmingly against office development on the site. Despite this, nearly 200,000 square metres of office space was approved because of the planning gains involved. In return for the go-ahead, the developers had offered land for public open space, the completion and improvement of a walkway by the river, 1,700 square metres of industrial space available for council nominees, a 920 square metres leisure centre, and a housing association scheme comprising 203 units, half of which would be available for council nominations. The developers also agreed to preserve and refurbish listed buildings.

After 'Riverborough' had resolved to grant permission, the applications were called-in by the Secretary of State and a public inquiry was held. The decision gave permission for 70,000 square metres of offices, shops, and 40 flats (24 two-person and 16 three-person) on three parts of the area. Permission was refused for offices and other uses on the remainder of the site, but provided certain criteria were met, a more favourable decision could be expected if these elements were re-submitted.

In the meantime, community groups had formulated a list of priorities for the future of the wharf, including family housing with gardens, the development of industry to suit the skills of local people, and open space. The Secretary of State indicated that while accepting the case of housing need in 'Riverborough', he was convinced that it would be wrong to develop 'South Wharf' with family housing, and that the type of housing sought would be out of place on such a prominent site. At the time the development was approved the Local Plan was at the options stage and, of the options, those backing none or limited office development were the alternatives which found public support. When the draft Local Plan was published it incorporated the developer's scheme, and the Secretary of State stressed the fact that the proposed development conformed with the development plan.

Planning Gain

It could be argued that the development should not have been incorporated in the plan since 'Riverborough' had a shortage of council and family housing and required homes not office development. The proposed gains may not even benefit locals. The riverside walk is a tourist feature and flats will not alleviate the shortage of family housing. These planning gains do not help solve the problems of the area, but are simply a way of justifying approval of profitable development. They have been allowed to influence plan-making, and this has acted against local needs.

Office Development, 'Northborough', London[17]
This case involved choosing a developer for council-owned land. The local authority produced a planning brief prior to calling for financial bids and design submissions from developers. The brief proposed both profitable office development and facilities for the local community. The design was to be of high quality and the development schemes were to include a maximum of 70,000 square feet of offices, as well as a community centre, shops, pub and restaurant, residential accommodation of 50 habitable rooms, preferably sheltered accommodation for the elderly, offices for the Citizens' Advice Bureau, public open space and public conveniences.

Three development companies accordingly prepared schemes, which were put on show for public inspection prior to the local authority determining which developer should obtain the lease. But the council did not choose the developer on the basis of the architectural quality of the various proposals or on the planning suitability of alternative schemes. What resulted was financial bidding, with developers increasing offers for the lease. The authority chose a development which was not the one favoured by a large majority of the public. Nor was it the scheme that the deputy leader of the council had publicly supported prior to developers trying to outbid each other. As a result an agreement was concluded with developers which allowed:-

1. Office development by the developer on land leased from the council.
2. Community buildings and public open space provided with funds from the developer.
3. The developer making funds available to finance other projects contained in the brief.

The scheme chosen was that which was the subject of the highest bid for the council-owned site, and the decision taken was not on planning grounds. It would appear that there was extensive secret financial bargaining prior to the granting of permission. Financial considerations had been allowed to influence the proper development of the site, contrary to local expectations.

Housing at Foxwood, York[18]
This example indicates how a local authority can negotiate an agreement which allows for the occupancy of private housing by people on the waiting list while, at the same time, limiting the price of units. Such conditions could not be placed in a planning consent as they would probably be illegal. The local authority felt that council-house sales and reduced financial allocations from government (restricting the level of new-build) meant that it was becoming more difficult to meet housing needs. The council also recognised an increasing demand from small households for smaller house types.

In 1981 the council decided to release two plots of land and enter into a partnership agreement with a developer. The agreement allowed for dwellings to be built by the developer, and for the council handing over the freehold of each plot to the house purchaser when the dwellings were sold. The developer would retain the money from the sale, but pay for the land by handing over an agreed number of dwellings to the authority for renting to people on its waiting list. The council would acquire 36 houses (32 flats, 4 two-bed houses), and another 158 houses would be sold privately. Priority for these houses would be given to people on the council's waiting list and to existing tenants.

The total sales value of the houses offered to the council exceeded the estimated market value of the land. The smaller house types allowed higher densities and produced lower house prices (approximately one-third below those of houses recently built in the area). Of the 70 houses in the first release, 20 were bought either by council tenants or by people on the waiting list, and eleven reservations were made by people living in council houses with their relatives. In all, 67 of the 70 dwellings were bought by first-time buyers or council tenants. People on the waiting list were

Planning Gain

also given priority for house-purchase in the second release.
It is probable that conditions attached to planning permissions which give priority to people on a council's waiting list would be unlawful. This effect, however, was precisely what the Foxwood agreement achieved, and a basic aim was also to set prices which might come within the reach of people on the waiting list. The developments were specifically aimed at an area of need identified by the authority, leaving the council to concentrate its own development on those unable to afford owner-occupation. In this case there had been co-operation with the developers to benefit the community.

By-pass at Broadbridge Heath, Sussex[19]

The need for a by-pass at Broadbridge Heath has long been recognised, and a route has been protected since 1962. Lack of funds, however, meant that, by 1980, the scheme was towards the end of the county council's ten-year programme. Land inside the line of the proposed by-pass was considered suitable for development, but traffic congestion and ensuing environmental problems in the village led the council not to allocate it. The district council, having decided that Broadbridge Heath was a suitable location for development, considered that it might be possible to absorb the cost of the road as part of large-scale development, and eventually included such a proposal in the Local Plan. This received widespread support from the residents who wanted the by-pass and the wider selection of house types that would be provided by development.
The major landowner also indicated that he would assist in bringing forward the by-pass. The land required for it was in five ownerships, and he was persuaded to negotiate with the remaining four owners so that acquisition by the county council (who had resolved to use compulsory purchase powers) could be avoided, with a subsequent shortening of timescale. It was hoped that the by-pass would be opened prior to other developments but, as a compromise, phasing which allowed for commercial needs and planning requirements was agreed, and the district council prepared a development brief. In 1981 agreements were signed by the various landowners, developers and local authorities, and outline permission for the by-pass, an industrial site, four residential sites, two areas of open

113

Planning Gain

space and a village hall was given. The major landowner, having acquired the necessary land interests for the road, agreed along with the industrial developers to construct the by-pass, with the proceeds from the sale of a 6.4 acre industrial site being used to finance it.

The development allowed for a £1.4 million by-pass for the village funded by the development of adjacent land. The agreements and permission also marked the implementation of a major proposal in the District Plan. The by-pass serves more than the new development and extends beyond the development sites. But this is not a case of acquiring planning gain by selling a planning permission. The district council wanted to release land for development, and it was only shortage of money to provide the infrastructure that prevented its allocation. Similarly, landowners and developers appreciated that further development in the village was out of the question until traffic problems had been overcome.

In entering into agreements with the private sector the planning authority had been able to bring forward a scheme, providing about 400 jobs and 350 homes in the process. Broadbridge Heath also had a solution to its planning and highway problems earlier than it might have done otherwise. There had been co-operation between private developers and the local authority, while at the same time the planning gains had not been in conflict with local requirements or the development plan.

Comments on Case Studies

The Foxwood and Broadbridge Heath cases demonstrate that an authority can successfully harness private investment to implement developments and meet local needs. Planners are frequently accused of being negative and obstructive, and of lacking understanding of the financial aspects of development. These projects demonstrate that local authorities can initiate development by negotiating planning gain. In these instances local authorities are co-operating with developers, but are not 'selling' unsuitable planning permissions. By contrast, the other case studies highlight how the negotiation of planning gain can be detrimental if it does not have local support, is not in line with previously-established policies, or is not meeting local needs. Of course, all four cases relate to areas where there is pressure for development,

Planning Gain

so that authorities have been in a position to negotiate.

CONCLUSIONS

Planning gain achieves community benefits from the development industry. There are those who feel that the 'buying and selling' of planning permission by negotiation of planning gain is of dubious legality, and has no democratic basis. Some decisions have been determined by the planning gains involved, and by offering planning gain developers can perhaps impose their wishes on an area. But critics have a narrow view of the planning system, and pay little attention to the economic forces from which planning gain arises, or to the case for recouping development profits. Land values influence the shape and direction of development (and in this way planning control can be undermined by market forces). Planning gain can be justified on the basis of attempting to 'claw back' some of the increases in development value, but if this is against the wishes of local residents then it is difficult to support. In the interests of democracy, planning gain must be seen to reflect the expectations of local residents. Planning gain is also a tool which can make planning more 'positive', and allow development to proceed which otherwise might not. To suggest that planning gain should not be part of the development process is to suggest that in some cases acceptable development should be refused.
    The mis-use of planning gain by both developers and local authorities can bring the planning profession into disrepute, but given care and appropriate consultations positive results can be achieved. Developers readily accept planning gain in these instances. Planning gain can be unobjectionable when it is planning-led, as opposed to being instigated by developers. When it becomes planning by market considerations the practice can be harmful. Planning gain can add to development costs, and it is possible that this cost will be paid by the community, since developers may try to retain their profit margins.
    In the present writer's view, the disadvantages of planning gain are outweighed by its usefulness. Six reasons justify the approach:-

    a. planning gain means that increasing land

115

values arising from development are partly recovered by the community;
b. planning gain is used by local authorities to tap external resources at a time of strict financial control;
c. it can be accepted by developers, while ensuring community benefits from the development process;
d. it brings together the development industry and local authorities in meeting both market considerations and social needs;
e. prohibition could result in more refusals of permission, and would deny local authorities the use of one positive feature of the development control system;
f. the practice is common, yet its mis-use is relatively rare.

As far as point (a) is concerned, the most important qualification is that agreements should not over-ride local interests. The negotiation of planning gain must be seen to reflect local needs. On point (b), planning agreements can mean that policy objectives are met despite the curtailment of public expenditure, and some works can be brought forward that would otherwise face long delays. This is especially important in the current financial climate.

To conclude this chapter, some comments will be made about future prospects for planning agreements within the context of the development control system as a whole. There are many ways in which that system might be adapted to help positive planning. Extending the scope of material considerations, for instance, could remove some of the legal problems surrounding various kinds of policies, and perhaps would make planning bargains less necessary. If, for example, a council could grant planning consent for office development subject to the development including housing to accommodate people on the council's housing waiting list, then the reason for some agreements would disappear. At present conditions of this sort would be contested by developers, who would argue they are not valid. Certainly there is a case for legislation to extend the scope of material considerations to include social and economic factors not directly related to proposed developments.[20] In the absence of this, however, planning gain will remain significant for achieving policy goals. Therefore it is important to view planning gain constructively, paying attention to consistency and openness, and seeing negotiations as an aid to positive planning.

Consistency and Publicity: Planning Gain in Development Plans and Development Control
The inclusion of planning gain policies in local plans is important for several reasons. As the RTPI puts it, 'the planning system should move as quickly as possible towards a situation where local authorities would not normally seek planning gain which is not mentioned in a development plan or brief'.[21] Development plan policies setting out the circumstances in which planning gain will be sought would 'enable developers to know in advance where they will stand, and the reasoning behind demands made during negotiation'. Ideally, structure and local plans should specify localities or instances where planning gain would be sought. One advantage of expressing planning gain requirements in a plan is that they can be subjected to public debate and to challenge at a local inquiry. It also means that developers are aware of the requirements, which they may take into account in their assessment of land values. Therefore some cost of planning gain is passed to the landowner by minimising possible increases in land values. There is also the argument that once a plan has been approved the validity of the policy is not so open to challenge. If the policy is included in a development plan then it is likely to add support to a refusal of an application by a developer unwilling to meet the requirements.

At individual development control case-level, having to publicise certain applications provides the opportunity for public participation. There can be confidential discussions, however, between the authority and the developer, and planning gain can be agreed before the public is aware of negotiations. The developer could offer community facilities in return for a speedy and favourable decision which is not in accordance with a local plan, yet there is no obligation to publicise these discussions. Local communities should be able to influence the negotiation of planning gain, and the types of planning application advertised should include any application where the applicant has offered, or the planning authority has requested, planning gain. Thereby, the secrecy which surrounds bargaining could be reduced, and with it much of the concern that the development control system is being mis-used. Information such as the expected profits from development and the cost of the planning gain being returned to the local authority could be provided. If these were made available residents would be able to decide whether the balance of private and community gain is one they can support.

Planning Gain: an Aid to Positive Planning

Development control is sometimes represented as a negative activity, but ideally the sanction of saying 'no' should be reserved for that which is either socially or environmentally unwarranted. In other situations planning should be an enabling activity and not a hindrance. There has been debate over how to adopt a more positive attitude. Planning should be more than a restrictive code, yet this can be how the public view the process. There has been growing awareness of the need for co-operation with the development industry to ensure that land is developed to the mutual benefit of the developer and the local community. Consequently there has been increasing interest in the possibility of achieving planning objectives through agreements rather than statutory controls.

The negotiation of planning gain brings together local authorities and the private sector. Local authorities therefore learn to work with the private sector. In doing so they recognise the different and often conflicting aims that motivate private developers. Planners have developed negotiating skills, become more involved in economic matters, and developed a better understanding of propertied interests. However, the success of the development industry must be judged against its failure to meet requirements in less favoured areas, with large parts of towns and cities being no longer of interest as far as developers are concerned. Government encouragement for building societies to become involved with inner city properties is indicative of how the development industry could become more responsive to areas of stress. Regrettably, housebuilders and property developers continue to seek locations determined by economic criteria, as opposed to any social criteria.

One way of bringing developers' and planning's priorities together is through agreements. Planners must acquire further understanding of private sector behaviour and motivation, in order successfully to promote development according to public priorities.

Planning authorities must know where to draw the line between bargaining on reasonable terms and on others too onerous. Officers therefore need to know the financial implications of development. The use of planning agreements must become more widespread, but this requires new knowledge and skills if the public interest is to be safeguarded.

NOTES

1. D. Heap and A.J. Ward, 'Planning Bargaining - The Pros and the Cons: or, How Much can the System Stand?', Journal of Planning and Environment Law, 1980, p. 631.
2. See J. Jowell and M. Grant, 'A critical look at planning gain', Local Government Review, 147, 25 (18th June 1983), pp. 491-3. Jowell and Grant list 11 reasons for the increase in bargaining.
3. Property Advisory Group, Planning Gain (Department of the Environment, HMSO, 1981), p.7.
4. Ibid., p. 8.
5. Heap and Ward, op. cit., pp. 631-7.
6. J. Jowell, quoted in Planning, 394 (14th November 1980), p. 4.
7. The Law Society, 'Planning Gain: The Law Society's Observations', Journal of Planning and Environment Law, 1982, p. 350.
8. R. Cowan, 'The cost of cheque-book planning', Town and Country Planning, 50, 6 (June 1981), p. 160.
9. Ibid., p. 161.
10. Jowell, op. cit.
11. The Royal Town Planning Institute, Comments on the Report by the Property Advisory Group (RTPI, London, 1982).
12. J. Underwood, 'Development Control: A Review of Research and Current Issues', Progress in Planning, 16, 3, p. 199.
13. Ibid., p. 198.
14. J. Rowan-Robinson and E. Young, Planning by Agreement in Scotland: The Law and Practice, Scottish Planning Law and Practice Occasional Paper (Planning Exchange, Glasgow, 1982).
15. M. Grant, 'False diagnosis, wrong prescription', Town and Country Planning, 51, 3 (March 1982), p. 59.
16. See Cowan, op. cit., and comments in Planning, 452, (22nd January 1982), p. 4, and 388 (3rd October 1980), p. 4, and in Community Action,

<u>60</u>, (January/February 1983), p. 5. Also personal correspondence between author and local authority. Relevant discussions may also be found in P. Ambrose and B. Colenutt, <u>The Property Machine</u> (Penguin, Harmondsworth, 1975).

17. See Cowan, op. cit. Also personal correspondence between author and local authority.

18. See comments in <u>Planning</u>, <u>419</u>, (22nd May 1981), p. 12; also City of York, <u>Particulars relating to the development of low cost housing Pilot Schemes on Council Owned Land at Foxwood</u> (The Council, York, December 1980), and personal correspondence between author and local authority.

19. See L. Durrant, 'How development can pay for a bypass', <u>Chartered Surveyor</u>, <u>114</u>, 7 (February 1982), pp. 396-7. The present writer and the editors are grateful to L. Durrant for permission to draw on his material on this case. Mr. Durrant is now Chairman and Managing Director of Development Planning and Design Services, Swindon.

20. Trends in central government advice, however, have been rather in the opposite direction.

21. The Royal Town Planning Institute, op. cit. For further details on how to control planning gain see M. Grant, <u>Urban Planning Law</u> (Sweet and Maxwell, London, 1982), pp. 374-7.

Chapter 7

DESIGN CONTROL

Philip Booth

INTRODUCTION

Perhaps no issue in development control inspires more debate than the subject of controlling design. The professional journals are full of the vituperations of planners and architects, while for the public at large design control is very often seen as the essence of development control. The ugliness of modern buildings is taken to be as much a failure of planners to carry out their proper functions as of architects to design. Yet at the same time some participants regard design as being an optional extra, nice but not absolutely necessary, and certainly less necessary in some places than in others. The debate, which in truth has not been especially productive, has tended to focus on two questions; namely whether design control is needed at all, and if so, who should exercise it.

Those in favour of control would say that, despite failures, some bad 'eyesores' have been prevented, and many a scheme has been improved. They would also argue that the public at large have a right to be consulted on individual development proposals which will have an impact on the areas in which they live and work. Those against design control may oppose it on the grounds that the quality of the environment has not been substantially improved since 1947 as a consequence. Some would go further, arguing that such control is an unnatural interference both with the rights of the individual, and the rights of the design professions to exercise the skills that nature, education and experience have endowed them with. A claim may be made, in addition, that control is notorious for failing to recognise true quality in architectural design, and thereby for stifling innovation and imagination, substituting for both a monotonous mediocrity. Critics would contend, finally, that design control is exercised by those least qualified for the task: lay committees on the one hand, advised by non-architect-planners on the other.

Although it raises important matters of principle, this kind of debate tends to obscure the issues. There are beneath the rhetoric three basic questions that need to be examined. The first is what actually constitutes the 'design' over which control is sought. The terms design or aesthetic control are used with some vagueness, and it is important to understand what people have meant or could mean by the phrases if we are to assess impact. The second question concerns how control over design has actually been achieved. A whole series of policy and control mechanisms may be discerned, devised with differing ends in mind. Thirdly, there is the question of what the effects of design control have been. Of the three this is by far the most difficult: anecdotal evidence abounds, but there is a dearth of hard data, with one or two notable exceptions. If analysis is to proceed beyond rhetoric, then these three specific questions need to be borne in mind. The present chapter aims to help readers come to terms with them, as well as with the issues of principle.

The discussion is arranged below under six headings. Firstly, a brief account is given of the historical background, and this is followed by a comment on statutory powers and policy. Then the chapter turns at greater length to the actual practice of design control, and subsequently to the particular topic of the design guides produced by local authorities. After this, the essay looks again at some of the objections to design control that were touched upon briefly in this introduction. Finally, some conclusions are drawn.

THE HISTORY OF DESIGN CONTROL[1]

Design control is not of course an invention of the 1947 Act; indeed it has been with us for several centuries. Before 1900, however, most design control was achieved through the exercise of covenants attached to leasehold agreements imposed by ground landlords. In theory there was a mutuality of interest in these agreements: landlords wished to secure the best possible building on their land to enhance the capital value of their property, while builders, concerned then as now to find purchasers for their houses, found it in their interests to build soundly and fashionably. The State did intervene, notably in the London Building Acts from 1666 onwards, and occasionally by direct intervention of the Crown, as at Covent Garden. Much of this intervention had to do with layout and building standards, but much, too, related to the staple of design control, elevational treatment.

The shift to public rather than private control of design came at a moment when State intervention in many aspects of social policy was becoming intensified. In the second half of the 19th century the theory of mutual interest between landlord and lessee was seen to be frequently flawed in practice. The Public Health Act of 1875, with the model bye-laws which it made possible, was one response of government, aimed at improving outcomes. The intention, it is true, was primarily sanitary rather than aesthetic, but the insistence on standards for roads and the spacing of buildings was intended to have an effect on the general amenity of residential areas. The inadequacies of bye-law layouts subsequently led the pioneers of the Garden City Movement to try to redefine the desirable qualities of good layout. Such was the success of Unwin and other advocates of low-density housing that the 1909 Town Planning Act gave local authorities the possibility of controlling both layout and external appearance of new development in town schemes. The scope of the Act was far wider than the old model bye-laws, and, as Punter notes, for the first time the word amenity is used to indicate a general sense of aesthetic propriety.[2]

Design control thus entered the statute books with an objective of promoting the development of sensuous well-being in the environment, and being concerned with external appearance of buildings in the context of the relationship of buildings to each other, the enclosure of space and the provision of gardens and planting. Since the early 1900s, however, there appears to have been progressive narrowing of focus on what design control should be about. Much of this appears to have been due to the reluctance of successive governments to let local authorities become too deeply involved. Bacon[3] notes that central government's attitude has been that the design of a building is held to be concerned chiefly with its exterior appearance which can be judged independently of its other features, and that such judgements are primarily aesthetic and subjective, requiring the skills of architects. In the post-1947 period the role of architects has been stressed on a number of occasions. In Circular 28/66, for instance, reference was made to the 'special professional responsibility' of the architect, and to the need to seek advice from a qualified architect (or perhaps an advisory panel).[4] It is worth noting that this circular urged authorities to consider very carefully before withholding consent on aesthetic grounds for 'buildings designed by an architect for a particular site'. Similar observations have been made in more recent years. Despite such reservations, however, and the recognition thus given to architects, there have always been potential conflicts about the control of exterior appearance, especially given the view that this could be judged independently of other features. Such a view was scarcely likely to endear itself to architects trained in theories of the Modern Movement, which held that there was an indissoluble relationship between the exterior of a building and its plan and section. Thus even the limited intervention that government nowadays expects local authorities to exercise can become a source of conflict. The longstanding emphasis on the need for architectural advice has not eliminated the difficulties.

STATUTORY POWERS AND POLICY

The statutes themselves offer little guidance on how design should be dealt with. Indeed the 1971 Town and Country Planning Act makes no specific reference to design in the general section on development control. Yet the phrase 'other material considerations' of S.29 is always taken to include aesthetics, and no doubt this was Parliament's intention. The 1947 Act and its successors were, we may argue, making design control universal in the same way as with control of the allocation of land use. When the statutes are explicit about design in relation to listed buildings and conservation areas, the word 'character' has appeared as the benchmark for control. The term is clearly capable of several interpretations, but again is recognised as being related to design, meaning external (or sometimes internal) appearance.

As far as the control of design in general is

concerned, government policy in circulars and advice notes has been less reticent and shows, as Punter[5] argues, considerable consistency from the inter-war to post-war years. We have already noted that the prevailing philosophy has been that design control has to do with external appearance, but that in controlling external appearance local authorities must not be too heavy-handed and must rely as far as possible on professional expertise (see above). Development Control Policy Note 10[6], which remains in force, succinctly summarises this view. On the one hand it is unequivocal about the need for design control: 'One of the objects of development control is to prevent bad design and encourage good. Planning is concerned with the environment in which people live and work, and this necessarily entails consideration of aesthetic qualities ...'. On the other it urges caution in taking decisions in such a 'subjective' area which in any case is the proper domain of the architect. Local planning authorities are particularly warned not 'to stifle initiative and experiment' or 'to favour the familiar merely because it is familiar.'.

Positive guidance in the Note is, however, limited. The main message is that the design of a building may fail either because 'the design is bad in itself; fussy, or ill-proportioned, or downright ugly' or because it does not fit in with its surroundings. Though there is limited development of this latter theme, the level of generality offers local authorities little real guidance in decision-making. The only other advice that is offered is that trees are 'a valuable, and sometimes necessary, adjunct to new development' and that the planting of new trees and the retention of existing ones should be a consideration in the determination of every application. The problems of layout - major concerns of design control in practice - and the wider problems of siting, landscape design, the creation of space and of a sense of place go unmentioned.

When Mr. Heseltine became Secretary of State for the Environment in 1979, changes in policy were expected and new statements of government intentions for development control in its entirety appeared in Circular 22/80. The Secretary of State's views on design control were already well known as a result of a speech to the Town and Country Planning Summer School.[7] The argument, which formed only a small part of the total speech, was familiar, but was couched in terms which had a compelling resonance:

Design Control

'Democracy as a system of government I will defend against all comers but as an arbiter of taste or as a judge of aesthetic or artistic standards it falls far short of a far less controlled system of individual, corporate or institutional patronage and initiative'. Apparently, design control had not really ever worked to produce a better environment, and the mechanisms for control were inappropriate and added to wasteful delays. The circular proved to be a good deal less radical than the bold words might have suggested. Authorities are urged once again to recognise the subjective nature of aesthetics and not to be 'over-fastidious in such matters as, for example, the precise shade of colour of bricks'. Local authorities must moreover be restrained in their control over design and must confine their concern to those aspects of design which are significant for the quality of the area. The important point, however, is that aesthetic control remains part of the development control process, and as if to underline the continuity of policy, Development Control Policy Note 10 was not withdrawn with the publication of Circular 22/80.

More recently, the DoE have circulated the draft of a new circular on Good Design and Development Control which is intended to amplify the guidance of Circular 22/80. Its tone is more positive than the earlier circular and it defines a clear role for local authorities in the promotion of good design. In the annex there is a checklist of six factors to be considered. The advice is a clear improvement on anything published earlier, although it still restricts design to the existing definition of the aesthetics of exterior appearance (see below, footnote 27).

It would be wrong, however, to assume that the DoE had not offered advice from time to time on layout to local authorities. The Design Bulletin Residential Roads and Footpaths[8] appeared primarily concerned to promote economies on adoption standards for highways, and a new approach to road and pedestrian safety. The effect is a good deal more revolutionary than the ostensible purposes would imply. The Bulletin accepts that roads and footpaths are a critical part of the external spaces of housing areas and need to be treated as part of the totality and not in isolation. The message is emphasised by references to design guides published by Essex County Council and Cheshire County Council, and to schemes such as The Brow at Halton, Runcorn New Town, all of which have an explicit urban design

Design Control

purpose in using reduced road standards. One final point about government policy on design control should also be noted. While acknowledging the role of local authorities in controlling external appearance, government has consistently refused to accept that internal layout was a 'material consideration'. In particular, local authorities were not expected to insist on Parker Morris standards, and matters such as private garden size or the provision of garages have also been considered to fall outside the scope of development control.

THE PRACTICE OF DESIGN CONTROL

Given that advice to local authorities from central government has been somewhat equivocal, we might reasonably ask how authorities have chosen to interpret it. At this point, however, it is hard to gain a clear picture of what is really happening. This is partly because the range of development a local authority deals with inevitably calls for a variety of rather different responses, and partly because local authorities may be so different from each other that approaches to design control are very varied. Nevertheless, there are features of development control powers and the discretion they afford, and of the development process that those powers are designed to regulate, that have an important impact on how all local authorities control design.

The first point is that development control is essentially a reactive process which has to deal with what is brought before it but, at least in principle, cannot initiate. The result has been that in spite of the wide discretion that 'other material considerations' gives, it has always been more difficult for local authorities to deal with anything other than detail. If on a residential development general land-use allocation policy has been complied with, and if the surveyors have been satisfied with the road provision, then local authorities traditionally found it hard to intervene on design except perhaps in terms of the choice of brick or maybe the detail of fenestration. In the case of residential development they would perhaps be reluctant to do more, given the frequently-repeated message from developers, that the standard detached house or 'semi-' was what the public wanted. Of course there have been exceptions (such

127

as attempts to encourage 'Radburn' planning[9]).

The second point about the development control process is that even when local authorities have felt that the output of the developers left much to be desired, precedent still made it hard to intervene. If permission had already been given for a housing estate or an office block in an area, it would be hard to argue later, at appeal, that another, similar scheme was unacceptable in design terms.

The third point about the process is that elected representatives often find it easier to grasp detail on matters of design than to deal with a scheme in its entirety: a big scheme may be very complex. It is often said from outside the system that this tendency is fuelled by the lack of professional design skills among local authority staff[10], because no-one in an authority may have the ability to advise on the totality of a scheme.

Officers, however, may be more interested in design factors in development than are elected representatives, and the problems that may face officers are then rather how to convince members and how to ensure the maintenance of standards of design in the absence of clear policy guidance.

A fourth point is that development control has to be concerned with far more than external appearance or even the more fundamental matters of layout and the creation of spaces. Design factors have to be juggled with what may be major land use policy factors, and design, however defined, may not be the most significant factor in the determination of given applications. Design may have to be dealt with fairly summarily.

We have therefore a system which has tended to militate against wholesale involvement in the design of development. Yet because design has been considered important, by central government and by the public at large, local authorities have tended to focus on detail in the belief (not entirely ill-founded), that the impact of detail is significant in the creation of a good environment. Another, less desirable, effect has been to encourage a reliance on quantifiable standards as a way into the design process which is reasonably resistant to the problems of precedent and the 'fait accompli'. The problem with using such standards has been graphically described by the DoE.[11] Inevitably, standards focus on those aspects of design which can be quantified - such as road widths, density, or spacing of buildings - and ignore those aspects

Design Control

which cannot. Then there is the problem that some standards, like density ones, have been developed to achieve a variety of purposes (not all of them design ones in the aesthetic sense). Finally, standards have the disconcerting habit of becoming ends in themselves, applied in ignorance of the original intentions, and often failing to secure any real improvement in environmental quality.

If it is inherently difficult for development control to deal with design in spite of the intentions of parliament and governments, the development process which it treats with has its own rigidities too. Any development that is built speculatively (which is the case with much commercial and industrial development and most residential development) exists within a process that actually discourages innovation. To ensure the profitability of a scheme, a developer is bound to keep to a minimum the time in which capital is not producing a return. Thus the effect will be to reduce the period between the point of purchase of the site and the ultimate sale or rental of the buildings that are put up on it, which will tend to reduce the time in which the design is prepared. Developers will also aim for the saleable scheme which will have been shown to have worked before and is likely to be bland and unoriginal (although there are some exceptions, notably with recent retail developments). Punter's study has shown this effect clearly in Reading where speculative office building was invariably less imaginative than those schemes which were purpose-built. The monotony and standardisation of much residential development can be ascribed to the same process. A second point is that intervention by development control comes at a point when many important decisions have already been taken, not least of which may have been the appointment of an architect. The problem of the 'fait accompli' is as much an inherent part of the development process as of the control process, which may make it psychologically difficult for local planning authorities to resist development even if the design is unsatisfactory.

The development process, therefore, reinforces the tendency of the control system to make design control marginal, a matter of detail, rather than encouraging a thorough appraisal of design in all its aspects. Yet local authorities are not wholly trapped by their constraints and many appear to have tried strenuously to come to grips with the difficulties. Certainly the understanding of development control as a negotiative process rather than a quasi-judicial one has been used to effect at least at Reading. Here lengthy negotiation, inter alia on design matters, has been used as a tactic to secure the slowing down of office development, but also has resulted in the authority's being able to resist some of the worst schemes. Elsewhere, negotiation resulted in one of the most spectacular urban design achievements of the development control process, the creation of the piazza in front of Westminster Cathedral.[12] Here the developer ceded the land between Victoria Street and the Cathedral and thus broke what would otherwise have been a continuous frontage to mirror the one on the opposite side of the street. Bargaining is, however, dependent on having counters to bargain with. We can be sure in the Westminster case that the creation of the piazza was compensated for in the total office floorspace for which permission was granted; and presumably the prize of development on that site was well worth the extra time spent in discussion and the added complexity of the design. The stakes are not always so high.

Negotiation also depends on the ability and willingness of the negotiators to develop a rapport, and on a shared view that design is a fit matter for discussion. The classic example of failure based on unwillingness to negotiate is cited by both Meades and Punter. The architect Michael Manser, later to become President of the RIBA, submitted a scheme for an office block in Reading, in an uncompromisingly modern style which was rejected by committee. Manser's response was to submit a further four schemes apparently aimed to demonstrate the virtues of the original proposal. However, the committee, predictably in Punter's view, chose the scheme with the most modelled facade which used brick as a facing material, and this was the scheme that was built. The result 'has haunted the architect, the developer and the planning authority ever since'.[13]

Local authorities also use their discretionary power to impose conditions to extract design improvements from developers and ensure a tolerable quality of environment. In a study of four districts, Beer and Booth found that conditions were extensively used on small-scale industrial and residential estate development particularly for 'landscape' (which in effect meant planting) and for materials. Use of conditions of course confirms the idea that design is a marginal consideration, an optional extra to be considered when other factors have been settled. But conditions also appeared to be an officer-led response to the lack of interest in design among elected representatives. If members do not see the importance of having a design policy, then at least conditions help to avert the worst results. Yet Beer and Booth concluded that conditions were not a very satisfactory way of ensuring design quality. Firstly, they were unsatisfactory because they treated design, and particularly landscape design, as an afterthought. Secondly, they often relied on subsequent agreement, which might in practice pass by default, and thirdly resources were inadequate to ensure that conditions had in fact been complied with. A belief in the psychological impact of conditions appeared ill-founded.[14]

Whether local authorities rely on negotiation to achieve design control, or on the statutory power to impose conditions, the problem of how to set design objectives remains. In fact the absence of anything other than an implicit (or at most a poorly-articulated) view about what design control should achieve is often striking. For instance, in Beer and Booth's study there was no district which had a clear policy base for using conditions, although one authority had prepared a check-list of design factors which was used in processing applications for development. There does, however, seem to be a widespread consistency in the kinds of factors that are regarded as important, a system of shared values which must be seen as something more than a question of what the system makes possible. Punter points to the concern for detail and appropriate materials and for buildings which are lively and yet repeat the street scene. The ubiquity of conditions which deal with landscaping in Beer and Booth's study, however inadequate they may have proved to be in practice, also suggests a widely-held belief in the importance of planting and site treatment.

The approach that central government has urged local authorities to adopt to get over this policy gap is to employ appropriate expertise. In practice this has meant particularly referring applications to architectural advisory panels whose members will be local practising architects. The underlying philosophy of such an approach is that the design training of architects gives them an innate and superior sense of what is required. But there are various snags to the theory. Firstly, consultation with experts almost inevitably comes too late in the process to make much impact on the finished product. Secondly, consultation relies on the development control officer responsible knowing when he or she requires guidance on design. Thirdly, architectural advisory committees will find themselves in an invidious position if they are called on to comment on schemes prepared by a local firm which may be well known to them. Their ability to contribute effectively to design control must therefore be limited. Punter saw such committees making a positive but essentially limited contribution to design control, while Hazan concluded that reliance upon them as the major source of design expertise was the least efficient and sensitive of the approaches to design control he studied.[15]

The first two problems identified with architectural advisory committees apply equally to consultation with experts, say, in the other parts of the local authority. At Reading, the Architects Department was consulted on office development, although the results were not very satisfactory. Elsewhere, technical expertise within the town hall appears to be tapped all too rarely, and Beer and Booth found that consultations might be with officials with inappropriate skills. In particular, in the absence of trained landscape architects, the Recreation Department might be consulted on landscape design. The advice, then, might come at the wrong time and might not even be the right advice. One way round this is the employment of design skills within the planning department. In practice this is probably possible only for larger urban authorities, or where county authorities can assist their districts, but it certainly allows architect planners to be involved with a project from its outset and not simply when the major options have been closed. In Hazan's study of seven local authorities those which employed design skills within the planning department were regarded as most successful in achieving high design standards in resulting developments.

Even so, securing the right skills must be only one part of the story. At least part of the problem of design control is that the basis for securing improvements to design is often not made explicit, and therefore actors in the process may be ignorant of the rules of the game being played. This absence of explicit rules is responsible for the repeated assertion that design control is capricious and at the whim of the planning officers and elected

Design Control

representatives (even though Punter demonstrates that at Reading at least there was a consistency of approach which did not suggest caprice). If developers and their architects have taken exception to the lack of clear guidance, so, too, local authorities have begun to perceive that a clear policy framework is likely to be of benefit to them in breaking the pattern of precedent for poor design to which they were tied. This awareness has given rise in the past fifteen years to the growth in use of design guides, policy documents geared specifically to the needs of development control. It is to these that we now turn.

DESIGN GUIDANCE

When Essex County Council published its now-celebrated Design Guide for Residential Areas in 1973, a very important stage in the history of design control began. There had of course been some (mostly rather timid) attempts at design guidance before 1973, with authorities like the Peak Park Planning Board trying to spell out what good or bad design might constitute. What was new in the Essex Design Guide was an attempt to cover the full range of design considerations in relation to one form of development. It quite decisively departs from the limited concept of design that is contained in Development Control Policy Note 10 and deals as much with layout and the creation of urban and rural space as with building detail. We have already noted its influence in this respect on central government policy as it emerged in Design Bulletin 32.

The Guide consists of a short section that deals with County policy and a far longer section entitled Practice Notes, which aims to show how the policy might actually be realised. The practice notes are founded on three important principles which are essential to a proper understanding of the impact of the Guide. The first is that residential development is held to have failed on both aesthetic and functional grounds. The second is the claim that a satisfactory environment is one which creates a 'sense of place' that is clearly related to local character. The third is that good design is not a subjective 'matter of opinion or taste' but based upon 'well-proven principles'.[16]

The first point is dealt with by an examination of layout to achieve adequate privacy and private open space, to provide a road network that is commensurate with pedestrian movement and the needs of small groups of houses, and to increase densities to achieve useful savings in the land-take for housing. But the issue of the creation of 'satisfactorily enclosed, contrasting spaces' is also taken as a criterion of equal importance, and one to be used in the assessment of development proposals.

The second point also relates to the satisfactory enclosure of space, and the integration of buildings in the landscape, and the concept of the spectrum of settlements is advanced as a way of ensuring that layout may be varied appropriately according to location. The use of local materials and to some extent local vernacular detailing is also encouraged as a means of creating a sense of place, and one which has a truly Essex identity. The authors of the guide have always insisted, however, that the Guide did not necessarily require the use of neo-vernacular architecture although the illustrations, and not least the cover, all show weather-boarded and brick-built houses with steep pitched roofs.

The third point emerges mainly in the guidance on architectural form which draws upon abstract principles such as unity, balance, visual strength and the avoidance of ambiguity. These are shown as being dependent on the placing of doors and windows, the ratio of solid to void and the disposition of principal and subordinate parts of the building.

Much of the advice contained within the Guide has a respectable pedigree, and for this reason no doubt the authors could lay claim to well-proven principles. The significance of the Guide lies, however, in its comprehensiveness and in its desire to tackle speculative housing in a consistent fashion. Certainly its publication created a predictable furore among developers and architects alike. Developers at least slowly came to realise that the Guide might actually be in their interests. For one thing, the Guide proved hard to resist because its principles were so clearly articulated, and even the argument, put forward by Federated Homes at an appeal on a site at Earls Colne, that the Guide made development uneconomic, was not accepted by the inspector.[17] For another, developers began to discover that Design Guide houses might come to have a rather special market appeal: the porches and the coy detailing that the Guide did not actually require seemed to catch the

Design Control

mood of a popular impulse.[18] By 1976 it was already clear that the Guide had begun to modify substantially the output of both the volume builders and the smaller regional firms.
The success of the Essex Design Guide and the unstinting efforts of Melville Dunbar (the Guide's principal author) to publicise the achievement led other local authorities to produce similar policy documents. Yet it was a hard act to follow. None has achieved quite the breadth of material or the attention to detail, although there have been some notable successes. Cheshire County Council's design guides laid emphasis on road layouts which usefully added to the options for roads proposed by Essex. Other guides have tended to concentrate on the architectural aspects of guidance, and here the sketches from Essex are sometimes reproduced, often without acknowledgement. The result has been a series of well-publicised private sector schemes that all draw heavily on parts of the Design Guide and all purvey what Maguire has termed 'the quality of contrived rusticity'.[19] The new townships at South Woodham Ferrers in Essex, Martlesham Heath in Suffolk and Bowthorpe in Norwich all show precisely this quality and use a similar palette of materials. Perhaps given that they are all in East Anglia, there is nothing wrong with that. More worryingly, the same idiom appears in the planning brief for a site in Alfreton, Derbyshire[20], although some working through in relation to a local industrial vernacular is attempted.
Not all design guidance is about new residential development, however, and there is now a wealth of other kinds of guides available in various parts of the country which usually have fairly limited application. Grimsby for example felt it needed to offer advice on alteration to the town's late 19th century terraces[21], Westminster City Council have issued cyclostyled guidance on details such as roof extensions and dormer windows, while many authorities have issued guidance leaflets for their conservation areas. Indeed, the establishment of conservation areas with their emphasis on 'positive planning' has encouraged the production of guides. Perhaps there may be much to be learned from some of the better local authority work in this sphere.[22]
Design guides have without question had an important impact, particularly upon residential development. There are reasonable grounds for asking whether the impact has been wholly

beneficial, however. There is first of all the question of whether design guidance is as inseparable from a neo-vernacular style as the Essex authors claimed. Twelve years on, the comment of architects to Robinson that the Essex Guide was a 'passport to Noddyland' seems rather more accurate than one might have hoped. Then there is the danger that the preparation of design guides becomes a form of dialogue between planners and developers in which each finds an advantage, to the exclusion of the needs of the users of the buildings.[23]

Of course, the use of design guides does not resolve all the conflicts, nor dispose of the more basic criticisms raised by opponents of design control. It is to these objections that we must now return, before drawing conclusions.

OBJECTIONS TO DESIGN CONTROL

Some possible objections to aesthetic control were mentioned at the start of this chapter. Many architects have traditionally objected to design control, and to their objections have been added those of developers who see control as productive only of delay. The arguments advanced have in the last analysis much to do with architects' dislike of outside interference in what they regard as their legitimate sphere of activity. Sometimes this attitude surfaces in a rather unsophisticated form, as for instance in a questionnaire circulated to architects in the RIBA's Southern Region. This, in spite of asking possibly loaded questions about 'undue' control of external appearance, nevertheless produced a fairly guarded response on aesthetic control and revealed an extensive ignorance among architects of the workings of the planning system.[24] Despite the limitations of much of the criticism, however, serious arguments have emerged about design control.

One concern expressed by various commentators[25] is that design control stifles innovation. The argument is either couched in hypothetical terms - would a planning committee have allowed Gibbs to build his Fellows' Building alongside King's College Chapel, Cambridge? - or with reference to particular instances of refusal, as in the case of a design for an artist's house in Chelsea by Piers Gough. Unfortunately, in such instances evidence is almost exclusively anecdotal. Gough's firm, for example, whose designs have

Design Control

invariably tweaked the nose of the establishment with a combination of wit and camp outrageousness, has managed nevertheless to complete many projects which tease and delight, notwithstanding the ranks of philistine councillors. Punter found little evidence that innovative schemes had been rejected in Reading, and felt that the problem was one of the fairly poor quality of schemes coming forward for approval. We are left, therefore, only with the consideration of likelihoods. Assertions based on the argument that certain types of innovative design 'could not have happened here' obviously cannot be substantiated. What we can say is that the discretion that is given to local planning authorities does allow them to reject the unfamiliar. The protection against arbitrariness is of course the appeals system, but the delay that appealing entails works against the interest of the developer. Nevertheless the studies that do begin to present firm evidence show that the problem for local authorities is not coping with the unfamiliar and the unusual, but dealing with the abundance of schemes whose design quality is very low, whether in office, housing, or industrial development.

A second argument that is advanced is that design control not merely stifles but actively encourages mediocrity. The theory is that architects respond to planners' insistence on 'keeping in keeping' by putting forward safe designs that do not offend the committee and do not therefore waste time. The argument is certainly plausible, but overlooks the possibility that the mediocrity of such developments is a product of the low level of design skills, and the stifling pressure of the speculative development system, as much as a response to planning committees. Certainly there have been instances of architects using the attitudes of planning authorities to exert leverage on their developer clients to secure improvements in design. Punter makes the point that design control may result in mediocrity not so much because of planning authorities' desire to play safe, but because the mediocre, as opposed to the really bad, is very hard to resist. This, again, is due at least in part to central government's policy to intervene only where absolutely necessary.

CONCLUSIONS

The major arguments proposed against design control

are difficult to substantiate, but lead us inevitably to ask to whom we should entrust the care of an environment. The nature of architecture as a public act must suggest that it is too important to be left to architects alone, and that there needs to be a mechanism for the involvement of those affected by the results. There must be a way of ensuring that a client's purposes in developing do not run counter to the needs and aspirations of the public at large. Design control is therefore necessary, but the evidence certainly suggests it could be improved. Three conclusions perhaps need to be stressed.

The first is that the very limited definition of design promoted by central government actually encourages local authorities to deal with design control as a matter of detail. If, instead, government were to recognise that design is more than a question of external appearance, it would be able to encourage local authorities to take a more responsible attitude to control. It would for example be able to urge the employment of appropriate skills at the right moment and to offer advice on the formulation of policy.

The second conclusion is that for the system to work equitably design criteria employed in control must be made explicit. Design guides may have inherent difficulties, but at least the 'rules of the game' are made clear. Many local authorities will need advice on preparation of policy documents, and a report like that produced by a joint RTPI/RIBA working party in Yorkshire is a step in the right direction.[26]

The third point is that architects and planners have to recognise their mutual responsibility to each other and to the public at large for the quality of the environment. So long as architecture exists for architecture's sake, and design control for the planning committee's, control will remain a source of contention. The co-operation of the professional Institutes at national and regional levels is healthy; it is moreover essential if progress is to be made.[27]

NOTES

1. For a recent treatment of some historical aspects see J. Punter, <u>A History of Aesthetic Control I: The Control of the External Appearance of Development in England and Wales, 1909-1947</u>, Working

Papers in Land Management and Development, Environmental Policy, no. 2 (Department of Land Management and Development, University of Reading, 1984).
    2. J. Punter, 'Issues in Aesthetic Control', Design and Development (Planning and Transportation Research, London, 1983).
    3. A.T. Bacon, Planning Control and the Design of Buildings (unpublished thesis, Leeds Polytechnic, 1980), cited in J. Punter, Office Development in the Borough of Reading 1954 and 1984, Working Papers in Land Management and Development, Environmental Policy, no. 6 (Department of Land Management and Development, University of Reading, 1985).
    4. Ministry of Housing and Local Government, Circular 28/66, Elevational Control (HMSO, London, 1966).
    5. Punter, Office Development, op.cit.
    6. Ministry of Housing and Local Government, Development Control Policy Note 10: Design (HMSO, London, 1969).
    7. Department of the Environment, Circular 22/80, Development Control - Policy and Practice (HMSO, London, 1980); M. Heseltine, Secretary of State's Address, Proceedings of the Town and Country Planning Summer School (Royal Town Planning Institute, London, 1979), pp. 25-30, 22/80 version.
    8. Department of the Environment and Department of Transport, Residential Roads and Footpaths, Design Bulletin 32 (HMSO, London, 1977).
    9. See for instance Ministry of Housing and Local Government, Selected Planning Appeals 1963, second series, 5 (HMSO, London, 1964), pp. 18-19.
    10. A. Beer, 'Development Control and Design Quality, Part 2: Attitudes to Design', Town Planning Review, 54, 4 (October 1983), pp. 383-404. For an earlier relevant contribution see A. Goss, The Architect and Town Planning (RIBA, London, 1965).
    11. Department of the Environment, The Value of Standards for the External Environment, Research Report 6 (DoE, London, 1976).
    12. Architects' Journal, 'Developing the Picturesque', Architects' Journal, 162, 50 (10th December 1975), pp. 1228-30.
    13. J. Meades, 'Aesthetic Control: Strangling Creativity?', Architects' Journal, 170, 51 and 52 (19th and 26th December 1979) pp. 1315-24; Punter, Office Development, op. cit., pp. 47-8.
    14. A. Beer and P. Booth, Development Control and Design Quality, Report 1, The Major Findings

(Sheffield Centre for Environmental Research, 1981).
  15. Punter, Office Development, op. cit., pp. 146, 179; J. Hazan, The Treatment of Aesthetics in Urban Planning, Planning Studies No. 2 (Polytechnic of Central London, 1979).
  16. Essex County Council, A Design Guide for Residential Areas (The Council, Colchester, 1973), pp. 190, 61.
  17. L. Robinson, 'Essex Design Guide', Architects' Journal, 164, 38 (22nd September 1976), pp. 534-52.
  18. J. Hamilton, 'Alan Reason's Rationale for the Essex Design Guide', The House Builder, 35 (September 1976), pp. 462-3.
  19. P. Maguire, 'Gnome Man's Land', Planning, 318 (18th May 1979), pp. 10-11.
  20. Derbyshire County Council, Broadmeadows Planning Brief (The Council, Matlock, 1974).
  21. Grimsby Borough Council, House Improvements and the Street Scene (The Council, Grimsby, 1975).
  22. Leeds City Council, Roundhay Conservation Area Policy Statement (Department of Planning, Leeds City Council, 1983; amended 1985).
  23. P. Booth, 'Housing as a Product: Design Guidance and Resident Satisfaction in the Private Sector', Built Environment, 8, 1 (1982), pp.20-24.
  24. Royal Institute of British Architects Southern Region, Questionnaire on Development Control, Report of Survey (RIBA, Winchester, 1983, mimeo).
  25. For example by N. Beddington, 'Mollycoddled into Mediocrity', Built Environment, 2, 12 (1973), pp. 688-9; M. Manser, 'Barriers to Design', RIBA Journal, 86, 9 (September 1979), pp. 401-3; and Meades, 'Aesthetic Control', op. cit.
  26. Royal Town Planning Institute and Royal Institute of British Architects Yorkshire Branches, Design Guidance (RTPI/RIBA, Leeds, 1984).
  27. Since the completion of the present essay, a new circular has appeared, setting out current policy: see Department of the Environment, Circular 31/85, Aesthetic Control (HMSO, London, 1985).

Chapter 8

PLANNING CONTROL AND THE CONVERSION OF PROPERTY FOR SMALL BUSINESS USE

Howard Green and Paul Foley

INTRODUCTION

The development of units for small businesses has received increasing attention since Coopers and Lybrand pointed to a shortage of premises for new or developing small companies.[1] Much interest has been shown in the possible conversion of existing redundant property for small business use following pioneering examples in Clerkenwell, Covent Garden and Rotherhithe.[2] With approximately 150 million square feet of industrial floorspace vacant, the conversion of buildings to provide small business units seems a particularly appropriate use of resources. The case for re-use is supported by the relative difference in costs between converted units (average cost £2.17 per square foot) and newly-built ones (average cost over £15 per square foot).[3] The increase in activity, in part initially stimulated by the 100% industrial building allowance on small workshop schemes, has involved a wide range of developers with differing motives. The conventional private developers and public agencies (including local authorities, English Estates and CoSIRA) are prominent in developing new units. With conversion schemes, however, there is an increasing diversity of participants, including enterprise agencies, community groups, the church, farmers, and companies with spare space. The increased activity has widened the range of individuals now encountering the planning system.
    Our concern in this chapter is chiefly with problems that arise when developers are dealing with development control, in relation to conversion schemes for small businesses. We will begin with a comment on the policies of central government. This

141

will be followed by a discussion of aspects of discretion, a consideration of use classes, and a section on standards. The chapter then turns to the specific question of conservation, where the special circumstances require separate comment: this leads to two case studies. Finally, we summarise and draw conclusions.

THE POLICY CONTEXT

Since the late 1970s attitudes towards planning, and its relationship with business development, have changed dramatically both centrally and locally. Central government has sought to develop an 'enterprise culture', and remove the shackles of a constraining bureaucracy, in an attempt to encourage economic growth: this philosophy was summarised in the White Paper Lifting the Burden.[4] Local authorities, particularly in the areas of the country most badly hit by recession, have seen the need to help business, and particularly small firms. This has led to interesting modifications to traditional central-local relationships, with many Labour-controlled councils pursuing the centrally-encouraged policies, and staunch Conservative authorities resisting the adoption of these policies (which may be seen as environmentally-damaging). Central government guidance has come principally in the form of circulars: especially since 1979, these have exhorted local authorities to adopt a more responsive approach to industry. The degree to which recommendations in circulars are followed is part of the rather ill-understood area of discretion within the planning system. Examples below will show that the exercise of discretion by planning authorities can have major implications for conversion schemes.

Circular 22/80[5] was the first major statement of the present government's attitudes towards development control. In addition to discussing the efficiency of the system as a whole, the circular directs specific attention to industry in a section entitled 'Planning and Business Activity'. Authorities are asked to prioritise those applications which they believe 'will contribute most to national and local economic activity ...' and 'should bear in mind the vital role of small-scale enterprises in promoting future economic growth'. Referring specifically to planning and small business, it suggests that rigid zoning policies can be counter-productive and that development plans should be framed to facilitate small business development. The circular notes that redundant property is an appropriate base for small start-up businesses, and that where possible local authorities should identify suitable buildings. Also, as Booth notes in Chapter 7, Circular 22/80 raises questions about the imposition of design standards. In addition, Annex B to the circular (Enforcement and Discontinuance Action against Small Businesses) suggests that if enforcement is necessary, as a last resort, 'it should follow a carefully planned timetable which will give the operator of the enterprise sufficient time to find, negotiate for, and move to other suitable premises without unreasonably disrupting the business'.

Circular 16/84[6] reinforces the views expressed in 22/80. With reference to existing structure and local plan policies, it argues that 'There may be potential for conflict between approved and adopted plans ... and the present needs of industry'. Specific mention is also made of development involving small firms. Authorities are encouraged to search their own information bases for land and property suitable for industry. At the same time, 'all authorities will recognise that the prospects for bringing into use vacant buildings and sites in any area could be jeopardised if unrealistic and rigid restrictions are imposed ...'. The problems posed by a rigid classification of high technology activities into specific use classes are stressed. Authorities are encouraged in an annex to grant permissions in terms of a number of alternative uses. Circular 14/85 [7] supplements these exhortations, with the reminder that there is always a presumption in favour of allowing applications for development.

The recent Circular, 2/86, <u>Development by Small Businesses</u>, emphasises the requirements of small firms, and stresses the need to look flexibly at speculative building for this purpose: 'It is for market forces to determine whether there is a demand for such premises'.[8]

Our brief review of recent advice about industry and employment-related development highlights current emphases that local authorities are expected to take note of when reaching decisions. The importance placed on local authority compliance is made clear in Circular 14/85, which advises that ministers and inspectors will 'have regard to the terms of this circular in dealing with planning appeals and <u>with any application that may be made to them for the award of costs</u>' (our emphasis). There are, within the broader context of the various government policy statements, several themes of particular relevance to the conversion of property. These are: <u>firstly</u>, flexibility in the interpretation of development plans when assessing applications; <u>secondly</u>, support for the re-use of redundant buildings; <u>thirdly</u>, local authorities taking a positive role in identifying buildings; <u>fourthly</u>, problems of mixed use are identified and guidance is given especially with reference to high technology industry; <u>fifthly</u>, the market is seen as the primary means for assessing need. If local authorities were to respond positively over these themes when dealing with conversions (and assuming implementation of some of the proposed changes to the Use Classes Order discussed below), then the current level of conversion schemes could be enhanced. However, local authorities may not be quite so responsive, and are likely to exercise discretion in their interpretations of advice, taking into account local conditions. This will now be considered.

DISCRETION IN DECISION-MAKING

Several authors have noted the importance of discretion at both officer and member levels in the operation of the development control system.[9] Variability between authorities is highlighted in Davies and Healey's caricature of contrasting stereotypes of planning authorities.[10] In one, planning 'is flexible, responsive and innovative ... it recognises the importance of statutory planning procedures but is not confined by them.'. In another, by contrast, 'planning is an isolated activity, dependent at best upon an uncertain relationship with political and corporate leadership'. Whilst the changing approaches to industry and employment are set out in the circulars, interpretation remains with local authorities: it is not hard to predict how differently the two contrasted kinds of authorities would react to a centrally-located conversion scheme.
    Discretion is important if total uniformity is to be avoided. It is also vital for economic development, because no two local economies are the same; a project which works in one local authority

Conversions

area may not work in another. Considerable
variation in the availability of space for small
firms has been demonstrated at the sub-local
authority area level.[11] Market areas for small
units are tightly constrained geographically, and
can soon become over-supplied. Several examples
exist where conversion schemes have taken
considerable time to let because of over-supply in
the local market. Many developers new to the small
unit market in general, and to conversion in
particular, are as yet unaware of this pattern of
demand. This is a sphere in which the market (in
the terms of the circulars) would be a far from
effective judge of 'need'.

The use of discretion, however, can at times be
confusing for the developer, particularly if similar
schemes in the same area attract different
responses. The issue can baffle and infuriate
smaller developers, unused to the apparent
contradictions. Nor is it only the town planning
system which is involved, for both mandatory
building control rules and fire regulations are open
to some interpretation. In this context, an
illustration may be provided by a case where a set
of layout proposals were shown to a group of
building control officers. Whilst in principle all
but one were satisfied with the layouts, all
required minor modifications and changes, not all of
which were common to the group.[12]

Discretion is present in judgements on all
major questions relating to conversion of buildings
for small business use. It is worth stressing three
related issues, which will be discussed one by one.

Local Authority Responses to Proposals
The attitudes of authorities in England and Wales
towards building conversions vary significantly.
Whilst most now accept that small businesses are a
key element of economic policy, not all share the
spirit of Circular 22/80. Although many councils
adopt a positive approach in encouraging provision
of low-cost space by conversion, others appear to
hinder the process, in the hope that buildings will
be demolished and new units built.[13] Where local
plans have allocated sites for residential use, some
authorities have acted flexibly, allowing conversion
rather than promoting redevelopment. Approaches may
vary both between different local authorities and
for different localities within a single authority's
area. It seems that the personal views of officers,

Conversions

and the approaches taken towards economic development, rather than other major variables, are most important in explaining differences [14] (see also comments below on case officers). Although local levels of employment might be thought relevant, there appears to be no simple association between such factors and attitudes to schemes. In one local authority, conversions may be positively encouraged to the point where almost anything - within reason - is allowed. Elsewhere, uncertainties create problems: the development process is prolonged, and often punctuated with delays while permissions are sought for initial and then subsequent stages.

Discretion and Standards
The question of standards is dealt with more fully later, but at this point it is worth noting the role of discretion here. The rigid imposition of standards in conversion schemes can make them non-viable. Whilst there are broad groups of buildings which are commonly converted for small business - mills, warehouses, schools and barns for example - each building is different in design and location. Several schemes have been abandoned because of over-zealous insistence on pre-determined standards which are impossible to meet. Flexible interpretation is thus preferable. In practice the use of discretion in relation to standards is not necessarily influenced primarily by objective assessments linked to a problem or to a set of criteria! Rather, the relationship with developers is all-important. The small local developer typically associated with conversion schemes is still regarded with suspicion by many authorities, and is seen as seeking quick profits or making 'efficient' use of tax surpluses. Other councils are keen to work with developers for the overall benefit of the community.[15] Where local authority resources are very limited this may be a necessity: elsewhere it may be on the clear understanding of partnership. In a few cases developers may be invited to put a case to the planning committee, and to answer any questions arising.

Varying Attitudes of Case Officers
To conclude our consideration of discretion, it is necessary to emphasise the importance of the individual officer. Many design details imposed on

Conversions

developments are those of case officers, a fact frequently not fully understood by developers. Where the officer changes, a different approach may be taken. A recent case studied by the present writers illustrates this; it involved a conversion scheme phased over a period of six or seven years. As development progressed, not only were 'higher' standards applied at each stage, but different environmental requirements were also imposed. In stage 1, brick was unspecified and no landscaping was required. Six years later, in the most recent stage, the planting of conifers was required and local brick was specified. The completed development will be a very disjointed collection of buildings set in a somewhat artificial landscape. On enquiring why these changes were needed, the developer was amazed to hear that the area development control officer had moved, and his successor held different views about the area, its potential and its needs. The planning officer seems to have been interpreting market conditions, which he believed indicated that as demand was buoyant the developer would readily accept the new conditions.

USE CLASSES AND CHANGE OF USE

Major problems have been posed for many conversion schemes by the Use Classes Order and its interpretation by planning authorities. It has limited the range of uses to which units can be put. If proposals arising from the current review of the order are implemented, this may remove some of the problems, although many local authorities see the changes proposed by the Property Advisory Group as removing the little planning control which remains.[16] Of specific interest for small unit development is the permitted change from Class IV (General Industry) to Class III (Light Industry).

Two major problems arise for the developer of small units: (1) determining the previous use of the building in the initial process of seeking planning permission; (2) obtaining approval for a mix of uses for which there is local demand. Initial planning permission is usually based on existing use. The majority of buildings to be converted tend to have 'light industrial' or 'general industrial' permissions, so that most types of industrial development will therefore be within the appropriate use classes. Where the use immediately prior to conversion differs from the original use of the building, a Section 53 determination will be necessary.[17] In older property this can often cause some surprises. Ownership and tenant changes commonly take place without consultation about permitted uses. Buildings now used predominantly for warehousing in inner city areas are frequently found to have permissions only for general industry or light industry.

Recently, as demand for small units has risen, alongside the increasing availability of varied types of buildings for conversion (including church halls, warehouses, schools and farm buildings), the problem of permissions and changes of use has become potentially more contentious. This is particularly the case in rural areas, where barns and outbuildings are being converted for small industrial units. As demand in rural areas increases in the next few years in line with recent trends[18], this particular problem may be exacerbated.

More significant are the difficulties caused by mixtures of uses commonly associated with small unit schemes. As the aim of the developer is to maximise rental income by keeping a development fully let, he or she must have units which will meet the requirements of several tenant groups. Although the current use classes do permit a range of particular uses within one class, this is not necessarily the 'basket of uses' appropriate to current market conditions. If the pattern of demand for small units is examined, some broad generalisations can be made. Firstly, both business and personal services are growing, and this is creating demand for 'office type' units at various rental levels. Secondly, there is growth in leisure and tourist-related uses (such as craft industries). Many developers, appreciating the demand for leisure facilities, are retaining parts of schemes to let on short-term leases. Thirdly, many small firms demand units in which a range of uses can be carried out. A manufacturer, for example, may require office, retail and manufacturing space. Sometimes the floor area devoted to office and retail use may be significantly larger than that used for manufacturing. Fourthly, there is increasing demand for office and storage space by firms whose predominant activity is wholesaling. Given these trends, a diversity of uses may occur in one building. Furthermore, a developer will wish to modify the mixture of uses as tenant demand determines. Most certainly, he or she does not wish to have to reapply for permission each time a use changes. At present, a planning permission cannot be granted for a number of principal optional uses which can be taken up by succeeding tenants, without the need for further planning applications. As Circular 16/84 makes clear, a permission can be granted for more than one use, but 'once the first occupier moves in that alternative permission does not extend to subsequent changes of use.'.[19] In many cases small units have become 'fossilized' because they do not have the flexible permission appropriate to a volatile market, and tenants have turned elsewhere, mindful of the uncertainty and delays of obtaining permission. For many prospective small business tenants even the normal eight-week planning cycle is unacceptable if alternative accommodation can be found.

The problems are at their most critical where change of use is required for a complete scheme, or a particular use is required for part of a scheme. This frequently arises with developments which are principally concerned with office use. Many councils are keen to maintain a strict zoning policy for offices, and retain a commitment to central area office locations. Applications for change of use to offices, for the whole or part of a conversion scheme, consequently may be refused. Several inner city conversion schemes have failed because of this. Office use is frequently one of the few activities suitable for the upper floors of multi-storey properties, where floor loadings may not permit industrial uses. The availability of rental income from upper floors may affect a scheme's viability. In other cases excellent office space remains unused because permission could not be obtained for offices other than as an ancillary or incidental use.

Interest in modifying the Use Classes Order has arisen especially from problems posed by high technology developments, where it is argued that office and manufacturing functions merge.[20] However, the needs of smaller businesses, and the mixture of uses associated with them, raise equally important questions. In its recommendations for change, the Property Advisory Group suggests a single class, 'offices, light industry and other business uses'. This might help developers, but still would not recognise the very heterogeneous nature of small business activity: warehousing is still omitted because of traffic generation, and the importance of retailing remains unacknowledged. What might be appropriate would be a 'mixed class', which for example included 'use for a combination of offices, research and development, light industrial and wholesale uses, where no one of these uses represents more than 50% of the whole'. Alternatively, the General Development Order might be amended, to take account of the characteristics and needs of small firms.

Whichever approach to re-classification is adopted, the issue of nuisance deserves particular thought, given the implicit link between use and nuisance. For many activities, especially when carried out by smaller businesses, the nature of nuisance caused is likely to differ little between uses (whether warehousing, office, light manufacturing, craft or even retail use). A more <u>direct</u> measure of nuisance, associated closely with the impact on the environment or negative externalities, might prove a better way of dealing with this issue in the future.

CHANGING STANDARDS

A wide variety of buildings in a range of locations are being considered for conversion schemes.[21] Some date from the nineteenth century, others are more modern; many will present difficulties associated with standards imposed by public authorities.

Parking, access and traffic generation problems associated with intensification are the most common obstacles to successful development in this context. Imposing contemporary standards in an historic site can restrict development, while relaxation of requirements can help towards successful schemes. Parking provision is the most frequently encountered problem, varying with the type of building, its site density, and location. Adequate provision often is possible where site densities are relatively low, as at schools (where playgrounds form ideal car parks), or with post-war industrial property. In the case of older industrial property, where site densities are often high, on-site parking may be difficult. A local authority thus may be presented with two alternatives: either to insist on selective demolition, or to allow on-street parking. Either option will produce problems. With the first, the developer will see the authority as obstructive, increasing development costs and reducing valuable lettable space. With the second, local residents or the highway authority will not be eager to see surrounding streets choked with vehicles (especially if road-widths are narrow). In many instances, the planning authority, on advice from the highways authority, has insisted on additional parking spaces because of existing restrictions on surrounding streets. Ultimately, however, these requirements may be advantageous for the tenant and his or her customers, for whom easy parking is important.[22]

Access poses a similar problem, where the intensification of use associated with subdivision will lead to greater vehicular movement both into and within the site. Questions are often raised by the highways authority about the suitability of surrounding roads for the traffic generated. When buildings open onto main roads, sight-lines are frequently inadequate for the intensified use, and the highway authority may insist on improvements. To ease problems of access many councils require a circulatory traffic system on the site, which will allow goods vehicles to turn round. High site densities can make this very difficult to achieve. The requirement may be relaxed on condition, for example, that vehicles must reverse onto the site so as to minimise difficulties and dangers when leaving. Implementation of such conditions, however, is frequently impossible, as it is the tenant or driver rather than the developer who would have to comply.

CONSERVATION AND CONVERSION

In addition to the general difficulties posed by planning law and procedures, specific legislation relating to buildings and areas of architectural and historic interest can create particular problems. Industrial decline is leaving behind an increasing legacy of unused old manufacturing and commercial buildings. Redundant mills and deserted storage premises on coastal and inland waterways are perhaps two of the most common examples. There has been a growing recognition that some of these older buildings are a valuable part of our industrial heritage. Demolition of redundant industrial properties was the usual course of action during the 1960s and 1970s. The pace of demolition encouraged groups such as SAVE to campaign for the conservation of many older industrial buildings,[23] and increasingly large numbers of such properties have been protected by 'listing' as buildings of historic

Conversions

and architectural interest.[24] This growing concern has paralleled the increasing realisation of the value of older industrial buildings among developers and others wishing to use them. With decreased finance available to develop new industrial premises, the number of new industrial buildings constructed has fallen.[25] Given their relatively lower costs, the re-use of older premises has become more attractive.[26] Despite common interests in the re-use of such buildings, however, developers and conservationists may differ in their views. Some refurbishment projects have not satisfied conservation groups. From a developer viewpoint, moreover, the legislation has created problems. Some of the difficulties will be illustrated in two case studies below. Before this, a brief review of the legislative and policy position will be made.[27]

Legislation, Procedure and Policy
It is desirable to distinguish between preservation and conservation. The former was the dominant element until the 1967 Civic Amenities Act introduced powers for the designation of conservation areas.

We will begin with preservation. Currently, protection of buildings of special architectural or historic interest is afforded under the Town and Country Planning Act of 1971, and related legislation. In order to guide local planning authorities in the preservation of such buildings, central government compiles lists. Buildings are classified into three grades in order of importance; Grade I, Grade II* and Grade II.[28] Under the 1971 Act it is an offence to demolish, alter or extend a listed building 'in any manner which would affect its character as a building of special architectural or historic interest' without specific approval known as 'listed building consent' granted by the local planning authority.[29] Such offences will incur penalties in the courts. In terms of the case studies which follow it is important to note that listed building consent is required for internal alterations and also for demolition. These, of course, are actions for which planning permission is not normally required.

Whilst the process of applying for listed building consent is very similar to that associated with applying for planning permission, it is more complicated and time-consuming. Local planning authorities are required to advertise applications for listed building consent for 21 days, and to take note of any representations received.[30] Applications for consent to demolish, or where grant assistance is sought, are referred to the Secretary of State. The former are also sent for comment to organisations such as the Georgian Society and the Victorian Society. In determining applications for listed building consent, the local planning authority or the Secretary of State must take into account a number of factors, including the importance and merit of a building, its condition, and its likely economic value after repair. In this context the alternative uses of a site have to be considered, together with the subsequent enhancement of the environment or the more economic re-use of other listed buildings.[31]

Circular 23/77 stresses the advantages of re-use of buildings, stating for example that,

> New uses for old buildings may often be the key to preservation. It may be justifiable to relax control over land use allocation, density, plot ratio, day lighting and other controls where this would enable an historic building or group to be given a new lease of life.

A later paragraph states,

> Preservation should not be thought of as a purely negative process or as an impediment to progress. The great majority of listed buildings are still capable of beneficial use...[32]

The concept of conservation is more dynamic than that of preservation. The idea of Conservation Areas is based on the premise that preserving individual buildings may be insufficient if the area within which they stand is deteriorating. The objective is not merely to preserve, but also to enhance the character or appearance of an area.[33]

In principal, central government preservation and conservation policies could be seen as supportive of the re-use of older buildings. There is much scope, however, for variations in interpretation at the level of specific cases. Policies and practices may not in reality always prove helpful. Both our case studies involved Grade II listed buildings which developers wished to

Conversions

demolish (to facilitate the further conversion of properties on their sites for small business use). The histories illustrate the delays and difficulties which sometimes arise over obtaining listed building consent. Names have been omitted for the place and participants in the first case, which was in Yorkshire. Both discussions are summaries drawn from research by the present writers.

Case Study 1: a mill
This involved a mill in a small market town within the administrative area of a metropolitan district council. The local authority had rejected applications for further conversion work because of inadequate car parking and circulation at the site. Given the site density, the only way to resolve this problem was selective demolition to provide more parking space. All the buildings at the site (except one that was still in use) were Grade II listed. The developer suggested demolition of one of the mills, a building which had been redundant for some sixty years, and was both unsafe and an uneconomic proposition for re-use. He also proposed demolition of other minor buildings nearby.
Initially the council opposed this proposal. This left the developer in a difficult situation. He was required to provide extra car parking space before further development of other listed buildings could proceed, but was unable to demolish the one building which was most appropriate for the purpose of providing this space. After two years of negotiations the local authority finally conceded that the mill in question was not of significant enough interest to warrant preservation. The developer's case was strengthened by the employment opportunities, and potential help for small business tenants, offered by the scheme.

The arguments advanced against listed building consent appeared to have been contrary to considerations inherent in Circular 23/77 (see our comments above). The council's attitude indicates the scope for local interpretations delaying developments. As a result of the difficulties experienced, and other problems similar to those discussed earlier in this chapter, the developer has subsequently proceeded with development without awaiting consents (although ensuring that all work would be of a standard normally acceptable to the authority). Applications have been submitted while work was being carried out. The developer's

Conversions

attitude now is that he is sure everything will be done satisfactorily, and if an enforcement notice is issued he is confident that the employment and economic benefits of his scheme will be enough to sway any appeal decision. It is difficult to know whether his dissatisfaction with 'planners' (and current processes) is representative for this kind of developer, but the response he adopted might become more widespread if there is not a more positive approach on the part of local authorities.

Case Study 2: Industrial Park, Halifax
Dean Clough provides an interesting contrast to our first case. It is an industrial complex of about 1,100,000 square feet. Mr Ernest Hall bought the site from a carpet manufacturing company in 1982, with the aim of converting it into an industrial estate for small business use. Calderdale Metropolitan District Council have assisted Mr Hall to obtain all relevant permissions, expediting the passage of planning applications. Given the size of the site and the important role it could play in regeneration of the local economy, this may not be surprising, although the authority has also actively helped other smaller developments.

Dean Clough is a densely-developed site with over fifteen multi- and single-storey buildings, mostly built between 1840 and 1870. To allow better circulation and additional car parking the developer proposed to demolish C Mill, a 74,000 square feet building of seven storeys built in the 1850s. This demolition would also allow direct access to an old listed Axminster weaving shed of 120,000 square feet, and facilitate the re-use of other listed buildings of about 200,000 square feet at the site.

The Council considered Mr Hall's proposals, and £964,000 refurbishment estimates for C Mill (only supportable by a £2 per square foot rental), and decided to support his application for listed building consent. They received a formal application in February 1984. Site posters, newspaper advertisements, and notification to statutory bodies of the demolition of a listed building, produced three groups which opposed listed building consent. These were the Ancient Monuments Society, The Victorian Society, and Save Britain's Heritage. A public inquiry was held in February 1985, one year after the initial application, and the report of the inquiry was sent to the Secretary of State on 1st March. The inspector was critical of submissions put forward by the main objectors. He felt that the representations of one organisation were founded on the concept of preservation of a listed building group as an over-riding consideration, with no regard paid to lack of reasonable prospects of restored use or lack of viability of rehabilitation. He was scathing about another of the organisations, which did not actually appear at the inquiry. He saw their views as badly constructed, and centred on an unsupported belief about the applicant's future demolition intentions (despite acknowledgement of a good previous record). The inspector concluded his review of objectors' representations by arguing that the success of the scheme depended upon maintaining momentum in providing and marketing a variety of space use options with good service facilities in financially realistic order. Time had been lost without good enough reason, and a speedy consent was now needed. Perhaps because of the strength of the inspector's view, listed building consent was then granted very quickly, on 25th April 1985. (This contrasts with three similar inquiries in northern England at the same period, where approximately one year passed after each inquiry before a decision was reached.)

CONCLUSIONS

An increase in the area of vacant industrial floorspace in the United Kingdom has led to a decline in the real price of industrial property, particularly in some parts of the market. A variety of types of developers have been involved in converting property for small business use. Conversion can offer an economically viable proposition for the re-use of many old buildings. Increasing recognition of the possibilities here has widened the range of individuals and groups undertaking such schemes, and thus encountering the planning system. This chapter has outlined many of the problems these developers face. Attitudes towards conversion schemes vary both within and between local authorities, and regulations and national policy guidelines are open to wide variations in interpretation and response locally. Major problems can arise with the Use Classes Order.

If buildings are to be re-used and to provide local employment opportunities, it is essential that the smaller developers who undertake much of this

Conversions

type of work are assisted sympathetically. This should not be taken as a recommendation that all standards should be reduced, but rather a suggestion that buildings be treated on their merits, with appropriate relaxations being adequately considered. As some of our illustrative material has indicated, there may be occasions when the planning process could be speeded up. This is especially important with redundant buildings, where each month's delay can be accompanied by increasing vandalism, and deterioration of the property. At present there is often little enough encouragement for schemes, particularly with the demise of the industrial building allowance. If smaller developers are not aided by a sympathetic and speedy development control response, many of the buildings they hope to convert could remain as deteriorating reminders of lost opportunities for re-use or conversion.

NOTES

1. Coopers and Lybrand Associates, Provision of Small Industrial Premises (Department of Industry, London, 1980); Department of Industry and Shell U.K., Helping small firms start up and grow: common services and technological support (Department of Industry, HMSO, London, 1982); D.H. Green and P.D. Foley, 'Subdivision of Industrial Premises', Local Government Policy-Making, 11, 2 (November 1984), pp. 57-66; D.H. Green and P. Foley, Putting Spare Space to Work (Small Business Research Unit, London, 1985); M. Ambler and S. Kennett, The Small Workshops Scheme: a review of the impact of the scheme and an assessment of the current market position for small workshops (Department of Trade and Industry, HMSO, London, 1985); Department of Industry, Small Works Scheme; Survey of the effect of the 100% allowance (Department of Industry, HMSO, London, 1982).
2. URBED, Recycling Industrial Buildings (Capital Planning Information, Edinburgh, 1981).
3. D.H. Green and P. Foley, 'Making Homes for Small Firms', Town and Country Planning, 52, 1 (January 1983), pp. 17-20.
4. Minister without Portfolio, Lifting the Burden, Cmnd. 9571 (HMSO, London, 1985).
5. Department of the Environment, Circular 22/80, Development Control - Policy and Practice (HMSO, London, 1980).
6. Department of the Environment, Circular

16/84, Industrial Development (HMSO, London, 1984).
7. Department of the Environment, Circular 14/85, Development and Employment (HMSO, London, 1985).
8. Department of the Environment, Circular 2/86, Development by Small Businesses (HMSO, London, 1986).
9. For example see J.B. McLoughlin, Control and Urban Planning (Faber, London, 1973); J. Alder, Development control (Sweet and Maxwell, London, 1979); P. McAuslan, The Ideologies of Planning Law, (Pergamon Press, Oxford, 1980).
10. H.W.E. Davies and P. Healey, British Planning Practice and Planning Education in the 1970s and 1980s, Working Paper 70, Department of Town Planning (Oxford Polytechnic, 1983).
11. D.H. Green & P.D. Foley, Redundant Space: A Productive Asset (Harper and Row, London, 1986).
12. Green and Foley 1985, op. cit.
13. B.C. Kataky, Redundant premises and economic development, unpublished thesis, School of Planning and Environmental Studies (Leeds Polytechnic, 1985).
14. M. Perry, The Provision of Small Industrial Premises: A Geographical Perspective, unpublished thesis (Plymouth Polytechnic, 1986).
15. West Yorkshire County Council, New Life for your buildings (West Yorkshire County Council, Wakefield, 1985).
16. Property Advisory Group, Town and Country Planning (Use Classes) Order 1972: Report (DoE, HMSO, London, 1985).
17. Section 53 of the Town and Country Planning Act of 1971 makes provision for application to the local planning authority to determine whether or not planning permission is required.
18. S. Fothergill and G. Gudgin, Unequal Growth: Urban and Regional Employment Change in the U.K. (Heinemann, London, 1982).
19. Circular 16/84, op. cit.
20. C. Brook, Planning for High Technology Industry (Clive Brook Associates, Leeds, 1985).
21. See typology in P. Eley and J. Worthington, Industrial rehabilitation: the use of redundant buildings for small enterprises (Architectural Press, London, 1984).
22. D.H. Green, B. Chalkley and P.D. Foley, How to Choose Business Premises (Kogan Page, London, 1986).
23. F. Charles, 'Conservitis in excelsis', Architects Journal, 40, 176 (6th October 1982) pp.

71-82.
24. J.N. Tarn, 'Urban Regeneration: the conservation dimension', Town Planning Review, 56, 2 (April 1985), pp. 245-68.
25. H. Smyth, Property Companies and the Construction Industry in Britain (Cambridge University Press, Cambridge, 1985).
26. Foley and Green 1983, op. cit.
27. For the legislation see Royal Borough of Kensington and Chelsea, Urban conservation and historic buildings: a guide to the legislation (Royal Borough of Kensington and Chelsea, London, 1984).
28. See D. Heap, An Outline of Planning Law (Sweet and Maxwell, London, eighth edition, 1982).
29. Town and Country Planning Act, 1971, Section 55.
30. The Town and Country Planning (Listed Buildings and Buildings in Conservation Areas) Regulations 1977, S.I. 1977/228 (HMSO, London, 1977).
31. Department of the Environment, Circular 23/77, Historic Buildings and Conservation Areas - Policy and Procedure (HMSO, London, 1977).
32. Ibid.
33. The objectives are indicated in Department of the Environment, Development Control Policy Note 7, Preservation of Historic Buildings and Areas (HMSO, London, 1976).

Chapter 9

COMPUTERS IN DEVELOPMENT CONTROL AND RESEARCH

Eamonn J. Judge

INTRODUCTION

A significant phenomenon in the last ten years, and especially in the last five, has been the spread in planning departments of various types of computer systems for automating the process of development control (D.C.). Apart from the presumed benefits that this has had or will have for the process of D.C. itself, it opens up the possibility of greatly extending the amount of research which can be carried out in related areas. This chapter will review the growth in computerised D.C. systems in this country, consider the merits and drawbacks of the data, and comment on the potential for research.[1]

COMPUTERISED DEVELOPMENT CONTROL SYSTEMS

A typical planning application - whether in a manual or computer-based system - will involve the collection of a large volume of information, on the application form or subsequently. This varies from authority to authority. Table 1 illustrates the kind of case information built up: the example is taken from the situation in the Plans Processing Unit of Wakefield City Council. Much of this information is generated after receipt of the application, by internal processes (map measurements, site visits, consultations), and recommendations by officers, committee decisions, appeals, etc. A series of letters to the applicant will also be required, as well as the addition of the application to the monthly register. Clearly many of these items of information are encodeable or capable of being produced in a standard form. Thus

Computers in D.C. and Research

TABLE 1   LIST OF ITEMS KEPT BY WAKEFIELD CITY
          COUNCIL ON EACH PLANNING APPLICATION
          (including details for Building
          Regulations)

1. Application number, applicant's name, agent's
   name, agent's address, description of
   development, and location. Codes for local
   plan area and parish. Grid reference. Date of
   receipt by planning department.

2. Codes for approval type (planning permission,
   building regulations, etc.), type of
   development (new, redevelopment, etc.), special
   development (listed building, conservation
   area, etc.), application type (full, outline,
   renewal, etc.), type of applicant (private,
   statutory undertaker, etc.), site allocation on
   town map (residential, etc.), green belt
   (in/not in), existing land use, proposed land
   use (including whether mixed use), ownership
   (local authority or not). Site area,
   floorspace, number of parking spaces, number of
   existing and proposed dwellings (if
   residential), cross-reference with land
   availability file.

3. Previous application number (if any),
   recommendation code (approval, refusal, etc.),
   recommendation date, departure code (re town
   map), planning decision code (approval etc.).
   Date of decision, conditions (entered by
   standard code or else as text), observations
   (whether received and from whom), comments.
   Building regulations decision code, date and
   conditions.

4. Expiry dates of planning and building
   decisions, start and completion dates of
   development, whether partial completion.

5. Appeal progress codes (lodged, upheld,
   dismissed, etc.), appeal decision date.

NOTE

Some data fields (e.g. pertaining to the Community
Land Act) are now redundant and not mentioned
above.

one might have expected that the potential for automating all or part of the administrative process would have been recognised and grasped early on. However, although it is now over twenty years since the application of computers to planning was first looked into,[2] the main areas of initial involvement were in strategic applications to forecasting and modelling (stimulated by the importation of land-use/transport studies from the United States), and the development of information systems (very much in line with the move towards corporate planning after the Bains Report).[3] Growth in the use of computers generally in planning departments was slow, and use in D.C. was not helped by the reorganisation of local government in 1974, which separated the previous intensive computer users in planning (strategic planners) from planners dealing with D.C. directly, in the districts.

The first important initiative in computerisation of D.C. processes was in Leeds. The LAMIS (Local Authority Management Information System) Project started in 1972 as a joint study between Leeds City Council, the Department of Industry, and International Computers Ltd.[4] The purpose was not to produce a D.C. processing system: that was a by-product of broader objectives related to developing a land charges and development monitoring system. After the LAMIS initiative, the next significant development was at Wakefield, following local government reorganisation. Here a system was developed based on mini-computers, rather than the large 'mainframe' computer system at Leeds. This system was specifically orientated to the operational tasks of processing planning applications and development monitoring, and was very much under the direct control of planning staff, an unusual situation for the time.[5]

Since these early initiatives there has been a substantial increase in the application of computers to the processing of planning applications and related functions. This has been documented in a number of studies.[6] After relatively slow growth up to 1979, when the number of systems installed each year averaged 5-20, the numbers jumped in 1980 and 1981, probably in response to Circular 22/80 stressing the need to speed up the handling of planning applications.[7] The focus of research here has moved on from documenting the growth of computer applications in D.C., and the reasons for this, to studies of the experiences and problems associated with installing new systems. Some key

points are considered below.
   The growth of computer applications is of interest not just for the numbers per se, but also for the approaches adopted by different authorities. Wide variations have occurred in the types of computers or 'hardware' employed as a basis for D.C., and in the programs, or 'software' which have embodied the characteristics of the D.C. system to be implemented on the computer system adopted. Clearly, at various points hardware and software considerations interact, as do software and D.C. system, although it will be convenient to an extent to discuss them separately. The first computerised D.C. systems were, as indicated above, installed on large mainframe computers typically shared with other departments in an authority, for which the planning department would have limited control and access. Later, mini-computers came into use, and more recently, as micro-computers became more powerful, flexible and cheap, these began increasingly to become a feasible basis for a system, even for the smallest local authority. Within this spectrum of hardware the dividing lines have become blurred, with increasing power at the 'bottom' (micro) end of the spectrum, and decreasing physical size at the 'top' (mainframe) end. Nevertheless, the choice of location on the spectrum is broadly between the greater power, facilities and access to software available on a mainframe - though with less departmental control - and the limitations of small machines in technical terms, but with more direct control by the planning department. A recent study[8] indicated that of 179 authorities (36% of the total) with computerised D.C. systems, 62 used mainframes, 69 used mini-computers, and 53 used a micro-computer or wordprocessor (five authorities falling into more than one category).
   There are three possible software approaches. Firstly, authorities may design their own programs suited to their specific requirements. Secondly, manufacturers may do this for them, providing a program system to run on the machine supplied. Thirdly, an authority may acquire an 'off-the-peg' package from those available, reconciling itself to the limitations of any particular package vis-à-vis its own 'ideal' requirements. In 1984, 117 local authorities had some type of 'off-the-peg' system, and 67 had a developed system (within the first two categories above).[9] Of the 'off-the-peg' systems, the ICL PLANAPS package was most widespread, being found in 63 (35%) of all the 179 authorities.

For the type of D.C. system embodied in the software, a number of possibilities can be identified,[10] although categories overlap. Firstly, one can point to some form of 'stand-alone' system, in terms either of a machine completely devoted to running a D.C. system, or software committed purely to D.C. and not tied into any other process or database. (These two senses can of course be combined.) Such systems have the advantage of independence for the planning department. Secondly, the D.C. system may be linked into other databases, most obviously property ones. Such systems hold information on every address in an area, and a D.C. system linked to, or part of such a system, is essential for keeping it up to date. This would logically be linked to an intermediary building control system, and also a land availability system. Clearly, the time spent building up such a system (the ICL LAMIS system being an early and well-known example) can be substantial, but as the data, or much of it, is common to several of the linked systems there can be significant economies. However, apart from initial set-up costs, such systems have the disadvantage of reduced independence for planning departments where parts of the database are the province of other departments. Thirdly, the D.C. system may not be linked to other databases, but to other authorities via some jointly operated arrangement. Most typically this will be some sort of county/district approach, and may in fact combine aspects of the two previous possibilities just discussed. This may be very limited in nature with districts and county pooling information on decisions for the operation of a decisions analysis system: each district may conceivably have its own stand-alone D.C. system, not linked to the other districts. (The JDAS system in Humberside is of this type [11].) At the other extreme the counties and districts may operate jointly a single D.C. system (such as the PLANAPS system in Cornwall). The economies of such a system are obvious, though there may be co-ordination difficulties between participants, and some reduction in independence.

It is now time to consider the reasons for the introduction of computerised D.C. systems. A number of studies have examined this topic [12]: the most frequently cited reasons for setting up such systems relate to the desire to improve efficiency in terms of speedy processing of applications, or savings in staff and other costs. The cost aspect has accentuated the advantage of stand-alone off-the-peg systems which can be implemented quickly on inexpensive machines without too much worry about potential link-ups with other databases. As Grimshaw[13] points out, however, such short-term advantages may be bought at long-term cost. Significantly, in practice, the use of computerised D.C. systems for management information or monitoring purposes is a minor reason for installation, and outputs for research purposes are an even less significant reason.

As one might expect, an emerging area of research covers the impact of computerisation in respect of efficiency gains. Early work here produced contradictory findings, with some research showing that the most efficient authorities (in terms of speed of dealing with applications) were not necessarily those with computerised systems[14], and some indicating that authorities with computerised systems had better than average performance[15]. More recently Farthing[16] has shown, in a case study of four authorities, that whether or not savings are achieved depends on a number of factors: organisational constraints may nullify potential savings, systems may take longer to implement (or be more troublesome) than envisaged, systems may not do everything expected of them (so that manual processes cannot be dispensed with entirely), and benefits in any case take time to build up.

We may now proceed from this short review of the development of computerised D.C. systems, to a consideration of the nature and uses of the databases that they generate.

THE VALUE OF COMPUTERISED DEVELOPMENT CONTROL DATA AS AN INFORMATION SOURCE

It is necessary to comment first on some general characteristics of D.C. data, and then to explore additional issues involved when these data are computerised.

Most observers assert that D.C. data are a valuable resource for various types of research. The information on each application is detailed, especially if taken in conjunction with other sources, such as building control data, and it is readily available. In theory there are numerous issues where this data could be used to cast light, yet it is 'an under-used resource'[17]. This may be

attributed partly to such factors as the low
research profile of the profession that generates
the data, and the lack of resources generally for
research in the planning system. However, there are
problems with the data which themselves may militate
against their use. An obvious one is the difficulty
of eliminating double counting. There may be
duplicate applications for the same development,
submitted by the same applicant, or outline and
detailed applications. The extent of double
counting has to be established, and its effects
eliminated. A second problem is that records in
such a database can vary substantially in
significance: an application for a single house
extension constitutes a record, just as much as one
for a major housing scheme. Clearly, applications
need to be weighted by some measure of their
importance before many types of comparative analysis
(especially between areas) can be undertaken. As
McNamara and Healey say, 'Decisions are not units
that can be compared readily one with another'.[18]
In Rydin's opinion, the worst problem lies in assign
-ing any significance to the statistics; i.e. the
interpretation of aggregations of characteristics of
individual D.C. cases.[19] Thus 'The number of
planning applications and appeals received can vary
with general economic conditions, with statements of
planning policy or with changes in administrative
procedures'. The percentage of applications
approved or appeals allowed can reflect the workload
of a local authority or the inspectorate, as well as
'environmental' factors such as the existence of
Conservation Areas, Areas of Outstanding Natural
Beauty, and so forth. Furthermore, figures for any
one year will include cases carried over from
previous periods. It is not easy to make causative
connections between, say, policy changes such as the
introduction of circulars, and changes in D.C.
statistics. In drawing conclusions from D.C. data,
therefore, reference must be made to 'supporting
arguments and a coherent framework within which the
results of analysis fit.'.[20]

Thus statistical data derived from D.C. records
can seldom be interpreted by themselves without
recourse to other knowledge. It is also worth
noting that data collected and maintained in each
record are seldom a complete statement of all the
information pertaining to each application. The
files on applications may contain important
correspondence, records of telephone conversations
or of meetings with applicants. Much information

may be only in the heads of D.C. staff. In fact, as observers have pointed out, informal contacts before submission of an application may be of great importance, so that the formal D.C. records may only register part of the proceedings. The original intentions of a developer may be modified through some kind of mutual adjustment.

All these various problems are compounded when one tries to make comparisons between areas, or to aggregate data between areas. While generalisation is feasible on the main lines of information which any local authority will collect on most applications, there is still sufficient variation on the form and range of information collected to make aggregation a complex task. These data difficulties are exacerbated when systems are computerised, as the variety of D.C. systems is combined with the variety of approaches to computerisation. It was this which prompted McNamara to make a plea for a centrally-organised system for collecting a core of comparable information on applications across the country as a whole.[21] He wrote before the current proliferation of computerised D.C. systems, but recognised that any national system would become increasingly difficult to organise as more authorities become entrenched with their own specific approaches.

A number of additional problems arise with computerised D.C. databases. Accuracy is difficult anyway: the average database is large and daily expanding. Ensuring that all items of data are entered accurately and checked is a major concern, and errors can never be eliminated entirely. Their presence, however, can undermine the value of the base both for day-to-day purposes and for longer-term research. Failure to record correctly even mundane items like grid references means that, for instance, a search for all the cases in a particular grid square can miss some out. The consequence for research is that, even after the problems of converting magnetic tapes from different machines to run on the researcher's machine have been overcome, and the compatible elements have been defined from different databases, there is still substantial work in editing the database to correct codes and where necessary to remove cases which are incomplete or irretrievably inaccurate.

A further difficulty for the researcher, although not necessarily for the D.C. professional, is that computerised systems not designed with research in mind may have built-in barriers to their

167

use for research. For example, standard conditions on planning consents are frequently codified: they can be entered in computer files or on letters simply by activating the relevant code number. A failure to enter on the computer file the code number itself means that it is impossible to search the database for cases with particular conditions, unless one engages in a daunting programming exercise to convert the strings of characters associated with each condition back into codes.

Having said the above, however, it is a lecture of caution, not despair. Much useful research is feasible, despite the difficulties. We will now review some of the possibilities.

COMPUTERISED DEVELOPMENT CONTROL DATA AND RESEARCH

It is not the intention here to review D.C. research in general (see the literature review in Chapter 2).[22] Nor is it the present writer's purpose to summarise the substantive results of research using computerised D.C. databases: space precludes this. Rather, the broad areas of usage of such databases will be outlined, along with some of the issues involved.

The potential range of research topics which could draw on this data source seems very wide. Thus McNamara[23], in making his argument for a nationally-organised D.C. database, suggested the following list: land availability; the effects of local authority planning policies across their boundaries; the operation of development processes at regional and national levels; the effects of local authority policy stances on development pressures at national and regional levels; and the level of development and land use change occurring in any one area or across the country as a whole. This list is not exhaustive. We have already referred to research on whether computerisation makes the D.C. process any more efficient, while the issue of delays in D.C. is one where computerised systems can provide basic fuel for the debate. The present writer's own interest in these databases arose out of a concern with the relationship between transport investment and spatial development, for which this data source seemed potentially useful.[24] This type of application is by no means novel, a study already having been carried out since 1977 on the impact of the Tyne and Wear Metro, using (inter alia) such data.[25] Some indication of the

range of uses may be gleaned from the fact that the 1985 report on the Humberside County Council Joint Development Analysis System lists some eighty different purposes for which the system has been used to provide information.[26]
Some of the research applications suggested by McNamara are not feasible simply because we do not yet have a national system of computerised D.C. data (and with the demise of the Metropolitan Counties one must have some qualms about the survival of some county databases). However, below a national level, the most obvious research application at a fairly operational level is in the wide variety of monitoring systems which have been developed by many local authorities.[27] These make use of data other than D.C. data, though the latter form a major input. It is not of course a pre-condition to the operation of a computerised or manual monitoring system to have a computerised D.C. system,[28] but where the two exist interchange of information is clearly more direct. The primary uses of such monitoring systems, and the D.C. component of them, are in the preparation of structure plans and local plans, and in the subsequent monitoring of their progress and review. As Anderson says, 'An analysis of development control data is ... the only practicable means of ascertaining the extent to which structure plan policies are implemented in development control decisions'.[29] D.C. system outputs are useful in updating other databases (such as property registers), and in providing advance indications of likely changes in employment and population. D.C. data within a monitoring system will also provide information for research for many other operational purposes, such as dealing with planning appeals or assessing the effectiveness of such initiatives as Enterprise Zones and Industrial Improvement Areas.
Much of this monitoring-related research quite properly has a very 'operational' flavour. It may be for internal consumption only, and more concerned with a local authority's ongoing activities and priorities than with a more general research interest in the planning system and its policies, or in the nature of urban and rural change. Nonetheless, there are many examples available of academic research using D.C. data. Even prior to the availability of computerised D.C. systems, there were some well-known studies: for instance Gregory's work appraising the effectiveness of green belt policies in the West Midlands.[30] Some more recent

studies, furthermore, have not depended on computerised systems, as witness Brotherton's work [31] on development restraint and planning control in national parks. However, the flexibility and ease of access offered to researchers outside local authorities by computerised D.C. databases is on the surface a major attraction. Acquisition of a database as a whole will be unusual, but such a system can be searched rapidly by the host authority for cases with particular characteristics, so that relevant data can be supplied on printout or magnetic tape in response to a specific research need. These data may be transferred to another machine and analysed using standard statistical packages. Alternatively, or additionally, the selected cases may be used to gain access to case files for more detailed manual work. Clearly the characteristics of the computerised D.C. system dictate what is possible here: thus a search of a file for permissions with specific types of conditions will be difficult if conditions are not held on file in both code and text form. Equally, research requiring data on adjacent authorities to build up an area-wide database may be hampered by variations in the range and form of data held by each, or by gaps in the field of interest caused by one authority not possessing a computerised system. (This has been the writer's own experience.)

There are a number of examples of academic research where data have been extracted from a computerised system and subjected to analysis alongside other data. Anderson's [32] and Blacksell and Gilg's [33] studies of planning control in Areas of Outstanding Natural Beauty are well known, and more recently there has been Rydin's work [34] on residential development in areas of differing population growth, green belt restraint, and public housing policy.

As an alternative to academic researchers extracting part of a computerised D.C. database, a copy of the database as a whole may be supplied on magnetic tape by the local authority. This may occur for a number of reasons. At a time of staff shortage it may be more convenient than meeting more specific requests, especially if the authority can gain something in return (such as analyses it has no time or resources to carry out itself, or the undertaking to make data available to other researchers). For the researcher this may be attractive, leaving him or her with tremendous flexibility. There are various obstacles to

Computers in D.C. and Research

overcome, however, which may present varying difficulties, depending on the computer expertise and facilities available to the researcher. The first problem is the conversion of magnetic tapes to run on another machine, with the writing of programs to read the data. The second (and more major) problem will be the checking of records to ensure that the database is free of illogical or erroneous data. The level of accuracy acceptable for day-to-day administrative purposes may be less than is necessary for trouble-free research: checking may be time-consuming and involve the loss of some of the data.[35]

On the whole, however, whether one is talking of access to part or all of a database, the amount of research at present being undertaken remains surprisingly small, given the volume of data accumulating (especially in computerised systems). One can only regret that McNamara's suggestion [36] of a standardised national system has not been taken up. The continued proliferation of different computer systems (for carrying out a fairly similar administrative process across the country) will continue to be a hindrance for any research that goes beyond the confines of one or two local authorities.

CONCLUSIONS

The spread of computerised D.C. systems has been one of the major changes to affect the work of D.C. sections and planning departments generally in the last ten years, bringing the information technology revolution down to the 'grass roots'. This chapter has presented an overview, drawing together a number of strands of research and discussion. The variety of approaches to computerisation has been considered, along with the motives involved. The essay has reviewed the process of computerisation in making data more accessible, the nature of this data, and the issues involved in using this source, both generally and in relation to computerisation. Finally, some of the modes of usage and areas of application of this computerised data have been considered in a research context. Notwithstanding the caution necessary, the potential range of applications seems scarcely to have been tapped as yet. It seems reasonable to expect a significantly increased research output from it in the next few years.

NOTES

1. A short review of this kind cannot be exhaustive. Interested readers should refer to some of the cited sources for further information, and to S. Barrett (ed.), issue on computers in planning, The Planner, 68, 4 (July/August 1982).

2. In July 1965 the Research Committee of the Town Planning Institute set up an informal group to investigate the application of computers to planning: see 'The use of the computer in planning', Journal of the Town Planning Institute, 55, 1 (January 1969), p. 27.

3. S.M. Barrett and P. Leather, Information Technology in Planning Practice, Environment and Planning Committee Paper no. 4 (Economic and Social Research Council, London, 1984).

4. H. Thornton, 'PLANAPS in Leeds', British Urban and Regional Information Systems Association Newsletter (BURISA), 37, (January 1979), pp. 4-5.

5. A. Ray, 'Computers and Development Control in Wakefield', in E. Judge (ed.), Local Authority Information Systems for Planning, Brunswick Environmental Paper no. 34, Brunswick School of the Environment (Leeds Polytechnic, 1982).

6. K. Bardon, C. Elliot and N. Stothers, Computer Applications in Local Authority Planning Departments 1984, Computer Applications Research Project, Department of Planning and Landscape (Birmingham Polytechnic, 1984); Local Authorities Management Services and Computing Committee (LAMSAC), Processing Planning Applications: The Role of the Computer (LAMSAC, London, 1982).

7. Department of the Environment, Circular 22/80, Development Control - Policy and Practice (HMSO, London, 1980).

8. Bardon et al., op. cit.

9. Ibid.

10. D.J. Grimshaw, 'Planning Application Systems', in J.R. England, K.I. Hudson, R.J. Masters, K.S. Powell and J.D. Shortridge (eds.), Information Systems for Policy Planning in Local Government (Longman/BURISA, Harlow, 1985), pp. 215-25.

11. Humberside County Council, Development Trends 1985 (JDAS) (Humberside County Council, Beverley, 1985).

12. LAMSAC, op. cit.

13. Grimshaw, op. cit.

14. National Development Control Forum, The determinants of efficiency in development control in

Computers in D.C. and Research

England (unpublished paper, 1982).
15. S. Boyes, Computer-Based Development Control Systems, unpublished dissertation, School of Planning and Environmental Studies (Leeds Polytechnic, 1983).
16. S. Farthing, 'The Impact of Computers on the Processing of Planning Applications', The Planner, 71, 11 (November 1985), pp. 17-18.
17. P. McNamara, 'Development Control Data: An Under-used Resource', unpublished paper, Oxford Polytechnic/School of Advanced Urban Studies Land Policy and Problems Conference, 1982, Oxford.
18. P. McNamara and P. Healey, 'The Limitations of Development Control Data in Planning Research', Town Planning Review, 55, 1 (January 1984), pp. 91-7.
19. Y. Rydin, 'Residential Development and the Planning System: A Study of the Housing Land System at the Local Level', Progress in Planning, 24, 1 (1985), pp. 1-69.
20. Ibid., p. 66.
21. McNamara, op. cit.
22. See also J. Underwood, 'Development Control: A Review of Research and Current Issues', Progress in Planning, 16, 3 (1981), pp. 179-242; and 'Development Control: Research Review', The Planner, 67, 7 (July/August 1981), pp. 100-1, 109.
23. McNamara, op. cit.
24. E.J. Judge, 'Regional Issues and Transport Infrastructure: Some Reflections on the Effects of the Lancashire-Yorkshire Motorway', in K. Button and D. Gillingwater (eds.), Transport, Location and Spatial Policy (Gower, Aldershot, 1983), pp. 57-81.
25. A. Humphries, 'Development Monitoring in Tyne and Wear', British Urban and Regional Information Systems Association Newsletter (BURISA), 55, (September 1982), pp. 12-13.
26. Humberside County Council, op. cit.
27. For a review of a selection of systems see I. Brown, 'Land Potential and Development Monitoring Systems', in England et al., op. cit., pp. 226-37.
28. The JDAS system for Humberside County Council and the constituent districts, for instance, is based on the extraction of information on applications from all districts, some of which do not have computerised D.C. systems.
29. M.A. Anderson, 'Planning Policies and Development Control in the Sussex Downs AONB', Town Planning Review, 52, 1 (January 1981), p.6.
30. D. Gregory, Green Belts and Development

<u>Control</u>, Occasional Paper no. 12, Centre for Urban and Regional Studies (University of Birmingham, 1970).

31. I. Brotherton, 'Development pressures and Control in the National Parks, 1966-1981', <u>Town Planning Review</u>, <u>53</u>, 4 (October 1982), pp. 439-59.

32. Anderson, op. cit.

33. M. Blacksell and A.W. Gilg, 'Planning Control in an Area of Outstanding Natural Beauty', <u>Social and Economic Administration</u>, <u>11</u>, 3 (Autumn 1977), pp. 206-15.

34. Rydin, op. cit.

35. An example of this process is discussed in T. Briggs and E.J. Judge, <u>Computerised Development Control Systems and Research: A Case Study of Wakefield</u>, Brunswick Environmental Papers no. 58, Brunswick School of the Environment (Leeds Polytechnic, 1986).

36. McNamara, op. cit.

Chapter 10

ENFORCEMENT: THE WEAKEST LINK IN THE PLANNING CHAIN

Jeffrey Jowell and Denzil Millichap

INTRODUCTION[1]

The layman's view that violations of law, if detected, are likely to be prosecuted is not borne out in relation to a number of offences. In the criminal law, for example, what are known as 'victimless crimes' (where the action is labelled criminal despite its being freely undertaken by both parties) may be enforced less rigorously than other crimes. Behaviour that is the subject of regulatory control also often differs from behaviour traditionally labelled 'criminal', because of the moral ambivalence surrounding it. Enforcement staff concerned with pollution control differentiate between polluters who are morally blameworthy (those who intentionally discharge pollutants) and those who are not (those who have taken reasonable steps to prevent discharges, but could still not prevent pollution). The morally innocent offenders are less likely to be prosecuted than the former.[2]

The breach of planning law - a regulatory offence - is, similarly, surrounded by a degree of moral ambivalence. Like many regulatory offences, discretion to enforce planning law is given to the enforcement agency itself. The statute gives local authorities power to enforce when they consider it 'expedient' to do so. Breach of the law is not itself therefore a crime. It is only a prohibited act. The decision to enforce will balance the cost of the harm occasioned by the law's breach against countervailing costs of abatement - such as the possible loss of local employment.[3] If the authority then decides to enforce against a breach it will normally issue an 'enforcement notice'. The violator who fails to observe the notice commits a criminal offence which may be

175

prosecuted in a magistrate's court. In between the issuance of the enforcement notice and the stage of criminal enforcement, however, the violator has plenty of time to appeal against the enforcement procedures to the Secretary of State for the Environment. The grounds of appeal may be technical (asserting that there was a defect in the notice), or legal (asserting that there was no 'development'). The appellant may also assert on grounds of policy that planning permission ought to be given for the development. Unless a 'stop notice' is issued, the breach of the law may continue all this time. Even after an appeal to the Secretary of State has failed, the violator may appeal the legal merits of the decision to the High Court.

This complex system of enforcement bends over backwards to protect the developer against decisions by the local authority that are technically or legally unsound, and allows the Secretary of State, through an inspector, to grant planning permission on appeal despite the breach. Consequently, it is perhaps not surprising that the system is little understood and less appreciated. Planners consider enforcement to be 'the pits of planning'[4], a fringe activity removed from their proper professional purview. A judge has been more forthright, calling enforcement:

> ... a subject which stinks in the noses of the public, and not without reason ... Instead of their trying to make this thing simpler, lawyers succeeded day by day in making it more difficult and less comprehensible, until it has reached a stage where it is very much like the state of the land which the plaintiff has brought about by his operations - an eyesore, a wilderness, and a scandal.[5]

THE ORGANISATION OF ENFORCEMENT

The status of enforcement in the hierarchy of planning functions is low. This status is mirrored in organisational terms.

Our research indicates that the organisation of the process may be seen in terms of four distinct categories. First, an authority may not employ anybody to deal exclusively with planning enforcement. In 1982 12% of metropolitan authorities and 18% of non-metropolitan authorities

Enforcement

fell into this category. The enforcement responsibilities are split among officers primarily concerned with other tasks - usually building control inspectors and planners. Here enforcement activity is sporadic. Cases can easily 'get lost' - and are only revived by vociferous public complaint. There is little continuity or follow-through. The various skills of enforcement (fact-finding, planning, legal and fact-presentation - in court and before inspectors) are inadequately covered and poorly integrated. Ineffective procedures are thus often grounds for findings of maladministration by the Commissioner for Local Administration.[6] Enforcement at this level may be 'legalistic' or 'retreatist'. If the former, then planners may routinely send cases that have received little attention to the legal department for formal action. If the latter, then the complaint is noted, letters sent and the matter put 'on the back-burner'. Only if the complainant vigorously demands action does further (limited) action take place. Authorities with this organisation structure realise its limitations. As one respondent said, 'we need a specialist enforcement officer to liaise with area planners, site inspectors and solicitors and to monitor progress of enforcement'.

The second category is characterised by the employment of an Inquiry Officer, exclusively devoted to planning enforcement. His or her main task is to deal with the fact-finding aspect of enforcement; visiting sites, tactfully inquiring about the developer's intentions, and reporting to a planning supervisor. Usually the officer will be an ex-policeman.[7] Once he or she has gained more experience of planning rules (much more complex than the black/white norms of the criminal law) the officer will take on more responsibility. Minor violations and clear-cut decisions will often be left to the Inquiry Officer. However, in more complex and controversial cases he or she will act as the eyes and ears of the planners who may also make site-visits to check on tricky legal planning issues, such as intensification, ancillary uses, etc. The Inquiry Officer may also serve notices on behalf of the council and generally 'make his presence felt'. The negotiating and fact-finding skills (learnt as a policeman) are valuable to the organisation, and allow the confrontation of contravenors not easily undertaken by planners.

Our third category covers those local authorities which appoint an Enforcement Officer.[8]

Often this category is a development of the second one. Planning skills have thus been acquired and are regularly exercised by the officer, who is competent to deal with more and more aspects of more and more cases. Perhaps he or she may write and present reports to committee, and draft notices. However, the officer's authority is still limited. A planner with overall responsibility for enforcement (who may also deal with appeals and other 'fringe activities') will have the final say on matters, although relying on the officer for basic information.

The fourth category is characterised by a specialist who combines all the enforcement skills, investigatory, negotiatory, policy and legal. Departmental chauvinism is thus minimised. The legal department will not be able to hold up action by claiming lack of resources or suggesting that technical problems rule out certain courses of action. The enforcement specialist, through commanding all the necessary skills, can thus deal effectively with cases. This then allows a broader picture of enforcement to emerge and a more 'proactive'[9] stance to be taken. The limitations of 'reactive' enforcement are thus combatted. Normally authorities adopt a reactive approach. Limited resources mean that they can only deal with breaches arising from public complaint. It is to the subject of public complaint that we now turn.

PUBLIC COMPLAINT

Public complaint invariably provokes the majority of enforcement cases. The other main sources from which breaches are revealed are liaison with building control and environmental health sections, and officer observation. Minor sources revealed by our research include: Rating Officer memos; solicitor enquiries on behalf of prospective purchasers; applications for retrospective approval of contravening development;[10] land-use surveys by the planning department; local press adverts (for car-breaking or mini-cab services); Goods Vehicle Operators' Licence applications - passed on from the Traffic Licensing Authority; monitoring of conditions and agreements; requests from administrative staff to inspect sites covered by (expired) time-limited permissions; referrals from other departments (for example highways).

The dominance of public complaint is mainly

attributable to the lack of resources for proactive enforcement. However this dominant position held by public complaint greatly influences subsequent enforcement activity. Thus the vociferousness of public complaint is felt to be the major factor affecting the decision-making of officers and (especially) members. Damage to amenity comes second. One London respondent said '... you get more aggro from complainants than [from] the contravenor'. As a result enforcement is pursued differentially in different areas. As one officer said: 'There's more enforcement in Highgate than in Hackney'. This differential enforcement mirrors the attitude of the judiciary in the field of nuisance law where a famous judicial dictum states that 'what would be a nuisance in Belgrave Square would not necessarily be so in Bermondsey'.[11] The planning system is in this way similarly biased by socio-economic distinctions. To overcome this bias resources should be allocated to more proactive enforcement. Unless this is done areas of socio-economic deprivation (where articulate complainants are less numerous) will continue to suffer from damaging attacks on their amenity.

Vociferous public complaint can be a burden,[12] creating defence mechanisms in officers. Examples were noted where officers investigating a complaint would stress to the complainant that attendance in court or before an inspector was necessary to ensure a successful conclusion of a case. Without evidence from aggrieved neighbours it is true that courts or inspectors often then take the view that no harm is being done, and thus favour the contravenor. However, some enforcement officers suggested that if they emphasised the 'court appearance' then complainants might be 'induced' to drop their complaint. Enforcement officers also suggested that if they noticed a minor breach while 'on the rounds' they would not bother to investigate and would wait for a complaint first.[13]

Public complaint is most marked in more salubrious areas. It seems closely tied to occupier-ownership and a concern for property values. One London authority recounted the tale of a couple moving into a house next to an established scrap-yard: the price of the house reflected its situation. The couple then tried to get the local authority to take enforcement action against the scrap-yard. The resources of the private sector thus get channelled into chivying the local authority to take action.[14] However, the latter, short of resources and encumbered by an unwieldy system, cannot easily take effective and speedy action. One reform thus might be to free the resources of the private sector and allow some form of private enforcement of planning controls. American planning practice is a precedent for such a dual system of enforcement, where the standard State Enabling Act declares that a violation of zoning controls is a misdemeanour punishable by fine or imprisonment. Civil penalties are also authorised and these can include injunctions and damages for nuisance. Standing to sue is commonly given to ratepayers, neighbouring property owners and those specially damaged.

One criticism of such a reform would be that differential enforcement, apparent in present practice, would be further encouraged by offering a sanction only of practical use to those with access to complaints machinery. However authorities thus relieved of some of their workload might be able to deal with the remaining cases more effectively. This would be enhanced if the reforms we propose below relegating the criminal law to a lesser role were introduced. The reformed arrangements would still operate within the general framework of enforcement which is, above all, negotiatory. Thus 17 out of 21 non-metropolitan authorities estimated that 80% or more of their enforcement case-load was resolved by informal enforcement. For metropolitan authorities the figure was 9 out of 11.[15] This emphasis on negotiation would still enable flexible responses to be adopted by the developer, complainant and planning authority. Minor breaches and breaches not causing harm would be regularised by permission and be resolved by non-adversarial procedures. However, the background option of effective enforcement would help to ensure a more speedy resolution of cases.

ENFORCEMENT CASES

Changes of use which involve little capital outlay, provide local services and are often located on the fringes of residential areas represent the main category of enforcement cases. The back-yard car-repairer is the bête-noire of enforcement officers. A recent study of enforcement appeals[16] produced the following data: caravan-related cases accounted for 13% of appeals; then came vehicle repairs (11%); vehicle storage and office uses (8% each); farm

Enforcement

activities, vehicle sales and amusement centres (5% each); gypsy sites and scrap-dealing (3% each). Our research suggests that vehicle repairs, especially if conducted in the street, are particularly difficult to control. Activities may fall between two agencies - here the planning authority and the police authority. In such a situation the absence of a clear division of responsibility hampers effective action.

Apart from these difficulties there is the more basic problem that enforcement in planning involves 'discrete' breaches of the controls. This is different from, say, pollution control breaches where the regulator and contravenor (pollution inspector and factory) normally interact in a continuing relationship of regular visits and discussions about pollution abatement measures. With planning enforcement the occasion for contact between regulator and contravenor is invariably based on breach. There will normally be no existing relationship between the parties that can help both in dealing with the problem. The nearest we can get to the 'relational breach' (rather than the 'discrete breach') is in mineral planning. Here the nexus between regulator and contravenor is normally based on a long-standing relationship. Hence a negotiated resolution to the dispute is more likely. Discrete breaches in the field of regulatory law can be more difficult to resolve. Respondents sometimes remarked that the people they deal with on enforcement cases are often the same people they dealt with when working for the police force. Stories of violence and bribes came out. Planning enforcement throws up cases of the 'little man' who, either through ignorance or calculation, breaches the regulations. The official who does not display tact may receive an indignant response and in some cases threats of physical violence. The everyday world of the enforcement officer is not easy - particularly in areas with powerful and vociferous complainants.

THE FORMAL TOOLS OF ENFORCEMENT

We have seen that local planning authorities alone have the power to enforce breaches of planning law, through the issuance of an enforcement notice when 'expedient' to do so.[17] The contravenor can however appeal[18] the notice and during the appeal continue the activities unless the authority issues

181

Enforcement

a stop notice,[19] breach of which is a criminal offence. Eventually, non-compliance with the enforcement notice is also a criminal offence, but our research shows that magistrates, before whom these cases are heard, are generally unwilling to impose on violators fines that adequately deter breaches. The developer can thus write off the fine as a minor overhead, a 'tax' on illegal development.

Another sanction for non-compliance with an enforcement notice is the power to enter the land and carry out the works required.[20] This power is however rarely used. Authorities in our study were wary of such high-handed treatment, and also suggested that the risk of counter-claims against a local authority for damage could embroil it in needless disputes.

CIRCULAR 22/80

Appeals against enforcement notices to the Secretary of State are common. As well as postponing operation of the notice such an appeal may also enable the contravenor to win substantive gains. Central government policy on enforcement (as outlined in Circular 22/80) stresses that, for the inspector, the effects on local employment etc. may outweigh the amenity concerns of local people. Paragraph 13 of the circular states that,

> The fact that an activity is a non-conforming use is not a sufficient reason in itself for refusing planning permission or taking enforcement action.[21]

The circular also stresses the need to give help to small businesses in locating their development in more suitable areas. Annex B of the circular states:

> The first step in considering whether enforcement action is necessary should be to explore, in discussion with the owner or operator of a small business, whether it is practicable to reach a compromise which will allow his activities to continue at their present level, or if necessary less intensively. In these discussions the value of any business in providing local employment, whether in inner city areas or in depopulating

Enforcement

or otherwise disadvantaged rural localities or elsewhere, should be considered. If it eventually proves impossible to reach a satisfactory compromise and enforcement action has to be taken in the last resort, it should follow a carefully planned timetable which will give the operator of the enterprise sufficient time to find, negotiate for, and move to other suitable premises without unreasonably disrupting the business.

Some authorities in our study did try to help contravenors with relocation. Many however said that suitable premises were not available and that often contravenors were reluctant to expend money and time in renting and travelling to a new site when they could manage reasonably well at home. The circular thus overlooks the realities of the situation. It also fell foul of members who were more concerned about (the votes arising from) protecting residential amenity and would not condone 'law-breaking' merely because Whitehall required it. The effect of Circular 22/80 was said largely to be to delay enforcement: authorities had to ensure that 22/80 considerations were addressed in the case-file and accept that inspectors were likely to increase the time for compliance. As one respondent said, 'We read it to find out whether we can get away with doing what we're doing. Members don't like the idea that law-breaking be tolerated in the interests of employment'.

The pressure on an authority could of course be directed equally powerfully from the developer's side. If a persuasive contravenor mobilised support from members then a complainant might have a more difficult time achieving results. On the other hand, if a complainant got to a member early, officers might find themselves with a committee authorisation of formal action with little groundwork having been done. In such circumstances they would have to hope for the best on appeal.

PROPOSED REFORMS

We see from the above that enforcement of planning law bristles with obstacles, delays, legalities and conflicting aims in the context of unwieldy procedures. We propose, therefore, a number of reforms to the system.

183

Planning Enforcement Tribunals

Since almost 100% of enforcement appeals are now decided by inspectors under transferred powers,[22] the reality is that planning inspectors are both hearing and deciding appeals without reference to the Secretary of State in virtually every case. Although guided by departmental 'policy', many of their decisions raise matters of little national policy import, dealing largely with the factual or legal question of whether or not a breach of planning law has occurred.

Because of the lack in practice of policy import in enforcement appeals, we feel that they should be considered by tribunals, with a legal chairman (who would ideally have planning law experience), and two other members, one a nominee of the land development industry and the other a nominee of amenity or environmental organisations. The tribunals should be appointed at a regional level. They would have the advantage over the present inspectorate of having local knowledge and possessing a range of expertise. They would be seen to be more genuinely independent than the departmental staff inspector. The Secretary of State would of course still retain influence over policy issues via circulars and could have a residual power to 'call-in' cases.

We think, too, that there is great merit in removing the possibility of planning permission being granted on this type of appeal. The issues of breach of law and the grant of planning permission are logically distinct. In the interests of legality we think that breaches of planning law ought either to be regularised (by encouraging the submission of an application for planning permission) or enforced against. Once enforcement proceedings have commenced it would probably be efficient to suspend the possibility of a planning application being determined through a different route of appeal. Since the tribunal will not be deciding policy questions, but only the technical question - based on law and fact or degree - of whether development has occurred, we do not think much time would be wasted by this course of action. On the contrary, we think that decentralised, expert tribunals deciding only the question of development would be more speedy, and more effective, than the present appeals system. Above all, however, we think that the adjudication of development alone is more appropriate to a tribunal than to an inspector, who, historically, was established with the purpose

Enforcement

of acting as a minister's 'eyes and ears' and advising on matters of policy or planning judgement. The above reform requires legislative action which may not be immediately politically attractive. Consequently, until such reforms are introduced we suggest that local authorities make better use of their existing powers. It is to this subject that we now turn.

Stop Notices
These are scarcely used.[23] Interviews established that planning officers and members generally regarded stop notices with excessive caution. The following statement from the Commissioners for Local Administration[24] notes a phenomenon apparent in our research:

> Officer E said that it is a matter of 'policy' not to serve Stop Notices. The council has since told me that a Stop Notice is regarded as a last resort in extreme cases, following a period of negotiation.

The 'policy' not to serve stop notices usually stems from the bleak picture of compensation liability that is painted by the legal department (and accepted by planners and members). One reason for this interpretation may be that the legal department has more pressing work - for example sale of council houses - and does not want to be bothered by technical and unfamiliar matters like stop notices. However, compensation is only payable when the enforcement notice, on which the stop notice relies, is quashed, varied or withdrawn on grounds other than that planning permission ought to be given. The other ground for liability is where the stop notice itself is withdrawn. Thus local authorities will be penalised for procedural errors and not because of errors about the planning merits. Furthermore, the quantum of liability is reduced should any loss be attributable to the developer's own failure to comply with, or mis-statement in regard to, a Section 284 notice[25] (requesting information on material interests in the land).

Injunctions
The case of Runnymede Borough Council v Ball and Others[26] permits a local authority to have

recourse to a civil law remedy, the injunction, when it can be shown that the processes of the criminal law will be ineffective to protect the interests of the inhabitants of the area. Lord Justice Purchas said:

> ... When considering whether or not injunctive relief should be given, in my judgement the controlling criteria must relate to the protection of the interests of the inhabitants, to the established and threatened disregard of planning control by the defendants, and to the inadequacy of the statutory remedies available otherwise to achieve observance by the defendants of that control ...[27]

We believe that an injunction brought in the civil courts is a far more effective method of countering breaches in planning law than criminal proceedings before magistrates courts. As we have said, magistrates - at least lay magistrates - are reluctant to impose fines on violators that are truly deterrent in their effect. The 'moral neutrality' of planning law, the frequent lack of an identifiable victim, and the complexity of the law account for the magistrates' reluctance in these cases. The injunction has the effect not of punishing the violator, but of simply putting an end to the violation - restoring the status quo ante.

We propose therefore that the injunction rather than criminal proceedings be the standard method of enforcing a breach of an enforcement notice. The injunction we think should be sought either in the County Court or High Court, depending upon the value of the land, or the value to which the land is enhanced by the breach. Applications in the High Court could be reserved to the Crown Office list for the attention of one of the panel of judges dealing with applications for judicial review, thus ensuring expertise in administrative legal matters.

In addition to the injunction we propose that the courts be given the power to order a penalty akin to the French remedy of 'astreinte'.[28] The French courts may order the payment of a certain sum of money for each day during which the defendant delays in complying with a judgement or order for specific performance. The daily penalty can be fixed in advance and either reflect the damage that will be caused by non-compliance or incorporate a punitive fine to induce speedy compliance in obstinate defendants. This kind of penalty should be much more of a deterrent than those currently imposed by magistrates. The defendant would thus be fined say £100 for each day the breach remained unremedied. The penalty may then be enforced by the plaintiff as a debt. In our situation the local authority could then enforce the penalty through garnishee proceedings, a charging order or sequestration of the defendant's assets, perhaps by means of a court-appointed receiver. Although novel, we believe this kind of penalty to be appropriate to this and perhaps other areas of regulatory law.

Planning Enforcement Tribunals might also be given the power to issue 'astreinte' orders. Figure 1 outlines the flow of enforcement procedures under these proposed reforms.

Organisational Improvements
An important way of improving enforcement is to adopt tactical approaches that make better use of the presently available powers, and enhance the likelihood of negotiated settlements. Enforcement officers said that giving an impression of having powers greater than those actually possessed could persuade some contravenors to comply. Speedy and 'official-looking' warning letters can help perpetuate the illusion. The 'catalyst' effect of the S.284 notice was purposefully employed by some authorities to secure compliance.[29]

One officer said 'We worry them to death'. Regular site-visits, or just driving slowly past, can (with some contravenors) speed up compliance. Surveillance via building inspectors can help prevent breaches (of the operational kind) when structures are being built. Landscaping provision can be more easily enforced when properly drafted conditions are used[30] and monitored by timely site visits.[31] Checking up on landscaping obligations during the planting season helps to remind developers of any relevant conditions or agreements. 'Being seen' is thus an important aspect of enforcement.

The organisation of enforcement should reflect the range of skills (fact-finding, planning, legal and fact-presentation) that are deployed. If these skills are inadequately performed and integrated then enforcement (both informal and formal) will suffer. The enforcement specialist (category four in our typification) offers a model of how these skills may be effectively employed. In such a situation

Enforcement

FIGURE 1

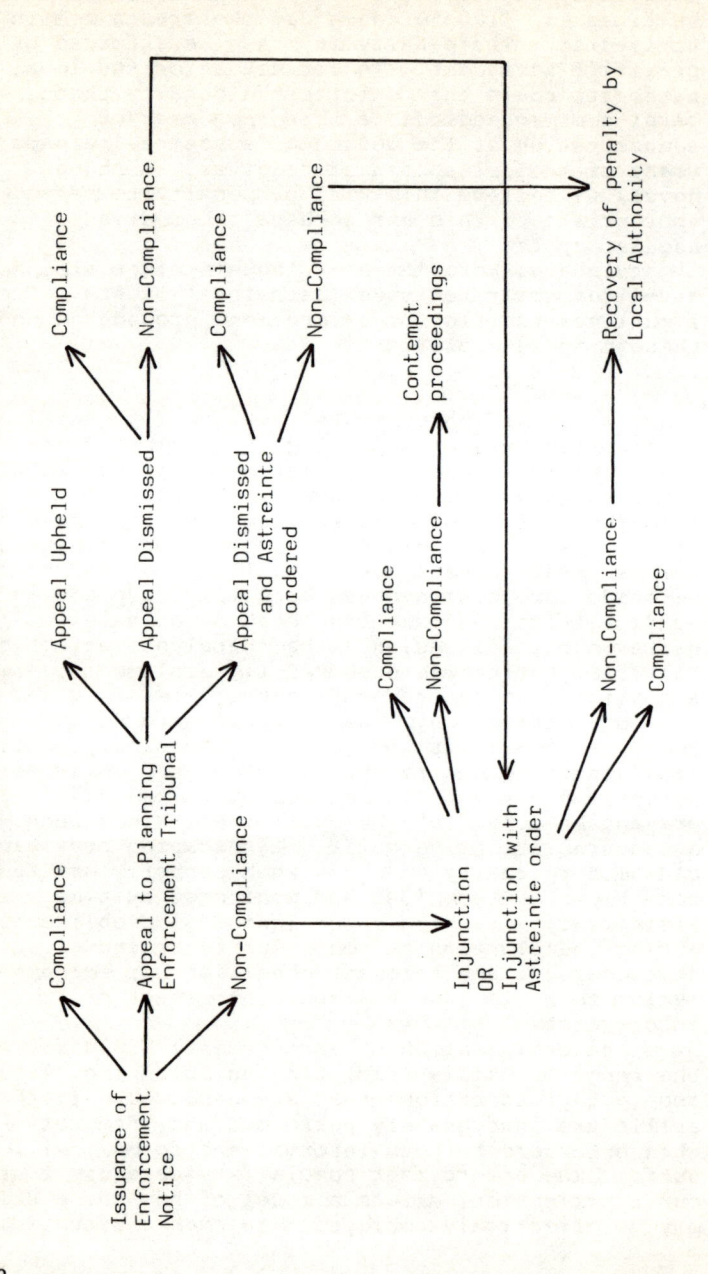

PROPOSED REFORMED ENFORCEMENT PROCEDURE

Issuance of Enforcement Notice
- Compliance
- Appeal to Planning Enforcement Tribunal
  - Appeal Upheld → Compliance
  - Appeal Dismissed
    - Compliance
    - Non-Compliance
  - Appeal Dismissed and Astreinte ordered
    - Compliance
    - Non-Compliance → Recovery of penalty by Local Authority
- Non-Compliance → Injunction OR Injunction with Astreinte order
  - Compliance
  - Non-Compliance → Contempt proceedings
  - Non-Compliance → Recovery of penalty by Local Authority
  - Compliance

Enforcement

enforcement takes on a more dynamic and strategic character. It can serve as a useful feed-back mechanism to forward planning and development control in cases where the policies and permissions generated within the limitations of the planning departments are found to be deficient. Superfluous, badly-drafted, conditions can thus be eliminated.[32] Even without the benefits of the enforcement specialist, authorities can still improve the liaison between departments and improve enforcement. Ombudsman reports indicate that bad liaison is often a source of maladministration. The building inspectorate should thus be involved in regular cross-checks of building and planning applications. Commencement and/or completion notices should be sent to planning departments: this would enable planning enforcement to be so organised as to check on operational development prior to its commencement. The planning department will also be able to disabuse developers of the notion that building consents also cover planning matters. The computerisation of building and planning work could provide automatic reminders to officers.

As regards elected representatives, consideration should be given to streamlining the authorisation process. Members need full and accurate information especially when the legal issues are unclear.[33] Our research indicated that enforcement powers were rarely delegated[34]: even when this was done officers still liked to confer with committee or experienced members. However it seems that with straightforward cases more delegation should be given. This might be balanced by regular reports (coinciding with the committee cycle) on all cases. When authorisation is given it is also a good idea to include authorisation for criminal proceedings - this saves time. Legal tasks should be performed (as far as practicable) by the enforcement section. A comprehensive guide to working arrangements - detailing options, responsibilities and preferred courses of action - should be produced. During our research, examples of these were found, the best of which contained the legal framework in a summarised and practical form.

CONCLUSION

The judicial description in 1964 of enforcement as a 'wilderness and a scandal' has been followed by some improvements in the system that, especially through the stop notice procedure, allow local authorities to put an end to the most blatant of violations. Nevertheless, the enforcement section is still the Cinderella of the planning system in organisational terms - poorly resourced, isolated, and lowly-regarded.

The informed violator is well aware of the delays and loopholes in a system that allows more opportunities for challenge on technical or policy grounds than can be found in any other area of law enforcement. At the end of the day he or she knows that there is a good chance that magistrates are likely to acquit, or impose only a nominal fine. The violator may also know that present central government policy is soft on breaches of planning law - despite the strong 'law and order' stance in other areas - especially in regard to small businesses. The interests of legality are obviously served by regularising breaches of planning law, by requiring a planning application to be submitted or by commencing enforcement proceedings. Naturally lack of staff resources will not allow this in all cases, but we suggest that the attitude of local authorities of relying almost entirely on public complaint before taking enforcement action skews enforcement action towards relatively salubrious areas or towards the protection of those persons who have the resources to complain.

Much improvement could be achieved by organisational changes that would unite a variety of the skills deployed in the cause of enforcement. We suggest that the time is ripe for more fundamental changes in the structure of appeals, and a move away from inappropriate use of the criminal law to the civil remedy of injunction. Institutional energies could then be directed not towards punishing the offender but to combatting unauthorised development in the shortest possible time.

NOTES

1. The authors are grateful to the Nuffield Foundation for funding this research, and to Sir Jack Jacob for his considered advice on procedures, to Roger Jowell of Social and Community Planning Research for his invaluable help with the questionnaire and research design, to Ray Walker, formerly of the AMA, for his co-operation and advice, and to Fred Simms of the Building Research Establishment for advice on sampling. The title

of this chapter is adapted from M. Grant, Urban Planning Law (Sweet and Maxwell, London, 1982), p. 383.

2. See K. Hawkins, Environment and Enforcement (Clarendon Press, Oxford, 1984).

3. G. Richardson, A. Ogus and P. Burrows, Policing Pollution (Clarendon Press, Oxford, 1982).

4. This and other quotations and information are taken from two empirical studies conducted by the authors. The first was a study of enforcement in London, published as J. Jowell and D. Millichap, 'The Enforcement of Planning Controls in London', Journal of Planning and Environment Law, 1983, p. 644. The second, a study sponsored by the Nuffield Foundation, will be published as J. Jowell and D. Millichap, 'The Enforcement of Planning Law: A Report and Some Proposals', Journal of Planning and Environment Law, 1986, forthcoming.

5. Harman L.J. in Britt v Buckinghamshire County Council [1964] 1 Q.B. 77, at p. 87.

6. In one case a Commissioner for Local Administration stated (report 667/H/80): 'I consider that the Council also have a responsibility so to arrange themselves administratively that they can check that the developer is meeting his responsibility even though they may be under no legal obligation to do so'.

7. Indeed the vast majority of personnel engaged on enforcement (apart from planners with supervisory roles) were ex-policemen. Their skills in fact-finding, tactful questioning and 'PR' are valuable. Normally, they were receiving a retirement pension: consequently they were on a low pay-scale. Enforcement was a source of 'pin-money' (as one planner put it). Another aspect was that (as a couple of enforcement officers remarked) the average officer is not particularly 'dynamic'. 'Gathering fat' was the phrase used by one ex-policeman. However, as most departments seemed content with inexpensive but tolerably competent enforcement officers there may be little call for more 'dynamic' personnel having the skills of an ex-policeman but also the strategic view necessary for improving enforcement activity.

8. Here the term is used with a specific meaning. Normally the term is used broadly to indicate personnel involved in enforcement duties. Context will indicate which meaning is implied.

9. Proactive enforcement refers to activity where the regulator actively seeks out violations in a systematic manner. Reactive enforcement is its

opposite and denotes a passive stance where violations are brought to the attention of the regulator by other people and organisations.
   10. Under S.32 of the Town and Country Planning Act, 1971 ('the Act').
   11. *Sturgess* v *Bridgman* [1879] 11 Ch.D. 852, at 865.
   12. In a study of enforcement in Scotland it was suggested that 20% of complaints were about matters not covered by planning control; J. Rowan-Robinson, E. Young and I. McLarty, *The Enforcement of Planning Control in Scotland* (Scottish Development Department, Edinburgh, 1984), p. 22.
   13. One interesting episode occurred during a wait for an interview in a rural authority. A member of the public approached the enquiry desk of the planning department and mentioned that his neighbour was building a wall of an extension one metre nearer their common boundary than was indicated on the plans. However, the assistant said that all the planning authority did was to approve the plans: breach of the plans was a matter for the inquiror's solicitors and not the planning authority. The inquiror then left.
   14. One might say that an 'unmet legal need' is apparent in such cases. Aggrieved neighbours want something to be done about an attack on amenity but cannot achieve the results they want because their access to effective legal sanctions is severely constrained.
   15. The following, from an Ombudsman case (628/H/80), illustrates the attitude of officers towards resolving enforcement disputes: 'The planning and legal officers have said that it is their practice to try and resolve all questions of planning control by negotiation before taking legal action. They emphasised the unsatisfactory results of an unsuccessful enforcement notice and the need to assemble firm evidence before starting legal proceedings ...'.
   16. R. Home, J. Bloomfield and N. Maclean, 'Trends in enforcement appeals', *Estates Gazette*, *276*, 6256 (October 1985), pp. 266-8. We would like to note our disagreement with the final two paragraphs of the study which bring together two conclusions from our London report and then suggest that Conservative-controlled local authorities are more likely to initiate enforcement action. Although areas of higher socio-economic standing can give rise to proportionately more complaints, we found that practically all authorities tried to

ensure that Circular 22/80 considerations did not prevent them from enforcing against unpopular breaches. Indeed, a Labour-controlled inner-London authority had started a revamped enforcement programme on the basis of election commitments to enforcement and the availability of resources arising from less development control work. The important factor is the practical awareness amongst the constituents of enforcement as a tool to protect amenity, and not the political complexion of the local authority. Indeed, Tory-controlled authorities may be more likely to cut down on 'inessential' staff and thus prevent effective enforcement action.

17. S.87 of the Act.
18. S.88(10) of the Act.
19. S.90 of the Act.
20. S.91 of the Act.
21. Department of the Environment, Circular 22/80, Development Control - Policy and Practice (HMSO, London, 1980).
22. See A. Barker and M. Couper, 'The Art of Quasi-Judicial Administration: The Planning Appeal and Inquiry Systems in England', Urban Law and Policy, 6, 5 (December 1984), pp. 363-376.
23. 65% of authorities did not issue a single stop notice in the two years to 1982.
24. 560/H/80.
25. S.177(6) of the Act.
26. [1986] 1 All E.R. 629.
27. Ibid., p. 638.
28. J. Jacob, 'Trends in Enforcement of Non-Money Judgements and Orders', International Association of Procedural Law, Lund Colloquium (June 1985), pp. 63-8.
29. S.284 of the Act empowers the local authority to secure information about the occupation of premises. See also Rowan-Robinson et al., op. cit., p. 52. Some authorities expressed concern that issuing a S.284 notice prior to committee authorisation was ultra vires. However these doubts seem to be unfounded. The Act authorises local authorities to issue and serve enforcement notices. It does not require that such notices be authorised (by resolution) by the council prior to issuing a S.284 notice. S.16 of the Local Government (Miscellaneous Provisions) Act 1976 gives a similar, but more limited, power to request information. The purpose for which the land is being used and when that use began cannot be requested.
30. See Department of the Environment,

Enforcement

Circular 1/85, <u>The use of conditions in planning permissions</u> (HMSO, London, 1985) for model conditions generally, and Appendix A, paragraphs 20 and 21 for landscaping.

31. In the provincial study we found that 29% of non-metropolitan authorities did not monitor conditions. For metropolitan authorities the figure was 20%. As regards agreements the figures were 67% and 60%. Non-monitoring of compliance has been criticised by the Ombudsman; reports 667/H/80, and 181/H/81.

32. Examples were found of standard conditions which were routinely attached with little regard for their need or enforceability. The imposition of a defective condition will be grounds for a finding of maladministration; 656/C/82.

33. Thus in one case where it was uncertain whether a use was ancillary or primary the Ombudsman said it was 'better to go to committee'; 254/C/81.

34. Delegation to officers (under S.101 of the Local Government Act 1972) was found in 5 out of 25 metropolitan authorities and 8 out of 98 non-metropolitan authorities.

Chapter 11

DEVELOPMENT CONTROL, PUBLIC PARTICIPATION AND THE NEED FOR PLANNING AID

Richard Mordey

INTRODUCTION

Planning aid is now, in effect, an integral component of the British planning process, a service provided more or less throughout the country. The Royal Town Planning Institute (RTPI) regards planning aid as part of professional planning activity, defining it as 'the provision of free and independent advice on town planning to groups or individuals who need it and cannot obtain it without an aid service'.[1] Planning aid emerged from the advocacy and public participation movements of the 1960s, in part inspired perhaps by examples from the United States. Blair, for example, wrote of advocate planners like Goodman, who in 1968 was working with students from M.I.T. in the streets of Lower Roxbury, Boston[2]: Goodman himself described how he and others formed an organisation called Urban Planning Aid.[3] This was a period when 'the environment' became a fashionable issue.[4] Pressure groups emerged in North America and Europe to fight a range of development proposals, and legislation in Britain began to allow for more involvement. In British planning a number of landmarks stand out in terms of formal provision for participation. The report of the Planning Advisory Group (PAG) of 1965 must be seen as a turning point in that it sought to ensure that the system served its purposes satisfactorily both as an instrument of policy and as a means of public participation.[5] The Town and Country Planning Act of 1968, which implemented many of PAG's proposals, introduced formal opportunities for consultation and involvement in the plan-making process. The Skeffington Report, published in the following year, was intended amongst other things to suggest practical ways in which local planning authorities could best implement public participation in the new development plan system.[6] Inevitably there was some scepticism: as one commentator remarked, 'The critics of Skeffington viewed the proposals as centred towards only one goal, namely, ensuring that planners can get on more quickly with their daily jobs'.[7] Nonetheless, there was to be at least a minimal requirement for participation in plan-making,[8] and the 1960s thus established citizen involvement as something to be catered for more positively. With increased scope for participation, of course, planning aid became a more urgent item on the agenda, in recognition of the difficulties members of the public can have when dealing with the planning system.

This chapter is concerned with development control (D.C.) in particular, and therefore explores the opportunities for participation and the scope for planning aid in that context. It begins by dealing with participation and D.C. under a series of headings, including third parties, planning appeals, the situation in some other countries, and applicants. The writer then turns to planning aid, considering needs, the development of the system, and its workings. Finally, the chapter concludes with observations on future prospects.

DEVELOPMENT CONTROL AND PARTICIPATION

In the 1960s D.C. seems to have been somewhat neglected as far as participation measures were concerned. PAG saw D.C. as essentially sound, and simply recommended improvements in the management of the system.[9] The Skeffington Committee pointed out that D.C. was not part of its brief, and merely stressed the need to inform the public of important planning applications, particularly departures.[10] Even proponents of participation argued that in D.C. procedures there was 'ample provision for the public to be fully aware of applications, and for them to make representations'. The keeping of planning registers, the advertising of certain applications, the circulation of lists of applications to residents, and their publication in libraries and other public buildings, kept the public informed (if they took the trouble to look) 'of all applications to be considered by the planning committees.'.[11] But have the public really been so well served, and how has the scope for D.C. involvement developed over the post-war period? To answer such questions it is necessary to examine the position of 'third parties', and of the less powerful applicant.

Development Control and Third Parties
Until 1959 a planning application was essentially a matter between applicant and local planning authority. Apart from the existence of the planning register, applications and decisions could in effect remain unknown to third parties, and even to owners of the land in question.[12] Section 37 of the Town and Country Planning Act 1959 resolved the latter problem by introducing the system of certification. Section 36 of that Act, furthermore, made provision for the advertisement of certain prescribed classes of development so that members of the public could, if they wished, make representations. At the time, the Minister of Housing and Local Government indicated that this procedure would only apply for 'very limited types of development which might be considered bad neighbours'.[13] The General Development Order of 1959 in fact prescribed five classes of development: this has not been substantially extended subsequently.[14]
For some the 1959 Act did not go far enough. The Council of the Law Society, for example, took the view that there were many other classes of development which might be just as objectionable.[15] By contrast, others argued that third party intervention was being encouraged 'in a matter which it is the duty of the Local Planning Authority to determine objectively ...': it was the job of the authority 'to do the planning', not to carry out development control 'in response to pressure' exercised by neighbours of proposed development.[16] This was probably not the general view, at least from those outside the system. A 1961 circular referred to the large number of representations received by the minister, seeking extension of publicity for planning applications.[17] Whilst the minister did not accept that all applications should be advertised, he did ask authorities to examine their publicity arrangements, suggesting that there were some applications where there was scope for increased publicity. The circular stated: 'The applications which the Minister has in mind are those which, if carried out, would affect the whole of a neighbourhood and which are therefore of

considerable interest to a good many people'. It went on to suggest that there were not many such applications, and they could not be legally defined: it was a question of judgement on the part of a local authority. This circular concluded by stating that although permissions would inevitably be given which were not generally popular, 'The essential thing in all these matters is that local authorities should keep the public and the press fully informed, and should enable themselves to take account of public opinion in reaching their decisions'. They might sometimes have to take unpopular decisions, even decisions to which there was strong local opposition. It was all the more important that they should be seen to have acted in the knowledge of public opinion and that their reasons for their actions should be fully understood.

It was some twelve years before this circular was superseded by that which is currently operative.[18] In this the Secretaries of State stressed that the basic principle should be that opinion 'should be enabled to declare itself before any approval is given to proposals of wide concern or substantial impact on the environment'. Arguments for neighbour notification and (widespread) site posting were dismissed on the grounds that the objective of planning 'is not the safeguarding of private property rights as such; nor, in particular, to protect the value of individual properties or the views to be had from them'. The continuing problems of delay and overloading of the planning machine were also mentioned. The circular opted for a discretionary approach, and indicated categories of development for which site notices were considered desirable. Despite this cautious approach, the opportunity for third party involvement was fractionally extended. It should not be forgotten that many authorities went (and still go) well beyond the statutory minimum in informing the public. This practice was commended in paragraph 11 of this circular.

A year later, Dobry's interim report was arguing for further publicity, involving site notices even for simple cases.[19] The proposals were pursued in more detail in the final report. The point was made that whilst there had been a great deal of research into participation in plan-making, there was a dearth as far as D.C. was concerned. Dobry also recommended a planning aid scheme, the cost of which should be at least partly met by charging for applications.[20] Dobry may

Participation and Planning Aid

have attempted the impossible - reconciling the need for speedy decisions with greater public involvement, and improvement of the environment - but it was a comprehensive report, although perhaps produced at an inopportune time.[21] Subsequently, the emphasis of government and ministerial pronouncements has been on speed of decision-making and avoidance of delay, rather than public participation. Nonetheless it is worth noting that the House of Commons Expenditure Committee, in its 1977 report, did put forward the proposal that site notices should be obligatory in all cases.[22]

In general, however, the interest of government at present is not in public involvement. Mr. Heseltine, in a York speech (labelled as 'notorious' in some quarters), stated that development control was the part of planning which most affected the ordinary citizen, and that it 'should not take away the legitimate rights of the citizen': but he made no specific reference to participation and publicity in relation to development control.[23] As Chapter 3 of our book points out, there are of course tensions between participatory processes and ideas about free markets (and the 'rights' of property owners). In any event, since 1979 policy and legislation have been concerned primarily with reducing constraints on the private sector, partly at the expense of participatory involvement. Circulars 22/80 and 14/85,[24] the 1980 Local Government, Planning and Land Act, amendments to the General Development Order, Enterprise Zones, Urban Development Corporations, and various current further proposals,[25] can only be seen as weakening the position of the public in the D.C. process, and in some instances removing opportunities for involvement. Members of the public, of course, still normally have opportunities for making representations on certain types of proposed 'bad neighbour' development; and for matters like listed building consent and schemes in Conservation Areas the public's position is clear and relatively strong. Even so, the extent to which members of the public are made aware of development proposals still generally depends upon the attitudes and performance of particular local authorities.

The Public and Planning Appeals

The question of the rights of third parties in planning appeal cases deserves separate treatment. The well-known 'Chalk Pit case' provides a useful starting point, for it indicates some previously established legal limits. Following an inquiry into an appeal against a refusal to extract chalk, there was an appeal to the High Court by a Major Buxton, a neighbouring landowner, who, with others, had appeared at the inquiry. The judgement was based on the principle that the purpose of planning legislation is to 'restrict development for the benefit of the public at large and not to confer new rights on any individual members of the public'.[26] It was noted that the statutory right of appeal to the court was restricted to those 'aggrieved by any action of the Minister', and that neighbours were not in fact aggrieved persons. This had ramifications for D.C. as a whole, in that it was ruled that individual members of the public had no legal rights to challenge the decision-making process of either the local planners or the minister.[27] As Lord Silkin pointed out, they (the neighbours) 'were not persons aggrieved in the legal sense because they had suffered no legal grievance ...': the minister had been under a duty to hear only the local planning authority and the person who had been refused consent. Any 'defect in procedure did not therefore constitute these persons aggrieved'.[28] The crucial point was that the planning process operated for the benefit of the public at large. It was the 'public interest' which had long been stressed,[29] rather than private rights of neighbours or objectors. Today matters are slightly different: as Chapter 4 points out (pages 60-1) third parties can and do challenge D.C. decisions in the courts. In policies, though, the public interest still tends to be invoked, rather than the needs of specific third parties.

Nevertheless, although third parties only have limited rights of representation in relation to D.C., they do have an administrative privilege to appear at a public inquiry on an appeal.[30] This is at the discretion of the inspector, but that discretion is usually exercised in favour of third parties.[31] Even so, over 80% of appeals are currently handled on the basis of written representations, so that the public's involvement may be limited. Whilst third parties may make statements in writing which are taken into account, there is not the opportunity for debate and cross-examination which occurs at a public inquiry.

Participation and Planning Aid

One or two Examples from Other Countries

To put procedures in this country in perspective, it is useful to examine briefly the situation in other places which have 'well developed' planning systems. The roles and opportunities of third parties vary quite dramatically.

Although changes are in the offing, France appears to have a very limited system in this respect. There is no specific appeal procedure, but public inquiries (or enquêtes publiques) are a routine part of decision-making; although there is no discretion, in that the categories of development subject to the procedure are prescribed by law.[32] In Switzerland planning applications are made to the local communes. Procedure is not standardised, but in many areas site notices are posted and there is a period for objections to which the applicant can respond. Interestingly, individuals may only examine planning application files if directly affected, and when the application is actually under consideration. In marked contrast to British practice, individual members of the public can call for a referendum to reject an application, or they can appeal against a planning permission. According to Gilg, the strength of Swiss planning lies in the close democratic control provided by the decentralised system of government, together with 'the highly developed sense of public obligation that the average Swiss citizen feels'.[33]

Although the planning system of the Republic of Ireland is based largely on that introduced in England and Wales in 1947, there are noticeable differences in terms of the rights of the public. In summary, persons wishing to develop must advertise the fact, either in an appropriate newspaper or on site. Any group or individual has the right to examine and comment on a planning application. Objections tend to be in writing, but it is not at all unusual for meetings to take place between an objector and representatives of a planning authority. Both applicants and third parties can appeal against a decision, 'third party appeals' being regarded as an important democratic right. Whilst the actual number is quite low, the proportion sustained (either wholly or in part) amounted to 76% in 1980.[34] Generally, the opportunities for public participation in planning control are extensive. Criticisms focus on the possibility that objectors may be seeking financial benefit, on the potential for delays, and on the point that some planning authorities appear not to

be as helpful as they might be in assisting either developers or interested members of the public.[35]
   The reason for looking briefly at one or two other countries is to help us assess the planning system here. Our illustrations suggest that British procedures for participation in no sense represent an extreme: the processes we are familiar with are not especially generous to interested third parties (this has a bearing on some of the arguments discussed in Chapter 2).

Development Control and Applicants
The applicant is of course the principal actor in the D.C. process. Superficially the applicant's position seems clear: there is a procedural framework, opportunity (usually) for preliminary discussion, and right of appeal. It might even be argued that as 'consumers' of D.C., applicants are reasonably satisfied, since over 80% of all applications are approved, the majority within the appropriate time limits. Furthermore, since 1947, there has been a presumption in favour of granting permission, and currently this is being emphasised strongly. The much quoted Circular 14/85 states categorically that the planning system 'fails in its function whenever it prevents, inhibits or delays development which could reasonably have been permitted'. There is therefore 'always a presumption in favour of allowing applications for development', having regard to all material considerations, 'unless that development would cause demonstrable harm to interests of acknowledged importance'.[36] In addition, whilst the number of appeals is rising, the proportion allowed is also increasing.
   Although the system thus apparently favours applicants, nevertheless it does not operate for their benefit, but in the 'public interest'. Given the legislation that has existed since 1947, ownership of land does not carry with it the right to develop, to build upon it, or to change its use.[37] McAuslan has suggested that planning law rests on three competing ideologies.[38] It protects private property, it exists to advance the public interest, and it serves to advance the cause of public participation. An applicant might identify with the first, but perceive the system operating in accordance with the second, with some reservations. Many developers and architects, whilst criticising the system, handle it with a degree of

Participation and Planning Aid

skill. A large number of applicants, however, may only become involved with the process once in a lifetime. To some of them perhaps 'the planning machinery appears mysterious in purpose and arbitrary in method'.[39] No matter that a planning officer has discussed an application at some length prior to submission: local government may seem as remote as Whitehall, and officers may be seen in terms of a 'them and us' situation.

If an applicant is not satisfied with a decision, and lodges an appeal, he or she may feel 'up against the system'. Written representations have their limitations, and Cullingworth has suggested that the fact that public inquiries are heard by ministerial inspectors often in local authority premises 'does not make for confidence in a fair and objective hearing'.[40] To add insult to injury appellants can be somewhat bemused to find that the representatives of the various parties — including their own — are known to each other, and are actually on friendly terms! Some years ago Grove wrote that a disturbing proportion of landowners 'tend to regard an adverse planning decision as the result of negligence, idleness, vindictiveness, corruption, or any combination of them', and the planning appeal as merely 'leading to the rubber stamp of approval being given to the decision'.[41] In these circumstances it would be wrong to assume that applicants will always be in a strong position, despite the presumptions of the legislation and national policies. There is a sense in which applicants — especially the 'small' ones — should be embraced by our notions of public participation, alongside third parties. Planning aid, therefore, can also be relevant to them.

PLANNING AID

This chapter will now focus on planning aid, in order to establish its merits and potential in the context of some of the issues raised above.

The Need for Planning Aid

A senior planning officer recently expressed the view that 'Development control is planning aid',[42] yet the same official helps operate a planning aid service. Some planners do argue that perfectly adequate advice can be obtained 'over the planning office counter': and given the checks and balances, and rights of appeal and objection, the need for planning aid might be questioned. Certainly third parties and applicants do have certain rights and opportunities for involvement, and planning departments can be extremely helpful. On the other hand, despite the success rate of applications, the planning application has been referred to as 'an argument between the applicant and the council'.[43] Many schemes never reach the application stage because property owners believe they would not receive permission because of some real or imagined restriction. An applicant may be advised that approval is likely, but then find his or her proposal rejected: clearly this will generate scepticism or hostility. Once an appeal is under way, the situation is definitely one of conflict, so that advice from officers may well not be seen as impartial. On the other side of the coin, objectors to a proposed development which is approved despite their representations will not be likely to turn to the planning authority for assistance.

In these types of situations advice is needed, and it is available from various sources. Local authority advice, as we have seen, has its limitations, but nevertheless, as Dobry suggested, 'the ordinary layman is entitled to receive at least some initial advice on any work he proposes to do on his own property before having to turn to professional advisors'.[44] He also made the point that the planning officer should not replace the professional advisor. As far as the RTPI is concerned, advice can be obtained commercially from over seven hundred consultant chartered town planners' offices which are registered with the Institute. These firms will, amongst other things, 'act for clients seeking planning permission, amenity societies and community groups wanting advice on the effects of planning proposals ... they can provide impartial advice and a fresh independent approach on issues that involve local controversy or a conflict of views between different interests'.[45] Architects, surveyors and others involved in one way or another with the planning process provide advice on a similar commercial basis.

But what of those who either cannot afford such advice or do not know where to find it? As long ago as 1971 Francis Amos, in his presidential address to the RTPI, commented:

It is a curious and discreditable anomaly of

British justice that a man can obtain free
legal aid to defend himself in a court of law,
yet a community or group threatened with
extinction or disaster can get no assistance
for its defence. It would do much to make the
planning process more democratic and more
sensitive to its effects if a free planning
advice service could be made available to those
in need.[46]

There are those who are affected or aggrieved in
some way or other by the planning process, but
cannot afford professional help. Here is the
rationale for planning aid.

The Development of Planning Aid

Whilst organisations like the Civic Trust or Rural
Community Councils may offer advice, the two
specialist bodies providing planning aid are the
Town and Country Planning Association (TCPA) and the
RTPI. The former was the first to establish a
planning aid service (in 1973). According to Lock
and Mackeith, the idea arose in a discussion of the
complexity of planning processes and issues, and of
the disadvantages of the poor or inarticulate 'when
confronted by the batallions of technical experts
and lawyers who crouch like spiders over the web of
planning'. The remit of the Association's Planning
Aid Unit extends beyond helping the public cope with
immediate D.C. issues. The Association has never
regarded its service 'as a cosy extension of the
professional practice of town planning, but much
more the practice of the language of the equitable
distribution of resources, opportunities and perhaps
political power'.[47]

Within the RTPI there was extensive debate on
the subject. Gardiner writes of the Institute
'wrestling with its conscience'.[48] In 1974 a
working party produced a report stressing the need
for planning aid.[49] As far as D.C. was concerned,
it stated firmly that 'failures of the system to
cope with public interest and involvement are clear.
Proposals to develop, in most parts of the country,
are not automatically widely advertised, causing
anger, distress, panic, and rumour to those
interested persons who learn of the proposals by
accident'. The working party also emphasised
certain professional issues that it considered
should be addressed by the Institute, particularly
problems arising as a result of local authority

planners working in planning aid.

There were undoubtedly problems of professional loyalty. Many senior planning officers considered an aid service to be inappropriate and unnecessary. Responses to a survey in 1975 of Institute branches indicated that there was certainly not a clear majority view in favour of establishing a service. The North-West branch was opposed, and 55% of Chief Planning Officers in the East Midlands branch were against the idea.[50] In 1976, instead of establishing a national service, the Institute recommended the support of local initiatives. Subsequently a number of branches developed services, and some were successful in obtaining funding.

The Organisation of Planning Aid
Gardiner has summarised the various approaches, emphasising the differences between the RTPI, TCPA, community action and consultants.[51] The RTPI service tends to be constrained because its volunteers are obliged to work within a code of professional practice, whilst the TCPA has stressed citizen self-help through education, and uses non-professionals extensively as volunteers. The Association tends to concentrate its efforts on assisting community groups, although almost half of its clients are individuals.[52] It operates through its Planning Aid Unit based in London. There are more than 150 volunteers throughout Britain. In order to make more effective contact with local communities a mobile unit was created in 1984.[53] Contact with the service is normally by letter and telephone, and many cases are resolved in this way. The TCPA works closely with the RTPI and other organisations such as the Association of Community Technical Aid Centres and Citizens Advice Bureaux.

In the RTPI, a national Planning Aid Panel has provided guidance since 1979. In 1985 a Practice Note and a new Policy Statement were issued.[54] The service now operates throughout England, Scotland and Wales. With the exception of the East Midlands, matters are managed through branch executive committees. Apart from one or two branches such as London and South Wales, the service functions entirely through a system of volunteer area co-ordinators and case-workers. Cases are generally referred either through Citizens Advice Bureaux or the TCPA, or are received direct by

Participation and Planning Aid

co-ordinators. All RTPI-handled cases must be the responsibility of a chartered town planner, although non-institute members can assist volunteers. As with the TCPA, many cases are dealt with by letter and telephone, although site visits are fairly common.

The Nature of the Case-Work
Whilst planning aid extends over a wide range of concerns, it appears that D.C.-related cases are particularly numerous. This is certainly so as far as the RTPI service is concerned.[55] Such casework tends to fall into four categories:

1. Providing information about procedures and rights for applicants, appellants and third parties.
2. Assisting with the preparation and submission of planning applications.
3. Assisting with, and advising on, planning appeals.
4. Advising on objections to planning applications.

The work is very varied, as may be illustrated by some brief case studies:[56]
Case 1. Advice was sought because a client believed that her neighbour's garage had been constructed so that it extended onto the client's land. This client was referred to a solicitor. Clearly this is the simplest type of case from the point of view of planning aid.
Case 2. A client contacted a co-ordinator by telephone, stating that she wished to extend a garage which had been built to specifications which allowed for later extension. She had been advised by the local planning advice centre that there was some possibility of refusal, due to the proximity of the proposed extension to the neighbour's boundary, and the effect on the neighbour's light. The client was duly advised by a volunteer to draw up a sketch plan showing the proposed extension in relation to her own and the neighbouring property, and then to seek an informal opinion from the local planning department. She could then decide whether to employ an architect to draw up detailed plans. The client was satisfied with the advice, and the case was closed as far as the planning aid service was concerned. This may be seen, perhaps, as a fairly typical type of case.

207

Case 3. An application for erection of a bungalow in the grounds of a large house had been refused, the main reason being that the site was located within an approved green belt. A subsidiary reason was that one of two alternative routes for a new road ran close to the site. The applicant sought advice on the likelihood of a successful appeal, raising the issue of precedent, in that a new bungalow had been approved and built nearby.

The volunteer suggested that much would depend on whether or not a precedent had in fact been established as a result of the permission for the bungalow nearby. Both sites were well within the green belt, but he felt that the existing bungalow was in a more urban situation than the client's site, being linked to neighbouring settlement by contiguous development. The proposed development would be relatively isolated, and this (he felt) was the crucial difference. The volunteer also suggested that the question of the new road had little bearing on the matter at that stage. If one of the new routes was selected, then it could be argued that the new road would create a logical limit to urban development in the locality, and therefore this could provide an additional reason for resisting further building. On the basis of these points the client was advised that an appeal was unlikely to be successful. The volunteer made other suggestions relating to the possible use of the land. The client accepted the recommendation of the volunteer, and did not proceed with an appeal.

Case 4. A residents' group had been formed to oppose a scheme for change of use of a former filling station to a restaurant/take-away. Initially, the planning application had been refused, but a subsequent application had been successful. There was considerable local opposition, and a public meeting was to take place, to be attended by the chairman of the planning committee and by officers. The question addressed to the aid service was, 'what could be done now that approval had been granted?'

The volunteer, having looked into the situation, was reasonably confident that there had been no malpractice in terms of advertising the re-submission. He suggested that the two applications should be compared on the register. The authority were initially somewhat reluctant to allow representatives of the objectors to see the register. The objectors were advised to cite the appropriate sections of the legislation and the GDO. This worked, but they were then informed by the authority that it was not necessary for the application to have been changed in any way for a different decision to be given. It transpired that improved soundproofing and fume-extraction equipment had been proposed, and this appeared to have been significant in persuading the authority to approve the new application.

The volunteer then advised that the group should press for a revocation of permission on the grounds that nothing had changed materially to justify granting of permission. The volunteer pointed out that this was a rare event, and if unsuccessful here they might seek a modification of the permission to reduce opening hours.

At the public meeting the planning committee chairman said that the authority would reconsider the application if written representations were submitted: the volunteer advised that this should be done immediately, as revocation was dependent upon building work not having commenced. As far as the planning aid service was concerned, this was the end of involvement, as there was no further contact.

Conclusions on cases. The variety seen in these examples of case-work is of course typical of the D.C. process as a whole. Cases, particularly some handled by the TCPA, can be more complex and larger in scale. There are also many problems referred which are not strictly 'planning' cases: for example, some relate to improvement grants or building regulations. Nevertheless, volunteers have endeavoured to direct enquirers in the right directions. Inevitably, as our third illustration showed, not all advice can achieve the desired outcome as far as the client is concerned. For volunteers too there may be frustrations, in that they do not always know the precise result of an objection or appeal.

Some problems
It is impossible to measure the effectiveness of the planning aid services, but a great deal of advice is being given. In 1984 there were over 1,100 clients referred to the RTPI services.[57] Over 75% of cases directly concerned D.C. issues: certainly members of the public do feel they require assistance outside the local authorities. Experience also suggests that the advice given is both competent and, in general, well received.

Participation and Planning Aid

There are, however, problems. These can be considered in three broad categories; 'need', finance and publicity.

One of the recurring issues is that advice is provided to clients who can probably afford to pay for a professional service. Many applicants, as property owners, certainly are in this position. Groups of objectors may sometimes be able to pay for advice but this is not always clear, and for many individuals payment of a fee is out of the question. The aid service was quite clearly established to help those who cannot afford to pay for professional assistance. On the other hand the RTPI sees planning aid as a means of involving the public in the planning process. By and large the decision to offer advice is left to the individual volunteer. Currently one or two branches are producing guidelines, and these tend to accord with normal practice. Initial advice is given to anyone: beyond that, advice is usually offered except where a person can obviously afford to pay, or where the potential client is likely to profit substantially as a result of a planning consent.

Of course, advice may include referral to consultants. There are advantages in retaining a consultant, particularly for a client with heavy investment in a proposal. A consultant should be able to devote more resources to a case than a volunteer working in his or her own time, who - being usually in full-time employment - may not always be able to respond quickly enough to a client's requests. Ultimately, therefore, paid consultants rather than volunteers ought to become involved unless there is evidence of 'need' on the client's part.

To an extent this problem is linked to the question of financial resources. Some limited funds have been made available for planning aid from various sources, including the Department of the Environment, the RTPI, the Greater London Council and the Manpower Services Commission. Much of this has been used to support full- and part-time co-ordinators. Certainly in London, the employment of paid workers has led to an increased case-load and allowed a more effective use of volunteers.[58]

The use of paid workers has also helped with the third category of problem, publicity. Many aggrieved members of the public may not know of the existence of planning aid, and may be unaware of the availability of consultants also. A number of services (particularly in London and South Wales) have made use of funding for publicity purposes. The RTPI's Planning Aid Panel have identified the need to promote the service, so as to increase awareness of its existence and functions, as a top priority.

THE FUTURE

Evans has discussed possible future developments in planning aid on a broad front, arguing that it should be seen as the 'social conscience' of the profession, and should be used to make planning more responsive to community needs.[59] D.C. is that part of planning which has an almost immediate impact upon members of the public. There may be many occasions when people feel that the process is operating against them and not for them, when certain individuals are benefiting at their expense. As the RTPI's policy statement on planning aid puts it, planning aid has grown out of a concern 'that despite the statutory duty of planning authorities to publicise planning proposals and invite public comment, the ability of some sections of the population to influence decisions is very limited'.[60] There may even be ignorance of what 'planning' is, and of what it can or cannot do. Whilst recognising the important role of planning authorities in assisting the public, the Institute acknowledges that there are limits: planning aid is thus seen as a complementary service for people when they feel that they need independent advice.

Various authors have commented on public disenchantment with the representative system of government, particularly in the big cities. It has been suggested that communications between members of the public and councillors tend to break down.[61] Clients of the planning aid services have on occasion found advice provided by local government officers difficult to comprehend, and some will have no dealings with their elected representatives. Although dominated by local government officers, the RTPI states, in paragraph 4 of its planning aid policy:

> The provisions in planning legislation for the role of the public are based on the twin assumptions that representative local democracy works effectively and that all sections of the population have equal access to knowledge and resources. Both assumptions are now generally

211

recognised to be unfounded in fact. Elected members cannot hope to adequately represent local views on specific issues. Experience has shown that the most articulate and resourceful sections of the population are most successful in having their views accepted.[62]

In this context, planners have long given advice informally as individuals: planning aid services have developed to put matters on a more organised basis. The legislative and administrative structures described in the earlier parts of this chapter do indeed provide some scope for participatory involvement, but these arrangements need to be supplemented by the active assistance of people with relevant skills and knowledge. If, as Chapter 3 implies, one of the more convincing justifications for D.C. lies in its role in interpreting the preferences of local people, then planning aid services have an important part to play.

Planning aid is here to stay. As far as D.C. is concerned, the way ahead for the service is quite clear and relatively simple. It needs to be more tightly organised and streamlined, but not to the extent that individual initiatives are stifled. More promotion and publicity are essential in order to make the public aware of the service. An increase in numbers of volunteers, and fuller geographical coverage are required. Inevitably, additional financial resources are needed, particularly to support full-time workers: obvious potential sources include the DoE and the RTPI. Without more funds the service will continue, operated by committed enthusiasts, but it is unlikely to maximise its potential.

NOTES

1. Royal Town Planning Institute, 'Policy Statement on Planning Aid', The Planner, 71, 7 (July 1985), p. 42.
2. T. Blair, 'Advocacy Planning. Human Factors in Urban Planning - 8', Official Architecture and Planning, 34, 2 (February 1971), pp. 131-4.
3. R. Goodman, After the Planners (Penguin, Harmondsworth, 1972), p. 60.
4. L. Allison, Environmental Planning (Allen and Unwin, London, 1975), p. 13.

5. Planning Advisory Group, The future of Development Plans (Ministry of Housing and Local Government, Ministry of Transport and Scottish Development Department, HMSO, 1965), p. 2.
6. Committee on Public Participation in Planning, People and Planning (Ministry of Housing and Local Government, Scottish Development Department and Welsh Office, HMSO, London, 1969), p. 1.
7. N.A. Roberts, The Reform of Planning Law (Macmillan, London, 1976) p. 111.
8. J. Ash, 'Public Participation. Time to Bury Skeffington?', The Planner, 65, 5 (September 1979), pp. 136-9.
9. Planning Advisory Group, op. cit., p. 4.
10. Committee on Public Participation in Planning, op. cit., p. 41.
11. J.L. Grove and S.C. Procter, 'Citizen participation in planning', Journal of the Town Planning Institute, 52, 10 (December 1966), pp. 414-6.
12. Roberts, op. cit., p. 203.
13. D. Heap, An Outline of Planning Law (Sweet and Maxwell, London, eighth edition 1982), p. 120.
14. The current GDO (The Town and Country Planning General Development Order 1977, S.I. 1977/289, as amended) specifies nine classes of development; Section 8, pp. 12-13.
15. Silkin, L., 'Third Party Interests in Planning', Town and Country Planning Summer School, Report of Proceedings, 1962 (Royal Town Planning Institute, London, 1962), p. 42.
16. L. Keeble, Principles and Practice of Town and Country Planning (Estates Gazette, London, fourth edition 1969), p. 310.
17. Ministry of Housing and Local Government, Circular 21/61, Public Bodies (Admission to Meetings) Act, 1960 (HMSO, London, 1961) paragraph 11.
18. Department of the Environment, Circular 71/73, Publicity for Planning Applications, Appeals and Other Proposals for Development (HMSO, London, 1973).
19. G. Dobry, Review of The Development Control System, Interim Report (Department of the Environment and Welsh Office, HMSO, London, 1974), paragraph 4.26, p. 41.
20. G. Dobry, Review of the Development Control System, Final Report (HMSO, London, 1975), paragraph 10.33, p. 116.
21. J.B. Cullingworth, Town and Country Planning in Britain (Allen and Unwin, London, eighth

edition 1982), p. 108.

22. House of Commons, Expenditure Committee, *Eighth Report*, Session 1976-77, *Planning Procedures, Volume I, Report* (HMSO, London, 1977), paragraph 71, p. xxxviii.

23. M. Heseltine, Secretary of State's Address, *Town and Country Planning Summer School, Report of Proceedings, 1979* (Royal Town Planning Institute, London, 1979), pp. 25-30.

24. Department of the Environment, Circular 22/80, *Development Control - Policy and Practice* (HMSO, London, 1980); Circular 14/85, *Development and Employment* (HMSO, London, 1985).

25. See especially Minister without Portfolio, *Lifting the Burden*, Cmnd. 9571 (HMSO, London, 1985).

26. Roberts, op. cit., pp. 201-2.

27. Ibid, p. 202.

28. Silkin, op. cit., p. 42.

29. Minister of Local Government and Planning, *Town and Country Planning 1943-51*, Progress Report on the work of the Ministry of Town and Country Planning, Cmd. 8204 (HMSO, London, 1951), p. 27.

30. Cullingworth, op. cit., p. 329.

31. Heap, op. cit., p. 252.

32. P.M.B. Chapuy, 'France', in R.H. Williams (ed.), *Planning in Europe* (George Allen and Unwin, London, 1984), p. 43; R. Macruny and M. Lafontaine, *Public Inquiry and Enquête Publique* (Institute for European Environmental Policy, London, 1982).

33. A. Gilg, 'Land Use Planning in Switzerland', *Town Planning Review*, 56, 3 (July 1985), pp. 315-38.

34. P. Shaffrey (ed.), *Your Guide to Planning* (The O'Brien Press and An Taisce, Dublin, 1983).

35. B. Grist, *Twenty Years of Planning* (An Foras Forbatha, Dublin, 1983).

36. Department of the Environment, Circular 14/85, op. cit.

37. D. Heap, *An Outline of Planning Law* (Sweet and Maxwell, London, third edition 1960), p. 14.

38. P. McAuslan, *The Ideologies of Planning Law* (Pergamon Press, Oxford, 1980), pp. 3-5.

39. L. Allison, 'Politics, Welfare and Conservation. A Survey of Meta-Planning', *British Journal of Political Science*, 1, 4 (October 1971), pp. 437-52.

40. Cullingworth, op. cit., p. 326.

41. G.A. Grove, 'Planning and the Appellant', *Journal of the Town Planning Institute*,

<u>49</u>, 5 (May 1963), p. 128.
42. Private conversation with the author.
43. R.J. Buxton, <u>Local Government</u> (Penguin, Harmondsworth, 1970), p. 176.
44. Dobry, 1975, op. cit., p. 115.
45. Royal Town Planning Institute, <u>Where to find Planning Advice</u> (RTPI, London, 1985).
46. F.J.C. Amos, Presidential Address, <u>The Planner</u>, <u>57</u>, 9 (November 1971), p. 399.
47. D. Lock and A. Mackeith, <u>The Planning Aid Experience</u> (Town and Country Planning Association, London, 1976).
48. H. Gardiner, in B. Evans and H. Gardiner, 'Planning Aid: Past and Future', <u>The Planner</u>, <u>71</u>, 7 (July 1985) p. 10.
49. Royal Town Planning Institute Planning Aid Working Party, <u>Planning Aid</u>, RTPI Planning Paper No. 5 (RTPI, London, 1974).
50. Royal Town Planning Institute, 'Planning Aid Debate', <u>RTPI News</u> (Spring 1976), p. 17.
51. Gardiner, op. cit., p. 11.
52. B. Curtis and D. Edwards, <u>Planning Aid</u>, School of Planning Studies Occasional Paper No. 1 (University of Reading, 1980), p. 24.
53. Town and Country Planning Association Planning Aid Unit, 'Planning Aid Goes Mobile', <u>Planning Aid</u>, <u>38</u> (RTPI and TCPA, London, September 1984).
54. Royal Town Planning Institute, Practice Advice Note No. 10, 'Planning Aid', <u>The Planner</u>, <u>71</u>, 7 (July 1985), pp. 39 41; 'Policy Statement on Planning Aid', op. cit.
55. Royal Town Planning Institute, <u>Planning Aid - Results of 1984 Questionnaire Survey</u> (RTPI, London, 1985).
56. The cases discussed are based on actual examples, but they have been modified and the names of participants have been omitted in order to maintain confidentiality.
57. Royal Town Planning Institute, Planning Aid - Results of 1984 Questionnaire Survey, 1985, op. cit.
58. Planning Aid for London, <u>Annual Report for 1983</u> (PAFL, London, 1984).
59. B. Evans, in Evans and Gardiner, op. cit., p. 12.
60. Op. cit.
61. For example, J.P. Reynolds (ed.), 'Public Participation in Planning', <u>Town Planning Review</u>, <u>40</u>, 2 (July 1969), pp. 131-48; G. Green, 'Politics, Local Government and the Community', <u>Local</u>

Government Studies, 8 (June 1974), pp. 5-16; J. Ash, op. cit.
62. Op. cit.

Part Three

SOME ISSUES FOR THE FUTURE

Chapter 12

CONCLUSIONS AND FUTURE PROSPECTS

Richard Mordey

INTRODUCTION

As Chapter 1 indicated, the development control system remained relatively untouched for over thirty years. From time to time governments responded to pressures and problems by making amendments to legislation, the GDO and the Use Classes Order, but by and large D.C. was felt to be doing its job. Keeble, whilst critical of bureaucratic procedures, suggested in the 1950s that it was 'sound enough, powerful yet flexible, firm yet affording every opportunity for the redressing of wrongs'[1], a view echoed by the Ministry of Local Government and Planning.[2] As late as 1965 the Planning Advisory Group saw the GDO and Use Classes Order as having stood the test of time. The Group's general conclusion was that development control was essentially sound and could work efficiently.[3]

Despite D.C.'s firm place in the planning system, however, the subject seemed to be virtually shunned in the professional and academic press until relatively recently. In one of the few significant publications McLoughlin made a number of pertinent remarks concerning the role and status of D.C.[4] He suggested that case-workers saw themselves as the 'Cinderellas' of planning. They tended to be less well qualified than colleagues in plan and design. Development control was regarded as being boring and bureaucratic, and less intellectually demanding than forward planning. In the last few years, however, there seem to have been changes of attitude among planning graduates, together with an upsurge in the number of writings on the topic. A useful perspective may be obtained by briefly considering planning education, where may be found perhaps part of the explanation for D.C.'s lowly status, as well

Conclusions

as indications of increasing awareness of its significance.

DEVELOPMENT CONTROL AND PLANNING EDUCATION

It is probably true to say that prior to the present decade the treatment of development control in the planning schools was minimal. Until the mid-1960s courses were dominated by design-based studio work. Control was usually handled very specifically within formal courses on planning law.[5] The influential Schuster Committee, whose report helped to open the doors of the profession to graduates from 'non-technical disciplines', appeared to regard D.C. as less demanding than other areas of work, arguing that those engaged in planning must include large numbers of officials performing minor routine duties of control.[6] From the late 1960s onwards there was of course a noticeable shift in planning education towards the social sciences, whilst at the same time quantitative techniques were absorbed from operational research and transport planning. Statutory planning experienced a number of changes during this period which led to concern at the shortage of planners to meet the new demands. A number of new courses were established, these being absorbed within the general expansion of higher education.

These changes led, perhaps inevitably, to new thinking about the nature of planning, and academics like Chadwick and McLoughlin attempted to build a more theoretical base for the subject. D.C. did not fit comfortably into the new developments, although McLoughlin made a valiant effort to fill the gap.[7] As Thomas points out, few planning teachers were interested in the subject.[8] Indeed there was a shortage of teaching staff with relevant experience and skills,[9] and some students seemed sceptical of practice generally.[10] It might also be argued that the kind of theory which was beginning to preoccupy the academics was likely to yield little for the study of development control. Interest in 'rational planning', 'systems', and abstract 'planning theory' led away from a focus on the procedural, socio-legal, political and administrative issues with which students of D.C. would need to be concerned.

By 1975, however, Mordey and Taylor were suggesting that there was a revival of interest in development control, which was seen by young

Conclusions

planners as action-orientated. To some extent this was coupled with disillusionment with structure planning.[11] Dobry also referred to younger planners realising that Control was of some interest.[12] In these circumstances more attention began to be given to teaching the subject.
One common view was that D.C. could only be properly learned through a process of apprenticeship.[13] Arguments developed, however, for the teaching of operational aspects of development control through case work.[14] Taylor and others went some way to meeting demand by producing a number of case-studies based on real examples. As Taylor put it, 'The cases represent a response to the neophyte student's development control question "how does it actually happen, eighty per cent of the time in planning practice?"'.[15] Judging by student response this teaching material has been successful. If this is considered along with the regularly-used role-playing exercises, the teaching videos produced at Sheffield University, together with more conventional approaches, then there has been a considerable advance. There has also been a healthy increase in the quality and quantity of publications and research on D.C. Even so, as recently as 1983 three teachers of planning were again advancing arguments - for the need to improve D.C.'s status - remarkably similar to those of a previous decade.[16] As Howes said, 'Development control ... is important; in one sense it is British Town and Country Planning. Paradoxically it has appeared to have remained ... the poor relation, the Cinderella, of not only the planning system itself but of planning education as well'.[17] Many practitioners may share this view: a recent survey of graduates revealed that of all the components of their education, the teaching of development control was felt most in need of improvement.[18] Case-workers continue to learn through the 'system of apprenticeship', gradually progressing to cases of increased complexity. To an extent this is appropriate, and probably inevitable, but it does not mean that formal education has only a minor part to play.

CHANGE, CRITICISMS, AND THE FUTURE

Practitioners are facing an increasingly uncertain situation. After thirty relatively unchanging

Conclusions

years, the D.C. process has become subject to a volume of criticism and changes which cumulatively may seem disturbing. One target has been delay (see Chapter 2), although in fact most decisions on planning applications have been made within the statutory period. More significant are the continuing changes to the GDO and Use Classes Order, particularly the recent proposed revisions to the latter. There is, more important still, the White Paper, Lifting the Burden[19], and its accompanying circular (14/85). Karski has suggested that 'the tenor of the circular is certainly anti-development control as we know it, anti-development plans and for a free and easy approach to letting development happen on its own seeming undoubted merits'.[20] Certainly many planners are concerned that they are now having to treat more and more applications primarily 'on merit'. There is also a view that the circular is having the effect of reducing the influence of structure and local plans, leading to a more pragmatic approach to decision-making.[21] We are being firmly reminded, furthermore, that there always has been a 'presumption in favour' of development. Seen positively, perhaps the circular is 'a mechanism for raising expectations of the planning system'.[22] Some D.C. staff, however, may be less than happy about the trends.

Times are no doubt difficult for the development controller, and there may be further changes, some more welcome than others. Change can be constructive, however, and we have tried to include in this book some discussion of possibilities. Pearce, for example, points out that there are those who argue for changing the basic structure of planning, and notes that we might need to evaluate some alternatives. Jowell and Millichap, Green and Foley, Purdue and Simpson all suggest changes in procedure or emphasis.

Perhaps it is also reasonable to argue for a re-examination of the basic elements of the 1947 structure, with its complementary plan and control system, or as Karski puts it, 'Perhaps we need a reminder of what the relationship between development plan and control should be'.[23] We did not need Circular 14/85 to tell us that many development plans were out of date. Purdue reminds us in his chapter that when the development control system was introduced it was assumed that the prime source of policy would be the development plans. The object of these plans was not 'to design or even to position every man's house but to provide a

Conclusions

framework of policy'.[24] With the benefit of such a plan (up-to-date of course), life for the D.C. case-worker could be much easier. The current Memorandum on Structure and Local Plans (see Department of the Environment, Circular 22/84) states that local plans are intended to provide a detailed basis for development control. Whilst undue weight should not be placed on them in relation to other material considerations, surely clear, up-to-date local guidance is a fundamental pre-requisite for effective D.C.?

Finally, there has been much change within the statutory planning system in the last few years. Echoing Chapter 5, a period of stability is required in order to monitor structure plans over a reasonable period, to prepare and implement local plans, and to give development control officers the opportunity to make sound and speedy decisions and recommendations.

NOTES

1. L. Keeble, Principles and Practice of Town and Country Planning (Estates Gazette, London, first edition 1952), p. 435.
2. Minister of Local Government and Planning, Town and Country Planning 1943-51, Progress Report on the work of the Ministry of Town and Country Planning, Cmd. 8204 (HMSO, London, 1951), p. 33.
3. Planning Advisory Group, The future of Development Plans (Ministry of Housing and Local Government, Ministry of Transport and Scottish Development Department, HMSO, London, 1965), p. 4.
4. J.B. McLoughlin, Control and Urban Planning (Faber and Faber, London, 1973).
5. See for example the Prospectus of the Leeds School of Architecture and Town Planning for 1955-56.
6. Ministry of Town and Country Planning and Department of Health for Scotland, Report of the Committee on Qualifications of Planners, Cmd. 8059 (HMSO, London, 1950), p. 51.
7. McLoughlin, op. cit.
8. K. Thomas, 'How to teach Development Control', Education for Planning Association Newsletter, 12, 3 (March 1983), pp. 13-16.
9. R.A. Mordey and J.L. Taylor, 'Training for Development Control', Proceedings of the PTRC Summer Annual Meeting, July 1975 (Planning and Transport Research and Computation, London, 1975).

Conclusions

10. Association of Student Planners, Aspects of Planning Education (ASP, December 1969, Glasgow).
11. Mordey and Taylor, op. cit.
12. G. Dobry, Review of the Development Control System, Final Report (HMSO, London, 1975), p. 45.
13. McLoughlin, op. cit.
14. Mordey and Taylor, op. cit.
15. J.L. Taylor, with J.A. Carpenter, R.A. Mordey, W. Parr and others, Development Control Case Studies (Local Government Training Board, Luton, 1977).
16. See Education for Planning Association Newsletter, op. cit.
17. L. Howes, 'Cinderella - or the Ugly Duckling of Planning', Education for Planning Association Newsletter, op. cit., pp. 16-18.
18. Thomas, op. cit.
19. Minister without Portfolio, Lifting the Burden, Cmnd. 9571 (HMSO, London, 1985).
20. A. Karski, 'Drawing the Sting in the Tail of White Paper', Planning, 656, (21st February 1986), pp. 8-9.
21. Planning, 'Anything Goes if Activity is Stimulated', Planning, 645 (22nd November 1985), p. 4.
22. Karski, op. cit.
23. Karski, op. cit.
24. B.J. Collins, Development Plans Explained (HMSO, London, 1951), p. 14.

ABBREVIATIONS OF LAW REPORTS, ETC.

ENGLAND AND WALES
All E.R.   The All England Law Reports.
Ch.D.   Chancery Division (Law Reports).
K.B.   King's Bench (Law Reports).
L.G.R.   Local Government Reports.
P. & C.R.   Property and Compensation Reports
Q.B.   Queen's Bench (Law Reports).
W.L.R.   Weekly Law Reports.

SCOTLAND
S.C.   Session Cases (Court of Session, etc., Reports).
S.L.T.   Scots Law Times (Court of Session, etc., Reports).
S.L.T.(Sh. Ct.) Scots Law Times Sheriff Court Reports.

SELECTED READINGS AND SOURCES

This list includes a selection of the relevant recent official publications, statutes, etc., together with other readings and sources which we feel will be particularly useful for students coming to the subject for the first time. For a fuller bibliography of official publications, readers may wish to refer to J.B. Cullingworth's Town and Country Planning in Britain (George Allen and Unwin, London, ninth edition 1985), which also contains good background material on the subject of development control. For specific topics, and for the specialist literature, see the individual chapters in the present volume.

SELECTED CIRCULARS, POLICY STATEMENTS, RECENT STATUTES, ETC.

Department of the Environment circulars: some also Welsh Office (WO).
71/73, Publicity for Planning Applications, Appeals and Other Proposals for Development (WO 134/73)
113/75, Review of the Development Control System: Final Report by Mr. George Dobry Q.C. (WO 203/75)
23/77, Historic Buildings and Conservation Areas - Policy and Procedure
22/80, Development Control - Policy and Practice (WO 40/80)
2/81, Local Government, Planning and Land Act 1980. Health Services Act 1980. Town and Country Planning: Development Control Functions (WO 2/81)
12/81, Historic Buildings and Conservation Areas
22/83, Town and Country Planning Act 1971: Planning

Bibliography

> Gain (WO 46/83)

28/83, Publication by Local Authorities of Information about the Handling of Planning Applications (also WO 23/83)
11/84, Town and Country Planning (Control of Advertisements) Regulations 1984 (WO 18/84)
14/84, Green Belts
15/84, Land for Housing
16/84, Industrial Development (WO 34/84)
1/85, The use of conditions in planning permissions (WO 1/85)
2/85, Planning Control over Oil and Gas Operations (WO 3/85)
14/85, Development and Employment (WO 38/85)
16/85, Telecommunications Development (WO 42/85)
31/85, Aesthetic Control (WO 69/85)
2/86, Development by Small Businesses (WO 8/86)
3/86, Changes to the General Development Order (WO 9/86)

Scottish Development Department circulars
20/1980, Development Control in National Scenic Areas
24/1981, Development Control

Other policy statements
Minister without Portfolio (1985), Lifting The Burden, Cmnd. 9571, HMSO, London
Ministry of Housing and Local Government, Department of the Environment, and Welsh Office (1969-1985), Development Control Policy Notes: (1) General Principles (MHLG/WO, 1969); (2) Development in residential areas (MHLG/WO, 1969); (3) Industrial and commercial development (MHLG/WO, 1969); (4) Development in rural areas (MHLG/WO, 1969); (5) Development in Town Centres (MHLG/WO, 1969); (6) Road safety and traffic requirements (MHLG/WO, 1969); (7) Preservation of historic buildings and areas (DoE, 1976); (8) Caravan sites (DoE/WO, 1974); (9) Petrol filling stations and motels (MHLG/WO, 1969); (10) Design (MHLG/WO, 1969); (11) Service uses in shopping areas (DoE/WO, 1985); (12) Hotels (DoE/WO, 1972); (13) Large new stores (DoE/WO, 1977); (14) Warehouses - wholesale, cash and carry, etc. (DoE/WO, 1974); (15) Hostels and Homes (DoE, 1975); (16) Access for the Disabled (DoE/WO, 1985)

Bibliography

Acts, orders and regulations
Town and Country Planning Act 1971 (Chapter 78)
Town and Country Planning (Amendment) Act 1972 (Chapter 42)
Town and Country Planning (Scotland) Act 1972 (Chapter 52)
Town and Country Planning (Use Classes) Order 1972, S.I. 1972/1385
Town and Country Amenities Act 1974 (Chapter 32)
Town and Country Planning General Development Order 1977, S.I. 1977/289
Town and Country Planning (Listed Buildings and Buildings in Conservation Areas) Regulations 1977, S.I. 1977/228
Town and Country Planning (Scotland) Act 1977 (Chapter 10)
Local Government, Planning and Land Act 1980 (Chapter 65)
Local Government and Planning (Amendment) Act 1981 (Chapter 41)
Town and Country Planning (Minerals) Act 1981 (Chapter 36)
Wildlife and Countryside Act 1981 (Chapter 69)
Local Government and Planning (Scotland) Act 1982 (Chapter 43)
Town and Country Planning Act 1984 (Chapter 10)
Town and Country Planning (Control of Advertisements) Regulations 1984, S.I. 1984/421
Local Government Act 1985 (Chapter 51)
Town and Country Planning (Amendment) Act 1985 (Chapter 52)

REPORTS, BOOKS, PAPERS, AND REFERENCE SOURCES

Alder, J. (1979), Development Control, Sweet and Maxwell, London
Amos, F., Storey, K., Brook, C., Palmer, M., Gilfoyle, I., Bocking, T., Long, J. (1980), Value for money in Development Control. A Series of Essays, Institute of Local Government Studies, University of Birmingham
Anderson, M. (1981), 'Planning Policies and Development Control in the Sussex Downs AONB', Town Planning Review, 52, 1, pp. 5-25
Barrett, S. and Healey, P. (eds.) (1985), Land policy: problems and alternatives, Gower, Aldershot
Beer, A. (1983), 'Development Control and Design Quality, Part 2: Attitudes to Design', Town

Bibliography

Planning Review, 54, 4, pp. 383-404
Blacksell, M. and Gilg, A. (1977), 'Planning control in an Area of Outstanding Natural Beauty', Social and Economic Administration, 11, 3, pp. 206-15
Booth, P. (1983), 'Development Control and Design Quality, Part 1: Conditions: A Useful Way of Controlling Design?', Town Planning Review, 54, 3, pp. 265-84
Brotherton, I. (1982), 'Development Pressures and Control in the National Parks, 1966-1981', Town Planning Review, 53, 4, pp. 439-59
Davies, H., Steeley, G., Finney, J. and Suddards, R. (1980), 'Policy Forum: The Relevance of Development Control', Town Planning Review, 51, 1, pp. 5-24
Department of the Environment, Scottish Development Department and Welsh Office (1976), Planning Control over Mineral Working, Report of the Committee under the chairmanship of Sir Roger Stevens, HMSO, London
Dobry, G. (1974), Review of the Development Control System. Interim Report, HMSO, London
Dobry, G. (1975), Review of the Development Control System. Final Report, Department of the Environment and Welsh Office, HMSO, London
Evans, B., Gardiner, H., Davies, M., Kirkham, R. and Chivers, D. (1985), Planning Aid 'feature', The Planner 71, 7, pp. 10-18, 39-42
Goodchild, R. and Munton, R. (1985), Development and the Landowner, George Allen and Unwin, London
Grant, M. (1982), Urban Planning Law, Sweet and Maxwell, London
Hall, P., Gracey, H., Drewett, R. and Thomas, R. (1973), The Containment of Urban England, PEP, George Allen and Unwin and Sage, London
Harrison, M. (1979), Land Planning and Development Control, Research Monograph, Department of Social Policy and Administration, University of Leeds
Harte, J. (1985), Landscape, Land Use and The Law, E. and F.N. Spon, London
Hawke, J. (1981), 'Planning Agreements in Practice: I' and 'II', Journal of Planning and Environment Law, pp. 5-14, 86-97
Heap, D., Brown, H. and Grant, M. (eds.), Encyclopedia of Planning Law and Practice, Sweet and Maxwell, London
House of Commons, Expenditure Committee (1977), Eighth Report, Session 1976-77, Planning Procedures, Volumes I-III (395-I, II, III),

Bibliography

HMSO, London
Journal of Planning and Environment Law (1979), Development Control - thirty years on, Occasional Paper 5, Sweet and Maxwell, London
Jowell, J. (1977), 'Bargaining in Development Control', Journal of Planning and Environment Law, pp. 414-33
Loughlin, M. (1984), Local Needs Policies and Development Control Strategies, Working Paper 42, School for Advanced Urban Studies, University of Bristol
McAuslan, P. (1980), The Ideologies of Planning Law, Pergamon Press, Oxford
McLoughlin, J.B. (1973), Control and Urban Planning, Faber and Faber, London
McMahon, M. (1985), 'The Law of the Land: Property Rights and Town Planning in Modern Britain', in Ball, M., Bentivegna, V., Edwards, M. and Folin, M. (eds.), Land Rent, Housing and Urban Planning, Croom Helm, London, pp. 87-106
Pearce, B. (1980), 'Instruments for Land Policy: a classification', Urban Law and Policy, 3, 2, pp. 115-55
Pearce, B. (1984), 'Development Control: A "Neighbour Protection Service"?', The Planner, 70, 5, pp. 8-11
Pountney, M. and Kingsbury, P. (1983), 'Aspects of Development Control, Part 1: The Relationship with Local Plans', Town Planning Review, 54, 2, pp. 139-54
Pountney, M. and Kingsbury, P. (1983a), 'Aspects of Development Control, Part 2: The Applicant's View', Town Planning Review, 54, 3, pp. 285-303
Royal Town Planning Institute (1979), Development Control into the 1980s, Final Report of the Development Control Working Party, RTPI, London
Rydin, Y. (1985), 'Residential Development and the Planning System', Progress in Planning, 24, 1, pp. 1-69
Simmie, J. (1981), Power, Property and Corporatism, Macmillan, London
Underwood, J. (1981), 'Development Control: A Review of Research and Current Issues', Progress in Planning, 16, 3, pp. 179-242
Vickery, D., Ray, T., Caddy, C., Haywood, I., Taylor, J. and Simmonds, D. (1978), 'Development Control, 1-6', The Planner, 64; 1, pp. 24-6; 2, pp. 56-7; 3, pp. 86-7; 4, pp. 124-5; 5, pp. 154-5; 6, pp. 186-7

Bibliography

Young, E. and Rowan-Robinson, J. (1985), *Scottish Planning Law and Procedure*, William Hodge, Glasgow

STUDY UNITS

Mason, R. (ed.), (forthcoming 1986), *Development Control. A Manual*, Oxford Polytechnic and Royal Town Planning Institute, Oxford. (See Chapter 1, footnote 14).

INDEX

amenity, 8, 46, 82, 84, 123, 179, 182, 183, 184, 204
anti-collectivists 33, 40, 41, 49
appeals 5, 7, 14, 17, 25, 60, 61, 63, 64, 66, 67, 74, 79, 80, 88, 94, 106, 128, 137, 144, 155, 160, 161, 166, 169, 176, 178, 181, 182, 183, 184, 190, 196, 199-200, 201, 202, 203, 204, 207, 208, 209
architects 121, 122, 124, 125, 129, 131, 132, 133, 134, 136, 137, 138, 202, 204, 207

bad neighbour development 83-5, 197, 199
bargaining 8, 41, 101-19, 130

case studies 4, 102, 109-15, 142, 152, 153, 154-6, 207-9, 221
change of use 5, 147-50, 180, 202, 208
Circular 22/80, 125-6, 142-3, 145, 162, 182-3, 199
conservation 6, 7, 124, 135, 142, 151-6, 161, 166, 199
Conservatives 8, 142, 192

consultations 12, 13, 14, 16, 79, 103, 104, 115, 132, 160, 195
courts 59, 60-6, 68, 69, 80-3, 86-7, 94, 102, 106, 152, 176, 177, 179, 186, 187

delay 7, 12-16, 66, 76, 79, 88, 104, 107, 108, 126, 136, 146, 157, 168, 183, 190, 198, 199
delegation 7, 13, 16, 189, 194
design guides 122, 126, 133-6, 138
development control policy notes 77, 125, 126, 133, 228
development plans 5, 7, 12, 13, 17, 18, 23, 24, 62, 63, 64, 65, 75, 76, 78, 79, 93, 101, 102, 103, 105, 107, 108, 110, 113, 114, 117, 143, 144, 145, 169, 196, 222-3
Dobry 11, 12, 16, 198, 204

enforcement 4, 8, 18, 81, 82, 83, 86-9, 143, 155, 175-94
enterprise zones 8, 17, 18, 19, 169, 199
externalities 41, 43, 47, 50, 150

233

General Development Order 84, 85, 150, 197, 199, 209, 219

high technology industry 21, 22, 77, 143, 144, 149
House of Commons Expenditure Committee 11, 12, 199
housing 20, 21, 22, 23, 24, 25, 45, 74, 82, 108, 110, 111, 112-3, 114, 116, 123, 126, 127, 128, 129, 133-5, 137, 166

infrastructure 19, 24, 102, 114
inquiries 7, 15, 18, 19, 48, 61, 83, 90-1, 110, 117, 155, 200, 201, 203
inspectors 12, 64, 65, 67, 68, 91, 134, 143, 155, 156, 176, 177, 179, 182, 183, 184, 200, 203

Labour 7, 8, 142, 193
landowners 13, 20, 21, 23, 39, 44, 82, 87, 101, 113, 114, 117, 200, 203
listed buildings 13, 110, 124, 151, 152, 153, 154, 155, 156, 161, 199
local needs 45, 109, 111, 114, 116

material considerations 16, 63, 64, 105, 106, 116, 124, 127, 202

occupancy 45, 48, 112
offices 7, 9, 21, 22, 104, 110-2, 116, 128, 129, 130, 132, 137, 148, 149, 150
Ombudsman 8, 15, 68, 177, 185, 189, 194

partnerships 22, 101, 102, 112, 146
planning agreements 19, 20, 89-90, 102, 106, 107, 112, 113, 114, 116, 118, 178
planning conditions 18, 19, 20, 82, 102, 106, 130, 131, 151, 168, 170, 178, 189
public participation 7, 8, 13, 16, 18, 46, 47, 48, 49, 50, 51, 63, 85, 103, 117, 195, 196-7, 198, 199, 201, 202, 203, 212
publicity 83-5, 93, 104, 117, 153, 155, 196, 197-8, 199, 201, 210, 211, 212

RTPI 104, 117, 138, 195, 205, 206, 207, 209, 210, 211, 212

second homes 45, 48
Secretary of State 59, 60, 61, 63, 67, 68, 73, 74, 75, 76, 78, 79, 81, 83, 88, 90, 91, 92, 93, 110, 153, 155, 176, 182, 184, 198
Section 52 89, 90, 101, 102
simplified planning zones 8, 16, 18
standards 8, 17, 19, 44, 45, 46, 48, 126, 127, 128-9, 142, 146, 147, 150-1, 154, 157
stewardship 35, 41, 47, 50

TCPA 205, 206, 209
third parties 8, 13, 15, 39, 60, 61, 68, 69, 196, 197-200, 201, 202, 203, 207

use classes 21, 142, 143, 144, 147-50, 156, 219

234